FOREIGN BODIES

FOREIGN BODIES

PERFORMANCE, ART, AND SYMBOLIC ANTHROPOLOGY

A. David Napier

University of California Press

Berkeley · *Los Angeles* · *London*

University of California Press
Berkeley and Los Angeles, California

University of California Press, Ltd.
London, England

First Paperback Printing 1996

The publisher acknowledges with gratitude the generous
support given this book from the Art Book Fund of the
Associates of the University of California Press, which is
supported by a major gift from The Ahmanson Foundation.

Library of Congress Cataloging-in-Publication Data

Napier, A. David.
     Foreign bodies : essays in performance, art, and symbolic
anthropology / A. David Napier.
        p.   cm.
     Includes bibliographical references.
     ISBN 0-520-20517-0 (alk. paper)
     1. Symbolism—Cross-cultural studies.   2. Symbolism
in art—Cross-cultural studies.   3. Mythology—
Comparative studies.   4. Ethnology—Philosophy.
5. Art—Philosophy.   I. Title.
GN452.5.N37   1990
306.4—dc20   90-34530
                                                  CIP

Printed in the United States of America
1   2   3   4   5   6   7   8   9

The paper used in this publication meets the minimum
requirements of American National Standard for Information
Sciences—Permanence of Paper for Printed Library Materials,
ANSI Z39.48-1984. ∞

For P. S. N., A. G. N., and R. N.

Non affirmo quod hic sit verus, ac certus et debitus rei gestae ordo descriptus, quia talis vix ab aliquo reperitur expressus.

I am not asserting that this is the true, certain and necessary depiction of the order of events, because anything of that kind which is clear can scarcely be found by anyone.

—Ludolph of Saxony
(trans. Charles Abbott Conway, Jr.)

Contents

Illustrations   xi

Introduction: Symbolic Imagination   xv

1. Anonymity and "The Arts Called Primitive"   1
2. Environment for an Animated Memory   34
3. Greek Art and Greek Anthropology:
   Orienting the Perseus-Gorgon Myth   77
4. Bernini's Anthropology: A Key to the
   Piazza San Pietro   112
5. Culture as Self: The Stranger Within   139

Epilogue: A Social Theory of the Person   176

Bibliography   201

Index   217

Illustrations

FIGURES

1. The Goddess as Void   xiv
2. Cows' afterbirths attached to milky-sapped tree   xvii
3. Ideographic story developed with imaginative preschool children   xx
4. Vanuatuan slit-gong   2
5. Jackson Pollock, *Autumn Rhythm*   4
6. Donald Judd, *Untitled*   5
7. Sidney Parkinson, *Patagonian Penguin*   10
8. Navajo zone-woven blanket   12
9. Dogon priest wearing checkerboard cloth   13
10. Carleton E. Watkins, *Mirror View of El Capitan, Yosemite, No. 38*   15
11. Vito Acconci, *Step Piece*   18
12. Cover, *"Primitivism" in 20th Century Art*   25
13. Jackson Pollock at work in his studio   27
14. Carl Andre, *Copper-Aluminum Plain*   28
15. Yoruba *ibeji* figures   30
16. Newton Harrison, *Portable Fish Farm: Survival Piece 3*   35
17. Vito Acconci, *Way Station*   38
18. Christo, *Valley Curtain*   40, 41
19. Richard Serra, *Tilted Arc*   43
20. Alan Sonfist, *Time Landscape*   46, 47

21. *a*, Salvador Dali, *Paranoiac Face*; *b*, *Face of Mae West Which Can Be Used as an Apartment*   60, 61

22. Edgar Rubin, figure-vase reversal; devil's tuning fork   62

23. *a*, "White Man," *Onyeocha*; *b*, White man emerging from ground, *Mbari*   63

24. Vito Acconci, *Following Piece*   67

25. Balinese trance: protection and encouragement   70

26. Balinese monsters devouring a cassette tape   71

27. Cover, *Eduardo Paolozzi: Lost Magic Kingdoms and Six Paper Moons from Nahuatl*   73

28. Cultural adaptation among Solomon Islanders   74

29. Attic black-figure eye cup by Nikosthenes   91

30. Gorgons with various forehead marks   92

31. *a*, Mastos; *b*, Black-figure eye cup by Nikosthenes   94

32. Attic black-figure kylix   95

33. *a*, Laconian black-figure cup; *b*, Laconian black-figure hydria   96, 97

34. Hindu holy man or *sadhu*   100

35. Piazza Obliqua, "Vatican Plan"   113

36. Gian Lorenzo Bernini, *Elephant and Obelisk*   116

37. Four hematite gems symbolizing uterus and altar or key   119

38. Piazza Obliqua, Foundation Medal III   120

39. A "Gnostic" view of the Piazza Obliqua   122

40. Statue of Saint Peter from within Saint Peter's Basilica   123

41. Lost medal employed by Bernini as a model for the baldachin at the crossing of Saint Peter's   127

42. Gian Lorenzo Bernini, *David*   131

43. Aerial view of the Piazza Obliqua   137

44. James Ensor, *The Bad Doctors*   144

45. "The Battle Inside Your Body"   149

46. Balinese masks   159

47. "Trail-blazin' for tax reform"   166

PLATES

(following page 138)

1. Kenneth Noland, *New Day*

2. Mark Tobey, *Edge of August*

3. Whirling Logs sandpainting

4. Alexander Buchan, *Inhabitants of the Island of Terra del Fuego in Their Hut*

5. William Hodges, *A View Taken in the Bay of Otaheite Peha (Vaitepiha)*

6. J. M. W. Turner, *Rough Sea with Wreckage*

7. Nancy Holt, *Sun Tunnels*

8. Giuseppe Arcimboldo, *Portrait of Rudolf II as Vertumnus*

FIG. 1.   The Goddess as Void (bronze, Rajasthan, ca.
1900): an anthropomorphic frame defines the symbolic
context in which the totality of the image is represented
by its absence. (Photo: Peter Cole)

Introduction: Symbolic Imagination

Jan Ch'iu said: It is not that your Way does not commend itself to me, but that it demands powers I do not possess. *The Master:* He whose strength gives out collapses during the course of the journey (the Way); but you deliberately draw the line.

The Analects of Confucius, trans. Waley, 6.10

There is an image well known among Tantrics of the last century, though not common now; one may call it an image for want of another descriptive term, for, in fact, it consists of no image at all—or, rather, it is an image of nothingness—since what is imaged is only an open frame, to which are attached a pair of arms and sometimes legs and ears (Fig. 1). As in some Eskimo masks, we find attributes attached to a periphery, only in this case that periphery borders an empty space. The empty frame, standing for all that is possible and impossible, represents for certain Hindus the Goddess as Supreme Void, a void that is specified by the frame that marks it out. Like the house in the *Tao Te Ching* (chap. 11), in which windows are defined by the empty space they enclose, the frame marks the bounds: it draws the line, it sets the limits within which meaning must manifest itself.

Every year on the Feast of the Ascension, the vicar of the Church of St. Mary the Virgin, a parish church of Oxford and the University's first building, ventures forth in solemn procession to a number of points that mark the boundaries of the parish. At each, whether it be in the quadrangle of an ancient college or in what is now the ladies' apparel department of a modern clothing store, a ritual known as "beating the bounds" is enacted. A prayer and a song by the choir begin and end the actual beating, in which the spot, already designated by a cross, is marked by thrashing it repeatedly. Why the bounds are *beaten* no one can precisely say (but compare Needham 1967), any more than we can now understand a similar "bumping" of the bounds that took place in Bristol up until the turn of this century; but the practice of ritually marking boundaries may be glimpsed in the earliest evidence we possess for what may be called human culture.

Both the above examples—the Tantric frame and the beating of the bounds—demonstrate how otherwise ordinary space may be delineated in such a way as to create a context wherein real actions take on extraordinary meaning. In the second case, the real character of the actions appears startling precisely because they mark otherwise unnoticed points in the real world; in the former—the few inches of bronze frame—a space no less real is set out despite our physical incapacity actually to occupy the tiny bit of air the frame marks out or the section of reality it visually frames. With these two examples, we perceive the difference between image and imagination, between those static objects that stand for something else and those stages upon which objects become marked images through imaginative acts. The distinction is clear, yet it is one that ritual forever attempts to resolve. In ancient China (Waley 1938, 64),

> the word *li* ("ritual") is expressed in writing by a picture of a ritual vessel. The original meaning is said to be "arranging ritual vessels"; and this may very well be true, for it appears to be cognate to a number of words meaning "to arrange in proper order," "to put in sequence," etc.

The ordering of vessels, thus, provides ritual meaning, so much so that the breaking of such vessels is, as one would expect, symbolic of chaos, much as in Hindu tradition, in which smashing a pot symbolizes loss of life in certain death rites. Naturally, part of the connection between a pot and a human life derives from what Tylor understood as the great principle of sympathy. In southern India one still ties the afterbirth of a calf to a milky-sapped tree to encourage it to give much milk in later life (Fig. 2). But sympathy here is not simply the result of recognizing that such trees are great containers for the life-giving sap (*rasa*) that is in everything that lives; it is part of the greater recognition that what we call symbols must be contextualized in order to achieve meaning. In this respect, the marking of boundaries results in no less an objective image than a line drawn on paper or a bronze statue of Śiva. However, what distinguishes the objective image from our

FIG. 2.   Cows' afterbirths attached to milky-sapped tree
(Madras, India, 1985): in the interest of securing a plentiful
production of milk, water buffaloes' afterbirths are wrapped in
bundles and attached to a tree known for its copious supply of
milky sap. (Photo: author)

traditional conceptualization of the process of imagining is that the drawing or statue is meant to stand for something else in all circumstances except when those images are ritually charged. In ritual, they may actually become something else if that other thing—god, demon, or other personified force—can be compelled to become identified through them; while, conversely, the ritual marking of boundaries sets the limits within which real objects become supernormal, where events take place that, otherwise, might have passed as a normal part of the real world or might even have gone unnoticed. The one imagines through the image of some thing; the other through the frame that isolates that thing. Between the two—between object and context—is the ritual activity that marks the connection; it is within ritual that objective images become contextualized and contexts become image-making or imaginary.

Thus, in ritual, objects and actions become contextual and connotative. They "identify" insofar as they demonstrate some absolute likeness existing between two things—a frame and the Void, a vessel and the world—and they represent insofar as each image is understood to be distinctive, a re-creation, something else. A symbol is, therefore, something that both stands in place of and represents something else while, at the same time, partaking of that other thing; and symbolic space provides the stage, the container, the vessel that delimits the ways a symbol may be manipulated. That a stage may be a vessel, or an empty frame the Void, is not merely a metaphorical correspondence, for the microcosmic symbol stands in sympathy with the larger phenomena that constitute what we call "reality"; the symbol becomes the basis for other sympathetic relations, so much so that actions occurring in the real, actual, or architectonic world may be inseparable from their symbolic content. Such inseparability is evidenced in nearly all images we recognize as symbolic, and it is in the very nature of symbolic images that they encourage this inseparability both through their archetypal character and their adaptability. When a Hindu is charged to pick out with the twigs of a milky-sapped tree the bones from a cremation pyre, the original image of the all-permeating fluid *rasa* is not merely certified; the action reiterates, through yet one more example, the correspondence between the symbol and events in the real world.

In the realm of symbolic language, the process of drawing a correspondence between a symbol and its context may be clearly observed in the construction and modification of ideographs. In refined and long-standing ideographic languages such as Chinese, the actual images may be transformed so greatly as to have made their original shapes unrecognizable, or, indeed, the shapes may have come to indicate phonetic values rather than visual ones. Difficult though recovering the processes may be for philologists, the mechanisms themselves may be easily observed elsewhere. I was astonished some years ago to find how readily children from about their fourth to their sixth year of age are able to create and sustain a complex symbolic vocabulary. Theirs is an ability that not only, once developed, can be maintained, but one that can be only very crudely learned if begun a few years later—after, that is, they have been conditioned to attach phonetic values to a written script, and after they have proceeded beyond the developmental stage associated with what Vygotsky called chaincomplex formation. At four years of age, a child is eager and ready to experiment with the fluid sympathy it perceives to exist between objects and their environment.

The experiment I employed is quite simple and easily replicated. Each child is given a piece of paper on which is drawn some arbitrary form. A circle, a triangle, even a line will do, though so will symmetrical shapes; at any rate, each child will before long be developing his or her own typology. One need only introduce the idea that a specific shape can have whatever meaning the child perceives it to have. Little encouragement is required for children to tell one what the form "is." The trick comes of their discovering that the shape can—like the empty Tantric frame or an Eskimo shaman's mask—become an image upon which attributes may be hung, and that the form of this image need not be disassembled before a new type is created. The child proceeds, to use the Chinese metaphor, to set up ritual vessels, to place similar modified shapes in sequence. What results is a story (Fig. 3) that the child has invented; but what is more significant is that the story can be read, developed, and modified. It can be "read" by one child to the next; it can be put away and its meaning recovered at a later date. The child has discovered a means of recording, conveying, and, most important, recalling a complex series of ideas. Without years of schooling the child has discovered the pleasure of reading and writing; it has de-

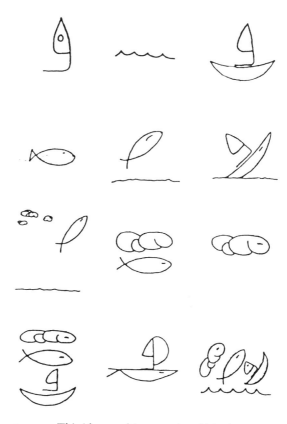

FIG. 3.   This ideographic story, in which abstract
images become sails, fish, and clouds, was developed in conjunction with preschool children, and illustrates how able they are to invent ways by which
conceptual categories may be merged, conflated, or
transformed. (1973; author's collection)

veloped a poetic imagination that will form the basis of a later love for
the manipulation of language. The child has suddenly and almost
spontaneously discovered how something may stand for something
else. At this point in its development, the mind is entertained by the
knowledge that symbols and events—and, indeed, all things microcosmic and macrocosmic—may be connected. It will be some time

before the child is resigned to the cultural demand that divisions and distinctions be part of knowledge, that nothing can be known, as Aristotle once said, except in its parts. For the moment, at least, children are still delighting in Aristotle's equally profound realization that what makes the world one will also be what makes a man.

It is with this last realization that the following five essays both begin and end; in fact, the penultimate essay literally ends with this dictum, as did the final paragraph of my *Masks, Transformation, and Paradox*, the study from which these essays stem. However, before saying more about the individual essays that make up this collection, it is necessary to make one point with regard to the fundamental connection between images and imagination; for a symbol is not only a microcosmic reflection of something macrocosmic, not just a distillation. It is, as importantly, an irreducible thing, the smallest atomic unit to which the macrocosmic may be reduced. It is the graphic point, the *bindu* of Tantrics and yogis, beyond which reduction of a greater image becomes impossible. Conversely, it is also the point where visualization begins. It marks, in other words, the birth of imagination. The moment at which we abandon a holistic view of the universe is precisely that moment at which visualization becomes impossible, where "imagination," in its strictest etymological sense, *disappears*; and the moment we let words—that is, not visual impressions—qualify as "symbolic," we make our first move away from what will qualify, in what is to follow, as "symbolic thought." The ability to visualize symbols, therefore, is directly commensurate with their ability to function in some atomic capacity. This is precisely why visualization is essential for symbols, and why the symbolic imagination becomes impossible in a world view in which the absolute correspondence between microcosmic and macrocosmic is not sustained. One obvious example of this loss of symbolic imagination occurs with the advent in science of the quantum-mechanical view, which Einstein so aptly criticized for its disjunctive way of treating phenomena and its consequent incapacity either to state its problems simply or to visualize them. There are many other examples of this devisualizing process, but what is important to emphasize is the exact correspondence between the loss of image-making capabilities, of imagination, and the abandoning of an atomic, microcosmic/macrocosmic world view.

The responsibility for explicating other modes of thought that are focused on a systematic and structural coherence between microcosmic and macrocosmic relations has frequently devolved upon anthropologists who have committed themselves, often tirelessly, to the systematic study of alternative categories of thought. The origins of this interest are, of course, much older than social anthropology itself, but at least from Durkheim onwards the discipline has been largely modeled on the notion that the "systematic combinations of collective representations" (Needham 1972, 158) are social facts and that, therefore, the higher forms of imagining and ideation are largely social phenomena, particularly when modes of thought function to elaborate categories of thought that provide a unique perspective on how images might be actualized—how, that is, human self-awareness relates categorically to the larger framework that we call the objective world. Thus, while Durkheim wished to distinguish the role of the social sciences from the domain of psychology, it is also the case, as Beidelman points out, that "it remains difficult to separate some forms of sociology from a 'higher' form of social psychology" (1986, 10) and that, in this sense, the systematic study of modes of thought involves the use of imagination as a kind of moral exercise (ibid., 2).[1]

What, we may ask, do ontological perspectives about object relations have to do with morality? As Simmel has shown, objectivity in and of itself may be the primary determinant of social freedom, since "the objective individual is bound by no commitments which could prejudice his perception, understanding, and evaluation of the given" (1950, 405). Conversely, in cultures for which one's perceptions are regularly guided by rules that govern microcosmic/macrocosmic connections, one's relations to objects are, likewise, more carefully established and nurtured. For this reason, anthropology has seen not only a resurgence in attention to the study of the social role of objects, but particularly an interest in the way that the "gift" (*le don*)—in the sense of something that is an extension of the giver—may be distinguished from commodities (i.e., from things that are "depersonalized" to the

1. By "moral," Beidelman also means *mos*, i.e., "a way of comporting oneself" (ibid.), a way of acting, of being a social person.

extent that they acquire an absolute value that is "replaceable").[2] More-over, when objects thus considered become vehicles for establishing the connectedness of things, rather than entities that by definition must be distinguished and separate, one can readily perceive how they be-come essential to culturally significant notions of hierarchy, and to no-tions, moreover, of how hierarchy may function in the development of canons, in the establishment of the very idea of culture and what distinguishes "our" culture from "theirs." In such a limited study as the present, it is possible only to intimate how these central and intim-idating problems of the discipline are related, and many of them, therefore, cannot be treated comprehensively; but it is my hope that the economy I have tried to introduce into an enormous topic will at least suggest how modes of thought that are particularly alien to post-Enlightenment civilization in the West can remind us that our concepts of culture—and, therefore, of the foreign—are intimately connected to how we envision symbolic thinking or how we understand it to function.

The following collection consists of essays in which symbolic cor-respondences are discussed with reference to notions of the foreign. In them, the "absolute likeness" that is part of identity is presented as the complementary opposite of a given notion of the foreign. The third and fourth essays show how specific symbols may be employed in seeking out, identifying, and encompassing the foreign, and how spe-cific symbolic forms are part of the same "image-making faculties"—to use again Aristotle's categories—through which we "identify" our-selves. That we understand ourselves by looking at the foreign is noth-

---

2. Of special significance here is the recent work of Weiner (1983, 1985); but see, among others, Appadurai (1986) and Stocking (1985), and references therein. See also my discussion of the relation of objects to modes of thought (1986). Note, especially, how the "replaceability" of commodities is mirrored by the shift in notions of identity from a focus on "selfsameness" to "the absolute likeness of two or more things"—things that may stand in for one another and that are, therefore, "replaceable" (i.e., objectified). That such commodifying does, indeed, have a moral dimension is, paradoxically, ap-parent in the degree to which we feel the need to introduce "morality" as a regulatory concept in contemporary cosmopolitan contexts. By contrast, I remember once hearing the current Dalai Lama describe Tibetan Buddhism as "amoral." What he meant, of course, was that Buddhism offered a release from self-conscious considerations that were explicitly about morality by providing a macrocosmic symbolic construct in which mo-rality was implicitly a part of all conscious and subconscious activity.

ing new, but it is my hope to show in these essays how specific symbols are at the foundation of our capacity not only to "imagine" the foreign, but to form an "image" of and for ourselves, a correspondence, an absolute likeness, an identity.

By contrast, the first two essays focus on a converse anthropological point—namely, that contemporary art must be willing to alter its traditional notions about artistic "identity" if it is to escape the loss of "imagination" that has characterized (as one now often hears) so much of modern art. My argument here is not that the art of the present has become too detached or avant-garde; quite the opposite. I argue that whatever loss of "imagination" or deterioration of the image-making faculties there may be is the result of the essentially conservative definition of the personality of the modern artist that modern society supports—a definition that, on its own terms, precludes artists from being innovative and, thereby, makes impossible their living up to the radical demands necessitated by a sustained and rigorous commitment to the avant-garde. I wish to show hereby not that the radical theses set down by earlier manifestations of the avant-garde in the late nineteenth and early twentieth centuries cannot be fulfilled, but rather why they have yet to be fulfilled. If I offer a view of contemporary art that represents it as too conservative, I do not do so as a disparager, but as an admirer and participant observer, as one who foresees a time when artists can gain an intellectual preeminence that they have, for various reasons, been denied and that, in turn, they have denied themselves.

Having alluded—albeit briefly and even, perhaps, cryptically—to the agendas of this book, it seems only fair that I should also state in more specific terms what motivated me to organize these five different arguments under a single title. The diverse domains of inquiry that form the subject of these five chapters and the Epilogue fall into two intellectually distinct groups. The first of these (made up of Chapters 1, 2, and 5, and including the Epilogue) sets out an argument about certain ways of imagining that are both largely neglected in the theoretical literature and relatively unexplored in those creative domains, or "art worlds" (to borrow Becker's words), that we sanction at the level of culture. In these three chapters (and in the Epilogue) I am largely arguing that there are specific techniques of knowing and of self-knowledge that we regularly mystify and, hence, "alienate"; and, furthermore, that these realms are, at least in part, knowable once we make the effort to demystify them by agreeing to approach them experientially, or, rather, once we realize the mystical potential in the ordinary, to paraphrase Goffman. I argue that, as a culture, we set up rules that proscribe any experiential venture beyond what is already known, and that we do so by distancing ourselves (intellectually, linguistically, emotionally) from those avenues that are actually quite close and readily available. I am not, therefore, treating the subject of "symbolic anthropology" as it is traditionally understood—that is, as a form of sociocultural anthropology that has evolved over the past few decades out of the work of linguistic theorists such as Pierce and Saussure. Rather, I am attempting to isolate domains of experience that are not as distant to us as our cultural canons encourage us to believe, and that, moreover, need not be as mysterious as the combined forces of rationality and Cartesian positivism suggest.

Though culturally disparaged, some of these experiential domains are, indeed, readily accessible to the inquiring mind, even though those that are closest to us are regularly denied intellectual status. Thus, while it may be the case, as Mary Hesse says of metaphor, that we must construct "a revised ontology and theory of knowledge" (1984, 41), the "radical challenge to contemporary philosophy" (ibid.) posed by such modes of thinking is not, as some philosophers would have it, only the result of how different are such ways of thinking; rather, the real challenge comes of trying to imagine these processes as having value comparable to other forms of thinking to which, as a culture, we have given prejudicial treatment. The challenge, in other words, is to credit readily accessible ways of thinking that are simply different. The *bricoleurs* and *idiots savants* are there before us whether or not we give them serious attention; and their ways of embodying, of understanding, are, I will try to show, at least partially accessible to us and may even come to be "known" through a concerted attempt to move within a meaningful social space to which we have been sensitized. I am talking here not only about "participation" in the classic sense first articulated by Lévy-Bruhl; nor is my argument simply one about "knowing through doing." Rather, I am arguing for certain forms of knowing that come to life only when richly meaningful social spaces are created—spaces in which new forms of experience can be approached and otherwise unrelated things can be formally juxtaposed or superimposed in ways that are creative.

It is also important to note that the dangers of engaging other ways of thinking are, as anthropologists well know, quite real, especially when they are not socially contextualized: it is no accident that any discussion of "modes of thought" regularly focuses on the symbolism of the left, on things often bizarre, and on mental states that are frequently unstable. These dangers are, moreover, evident in the degree to which culture steers us away from such modes of thinking by "alienating" them and identifying them exclusively with the dangers of losing one's self. However, if it is true, as I argue in what follows, that the ways of thinking described in this book are closer to us than we often think them to be, we need only look before us before taking the first steps. Moreover, if we are to believe what anthropology has taught us about rites of passage, it may also be the case that the very symbolic forms that empower such experiences can, if carefully constructed, also protect those who experience other, new modes of thought by offering a bounded and ordered symbolic domain, an experimental social context for exploring different instruments of cognition. Within such arenas, new images can be created through the connection (conjunction, juxtaposition, superimposition) of things that are otherwise unrelated. The results are not mere imaginary "collages," but images whose creative potential is not predetermined; and the imaginative character of, literally, seeing things differently becomes not merely a destabilizing experience.

The role of Chapters 3 and 4 is meant to be exemplary. They not only, therefore, offer historical studies of "otherness," but provide two specific and detailed examples of how a new approach to an old problem was generated by what was in my own initial thinking an unlikely juxtaposition of images or ideas in a regulated symbolic context. These chapters are not only arguments about theories of the foreign but the outcome of a particular method that works from a regulated context to a possible thesis, rather than from fact to fact. (Indeed, the thesis in Chapter 3 began as a rumination over a false etymology, while the dominant image discussed in Chapter 4 literally took shape at an introductory art lecture during which I imaginatively superimposed an image I had been reading about the day before on the one projected by the lecturer.)

Thus, whether my conclusions in these chapters are right or wrong, at least I hope to convey that the method (and it is a method) by which the solutions were arrived at had, at least initially, less to do with deductive reasoning than it had with the unlikely comparison of two things bearing in the beginning a similarity that could only have been described as "superficial." My comparison of the Greek Gorgon with Indian demons in Chapter 3, and of the Piazza San Pietro with a Gnostic intaglio in Chapter 4, both originated in the technique of submitting elements to a comparison, despite their unlikeliness on anything but a superficial level; indeed, I will even argue in this book that it is precisely the superficiality of each example that made possible a reenvisioning of what the symbols considered might actually mean. In each case, I offer a novel solution to an old puzzle; whether, therefore, either solution finds general acceptance is, on one level at least, secondary to the fact that each provides a demonstration of how a symbolic context governed by an attention to microcosmic–macrocosmic continuity establishes a place for an active hallucination to be contextualized.

In the spirit of just such a juxtaposition, I should, first of all, like to express my deep thanks to Jiří Kolář for providing many years ago the arresting image, *La Soif du passé*, for the cover of this book. At a time when I was myself actively engaged in the creation of a kind of art characterized by unlikely juxtapositions, the discovery of his work was, as it still is, an invigorating experience. But I should also like to thank at this juncture the many artists I discuss herein; for, regardless of whether or not what I have to say about their efforts is flattering, they have for the most part been extraordinarily kind and cooperative in providing photographs of and additional information about their works.

Among those who have directly influenced the critical content of this book, I would like to thank Gregory Nagy for inviting me to formulate my views on the Perseus-Gorgon myth for his seminar on myth and myth theory sponsored in 1984 by the National Endowment for the Humanities. I would also like to thank the other members of the seminar, and particularly John Hamilton, S.J., for their enthusiasm and interest in what has now become the third chapter of this book. This chapter has also benefited by the suggestions of many others who have read it in draft form. Of them I would particularly like to thank Walter Burkert, Diskin Clay, Alan Entwistle, Nanditha Krishna,

Glenn Markoe, Richard Seaford, and Jean-Pierre Vernant. For the first and second chapters, I am most grateful to the Belgian artist Constant Lambrecht for weaning me away from postgraduate work in philosophy and toward the artist's life I followed for some years before deciding to think and write about art cross-culturally. Jonathan Benthall and Andrew Duff-Cooper also deserve thanks for their thoughtful comments on this part of the book. For the fantastic thesis offered in the fourth chapter, I take full responsibility, though I should like to thank Leopold Ettlinger, John Hunisak, and Irving Lavin for criticisms and the encouragement required by anyone who undertakes a topic as baroque as Bernini's iconography. Here, credit is also due to the editors of *Res* for publishing this essay in an earlier form. To the American Institute of Indian Studies, I owe thanks for inviting me to India to study the role played by Indian religion and art in traditional Balinese notions of the foreign. While that research will become part of my ongoing work on traditional Balinese culture, the leave of absence from my teaching duties provided me with the opportunity to present my interpretation of the Perseus-Gorgon story to several audiences in India; indeed, the enthusiasm of these audiences, as much as any of my own research, provided the catalyst to pursue the publication of this work. To Middlebury College I am grateful for providing the release time to take up the American Institute of Indian Studies fellowship. Not only was my work in India invaluable for revising Chapter 3, but the fellowship also provided me with the opportunity to write this Introduction, to organize the essays into book form, and to experience personally several new notions of the foreign. Another fellowship, from the Andrew W. Mellon Foundation, made it possible for me to participate in a faculty seminar at New York University on Marcel Mauss and symbolic exchange, and I would like to express my thanks to Annette Weiner for inviting me to participate in that 1986 seminar and for the several discussions we have shared about our work since then.

Though there are many others to whom I owe thanks, Cynthia Atherton, R. H. Barnes, Judy Barringer, T. O. Beidelman, Hubert Decleer, Wendy Doniger, James Fernandez, Eric Frank, Ashraf Ghani, Byron Good, Mary-Jo Del Vecchio Good, Guy Hedreen, David Kessler, Arthur Kleinman, Donald Lopez, Emily Martin, Partha Mitter,

David Nugent, John Palmer, James Peacock, David Pocock, and Paul Stoller deserve special thanks for their comments on various parts of the manuscript, and my copyeditor, Paul Psoinos, deserves a double thanks, as it were, for his two careful reviews of the typescript. For research assistance I am grateful to Lyssandra Barbieri, Elisa Barucchieri, Kara Hordlow, Lou Murrin, Stephen Plum, Michael Rhum, and Fleur Laslocky and the staff of Middlebury College's Interlibrary Loan department, and likewise to Megan Battey and Guanlong Cao for photographic work. To Francis Huxley, Rodney Needham, and my wife, Elizabeth, I am especially indebted—not only for urging me to bring these studies together under one cover, but for encouraging me to pursue topics on which, despite their disparities, I was intuitively led to reflect.

Anonymity and "The Arts Called Primitive"

When I looked around, I saw and heard of none like me.
Mary Shelley, *Frankenstein; or,*
The Modern Prometheus

I. "THE ARTS CALLED PRIMITIVE"

It has been nearly four decades since Isamu Noguchi wrote his review article on the Museum of Primitive Art (Noguchi 1957), the museum that housed the astonishing collection of objects that did not, in Nelson Rockefeller's lifetime, find its way into the halls of the Metropolitan Museum. It was not until two decades after Noguchi's article that these works were embraced by the Met and that others, sent off to the tombs of the Museum of Natural History, were brought back to the Met to become seminal works in what is now known as the Michael Rockefeller Wing of the Metropolitan Museum of Art. Many who have experienced the stunning atmosphere of the Met's addition (Fig. 4)—Vanuatuan slit-gongs against the silhouette of Manhattan—have no doubt wondered about the relativistic character of so much of what passes for "great" art. Yet, oddly, our witnessing the influences of fashion and the effects of time seems always to widen the gulf between those parts of culture with which we are comfortable and those that, at a certain time, appear to us as entirely foreign and otherworldly.

On the surface, it appears that the gulf that separates Western art from so-called primitive art is enormous indeed. A long series of associative steps, it seems, is required to advance from a study of those areas of thought considered most alien to the Western intellectual tra-

FIG. 4.   Vanuatuan slit-gong (New York, Michael Rockefeller Wing, Metropolitan Museum): with the Manhattan skyline outlining the background, the juxtaposition of "primitive" and "modern" is perhaps nowhere more clearly seen than in this display. (Photo: *New York Times Sunday Magazine*)

dition to those areas so deeply entrenched within it. Not so distant are the two enterprises when approached from the vantage of discovery— from constant confrontation with the exotic, the fascination of learning how something that at first seems completely incomprehensible gradually reveals a complex matrix of associations that can be grasped. This sense of confronting the exotic applies, moreover, to the question of why so much contemporary art has focused on reestablishing some contact with things primitive.

What is troubling in this latter association, however, is that while people constantly associate the expressionistic spontaneity of much of the Western art of this century with the material artifacts of non-Western cultures, the former, when looked at anthropologically (that is, from the viewpoint of accepted tradition), often exhausts rather than astonishes. Why do so many people, for example, when viewing Jackson Pollock's *Autumn Rhythm* (Fig. 5) of 1950, still find it difficult, even inaccessible? Perhaps because of the problem of establishing some criteria of evaluation;[1] but perhaps even more because, whether it does so or not, people feel that it purports, as Isaiah Berlin once said of bad metaphysics, to describe through an accepted convention (in this case, painting) something that is alleged to transcend normal experience and to be outside and beyond any kind of analogy with it (1968, 34). "In the last century," as Harold Rosenberg pointed out several years ago in a now-famous article in the *New Yorker*,[2] "it was believed that the exclusion of subject matter (landscapes, people, family scenes, historical episodes, symbols) from painting would disentangle the image on the canvas from literary associations and clear the way for a direct response of the eye to optical data. In becoming more and more abstract, art is supposed to have attained, or have been reduced to, speechlessness. . . . [Yet paradoxically] if a work of today no longer has a verbal correlative, it is because its particular character has been dissolved in a sea of words . . . [in which] the place of literature has been taken by the rhetoric of abstract concepts." "Of itself," Rosenberg continues, "the eye is incapable of breaking into the intellectual system that today distinguishes between objects that are art and those that are not" (1969, 110). Rosenberg argues here that in order to qualify as a member of the art public, one must be willing to learn the new and ever-changing vocabularies and contexts of contemporary theory, to adjust one's intuitions to the rhetoric of abstract concept, to the cant of the initiated. Even though our eyes may suggest to us that a work by Kenneth Noland is a fabric design (Pl. 1),[3] or one by Donald Judd a stack of metal

1. See Kuspit 1979, 125–27, for a brief overview of how critics have fared with Pollock's work.
2. This is an article of which Tom Wolfe made much in *The Painted Word* (1975). For a detailed scholarly argument, see Danto (1964, 1973).
3. See Masheck's discussion of flatness (1976)—of how Albers, for example, thought his paintings might be read as textiles, or how Aldous Huxley did, indeed, read Pollock's *Cathedral* as wallpaper.

FIG. 5.   Jackson Pollock, *Autumn Rhythm* (1950: New York, Metropolitan Museum; George A. Hearn Fund, 1957, no. 163352): though this painting is something of a landmark in the history of modern art, viewers regularly comment on its inaccessibility. (Metropolitan Museum of Art; all rights reserved)

bins (Fig. 6),[4] we would be considered rather unenlightened were we to say so.[5] Yet, year after year, in introductory courses in modern art history instructors confront these same apprehensions. On one occasion a student of mine asked, quite seriously, if the burlap partitions on which works of art were hung in a college gallery were works of art

4. "One could say that if one of Judd's box forms was seen filled with debris, seen placed in an industrial setting, or even merely seen sitting on a street corner, it would not be identified with art. It follows then that understanding and consideration of it as an art work is necessary *a priori* to viewing it in order to 'see' it as a work of art" (Kosuth 1969a, 137).

5. More recently, Judd has encouraged a kind of "literalist" reading of his work by offering titles that affirm rather than deny such impressions. For example, a piece entitled *Armchair* (1984) looks for all the world like a minimal—and most uncomfortable—armchair. As Danto says, "To mistake an artwork for a real object is no great feat when an artwork is the real object one mistakes it for" (1964, 575).

FIG. 6. Donald Judd, *Untitled* (1965): Judd's minimalist boxes and cubes are designed to appear as anti-illusionistic as possible. In having the works fabricated by others, moreover, he distances himself yet farther from them. (Artist's collection)

themselves. Outrageously philistine, some might say, but so very true to the eye.

However, abstraction *per se* is anything but untrue to the eye if it involves a reduction that is also a distillation. Though we readily admit this of caricature, we are often disinclined to invoke the same process when viewing art of a more serious sort. Yet, every time I look at Mark Tobey's *Edge of August* (Pl. 2), for example, I cannot help thinking that what makes it, to my mind, a great painting is the fact that it reminds me of an explosion of pollen filling the atmosphere at the edge of August—that I can, in other words, make contact with the work without engaging in the tedious process of learning a new vocabulary that, as the French philosopher and anthropologist Lucien Lévy-Bruhl pointed out many decades ago, demands "a constant and excessive effort" that tires and repels a reader because "it recalls more or less closely the traditional terms to which a new sense is attributed" (Lévy-Bruhl [1949] 1975, 65). Tobey's painting astonishes, in other words, by simple analogy rather than by—or in addition to—abstract concept, and it is by simple analogy that I am able instantly to locate this image in the realm of the sublime. It astonishes me because, regardless of Tobey's own personal commitment to the abstractions of Buddhism, and regardless of the critical campaign that would chastise one for seeing pollen rather than just real paint, I see that scattered pollen every time I look at the work; I make, in other words, a specific metaphysical connection between experience as I know it and an acknowledgment of something greater. This symbolic character—which I, as viewer, ascribe to the work—is the first important point of contact between Western art history, be it contemporary conceptualism or Baroque revisionism, and what Noguchi referred to as "the arts called primitive."

If, in fact, symbolic associations can be made between contemporary art and the art of alien or exotic traditions, why should there be any problem with Jackson Pollock's equating the performative nature of his technique with the psychic participatory quality of Navajo sandpainting (Pl. 3)? The trouble, perhaps, stems from the sort of reaction that Kenneth Clark had to Roger Fry's glorification of African art—"the art of a people with whom," as Clark says, Fry could have had "no single idea or association in common" (1939, xxv). Though we may, indeed, find Clark's reaction as uncompelling as the assumptions about the primitive that he questions,[6] it is important to remember that the remark does not concern esthetics alone. In fact, it has little to do with whether one likes or dislikes Pollock's work; nor does it have anything to do with our finding it compelling or uncompelling. Rather, it has to do with the question of accessibility, and with our idea of what discovery involves. Even assuming that Pollock, in some obscure way, was led to his canvas by a reaction to the landscape of the American Southwest that was akin to what a Navajo indeed might perceive, one could still easily be troubled by the association for reasons that are not a function of Pollock's point of view as much as they are presuppositions of the Western tradition out of which he emerged.

Yet at the very heart of Western tradition we can see how absolutely contrived is the romantic opposition of neoclassical and primitive. In his "Personification as a Mode of Greek Thought," Webster says that in order to understand something of the character of the ancient Greeks' thinking, one has to realize that, for them, "the world is in some sense personal and that the human mind is a person" (Webster 1954, 16). In other words, a direct metaphysical connection exists—at least in early Greek thought—between one's sense of oneself and one's sense of the visible world. In ancient Greece, a man may even wed a goddess, and mortal women may have offspring by gods. The metaphysical world is, in this view, an extension of the physical man, while the metaphysical itself may be embodied in the physical, even in what we would recognize as the inanimate. At issue here is not simply what used to be called "animism," but an ontology, a system of connectedness by which an individual's awareness of self is predicated on a system of reciprocal exchanges in the visible world. In a universe of relations governed by Mauss's archaic notion of the gift—in which

6. Of course, such assumptions about the crude or direct or responsive character of the primitive are in no way restricted to Fry, but are pervasive in the works of painters and sculptors from Gauguin through Picasso to the present day. While art historians generally trace an active interest in things "primitive" to Gauguin (or, perhaps, Van Gogh, depending on how one defines the term), it is with the supposed "discovery" of African and Oceanic art in 1906 (by Derain, Matisse, Picasso, and Vlaminck)—and, particularly, with Picasso's *Les Demoiselles d'Avignon*—that primitivism proper gets under way. But Picasso's transforming whores into African masks is only slightly less offensive and provincial than Gauguin's use of the terms "primitive" or "savage" to describe artifacts from India, Egypt, or Java. In Romantics from Rousseau onwards, the same tendency is evident, but in our own century we may especially see how the primitive is employed as an anticlassical weapon by writers such as Lawrence.

individuals "know" themselves by actually exchanging with others those objects by which they are "identified"—knowledge can exist in the absence of intellectualism, since much of what is worth knowing is quite literally self-evident. The self, in other words, becomes evident through a visible demonstration of its connectedness.

For us, of course, the case is quite different. We have an omniscient God (or the intellectual remnants of one), an entity who is all-seeing, absolute, and often intangible. And insofar as the universe is the sum of God's work, it too—though natural—is beyond our complete knowledge. Like the soul encased by a body, the character of nature is not self-evident. In this sense, whether one considers oneself religious or not, this view of the universe demands a set of radical categories in which the world of human knowledge is juxtaposed to the infinite character of the universe, even though that universe is part of a nature that humans share. The very idea of "going out into nature" is, like-wise, by definition and contrast, an exotic enterprise in which self-awareness is predicated upon a need to discover something presently *unseen*, where things that are seen do not provide evidence of the self, where barriers against natural resemblances reassure each of us that we are unique. Indeed, the entire Age of Discovery, the voyages of the fifteenth to the nineteenth century, may, by this line of thought, be understood as an age of self-discovery wherein discovering exotic lands becomes synonymous with discovering the exoticism of the self—with realizing the irreconcilability of one's physical presence to post-Enlightenment metaphysics, if not to Christian Platonism in general.[7]

It is almost impossible, in a sense, for the Platonic thinker—or for that matter any monotheist—to "go out into nature" without a very heavy rucksack indeed. If one considers, for example, the voyages of Captain James Cook in the eighteenth century, one easily senses the problems involved in relating preconceptions to the experience of what is by definition unknown. Not that each of Cook's vessels was neces-sarily a floating microcosm of Western thought or that the question of preparedness was ever looked at in this way by Cook; but, considering

---

7. See Chapter 5 for a discussion of the relationship between "enlightenment" and notions of psychological pollution.

that such expeditions left Europe each time with an anticipation of confronting the unknown, one can readily imagine the difficulties inherent in having to decide, in advance, what one's criteria might be for representing something of which, at present, one has no experience—that is, for apprehending the exotic. When Joseph Banks was charged by the Royal Society to find illustrators for Cook's first voyage to the Pacific in 1768, he resolved the problem as both the scientist and the gentleman that he was. He would have one illustrator, Sidney Parkinson, provide faithful copies of plants and animals (Fig. 7), and another artist, Alexander Buchan, provide him with pictures of savages and scenery that would delight his friends back home (Pl. 4). In order to have a full experience of the exotic, in other words, Banks would have to satisfy both the needs of science and those of the Grand Tour, so that when Buchan suddenly died on the voyage, Banks wrote in his *Journal*, "His loss to me is irretrievable. . . . My airy dreams of entertaining my friends in England with the scenes that I see here have vanished" (1896, 79). Interestingly, this problem was worked out on Cook's second voyage. As it happened, there was a keen interest in atmospheric studies among the scientists on board—a situation that gave the ship's painter, William Hodges, a unique opportunity to attempt the reconciliation of scientific description and the sensations that would satisfy the gentlemen of the Grand Tour. Clearly, it is no coincidence that the challenge of providing a unified view of the atmosphere for both science and pleasure led Hodges to be the first to express the European vision of the South Pacific in a unified statement (Pl. 5); however, Hodges' *atmospheric* paintings also point to just how distanced was the portrayal of simple forms to the English conception of the totality of nature. Despite, for example, what in art-historical terms is the originality of the paintings of William Turner, one must surely accept that some measure of their immense popularity stems from their evocation of a natural world in whose nebulous monumentality characters dissolve (Pl. 6). In such "atmospheric" painting, objects become spiritual in every sense. They even become intangible. The lack of concrete symbols, and especially of human forms, in both Turner and Pollock does indeed make the environments they wished to explore intensely exotic—a result for which they cannot be faulted, for theirs are the presuppositions of an entire cultural mode of thought about human iden-

FIG. 7.   Sidney Parkinson, *Patagonian Penguin*: Parkinson's drawing was engraved and published in the *Philosophical Transactions* for 1768; his skill at depicting both flora and fauna resulted in his being selected as an illustrator on Cook's first and second voyages.

tity and its relation to the physical world: about, that is, how the *self* equals *the absence of connectedness*.

II. AVULSION

Implicit in the overwhelmingly atmospheric painting of Hodges (or Turner), in other words, is a covert thesis on the nature of physicality, and, by extension, a reflection on the Platonic idea of the human body.[8] In the contemporary setting, art cannot be referential (or, at least, innovative art cannot be so), because "things" are distinguished by the *absence* of connectedness; the more they *look like* something else, the less they are themselves. Art becomes enslaved to an exaggerated individualism; today's Jackson Pollocks remain trapped in self-reference.[9]

For the Navajo, to whom Pollock looked for a kindred sensibility, nature is not—and cannot be—exotic; humans are truly a part of nature, but they are so because the world does not exist if it is not, quite literally, spoken by them. The Navajo blanket (Fig. 8) is woven because, in the weaving of it, a stable relationship between words and objects is certified. As with the checkered cloth among the Dogon of Mali (Fig. 9), the words are spoken into the blanket by women as they weave. The blanket that covers the body *is* the Word, for, as the Dogon themselves say, "to be naked is to be speechless" (Griaule [1948] 1965, 82). As Gary Witherspoon points out in *Language and Art in the Navajo Universe*: "Beauty is not 'out there' in things to be perceived by the perceptive and appreciative viewer; it is a creation of thought. The Navajo experience beauty primarily through expression and creation, not through perception and preservation. Beauty is not so much a perceptual experience as it is a conceptual one" (Witherspoon 1977, 151). In

8. This is not the place to discuss Platonic notions of the human body-image, but the point can be easily made by recalling a famous incident that occurred to the missionary and ethnologist Maurice Leenhardt in New Caledonia. Asked whether he finally understood the Christian concept of the soul, one of Leenhardt's disciples replied, "No, Reverend Leenhardt, it was the idea of the body that you brought to us; we have always known the soul" (Leenhardt 1970, 195).

9. This radical tendency had already reached its absolute statement in Duchamp's notion of the intelligent artist as one who has found a way to get away from influences. But self-reference becomes completely problematic with minimalism, and especially in Judd's informed reductionism, in which "wholeness" is synonymous with a kind of separateness—a wished-for clarity that has led some critics (Fried [1967], for example) to accuse him of an overly contrived and degenerate theatricality.

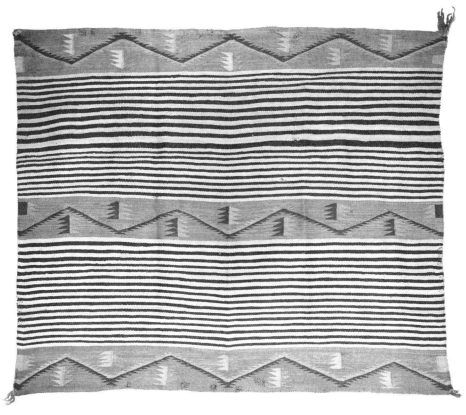

FIG. 8.   Navajo zone-woven blanket: for the traditional Navajo weaver, beauty is realized more through the creative activity of weaving than through the material artifact resulting from such activity. (Photo courtesy Museum of the American Indian, Heye Foundation, no. 29972)

FIG. 9. Dogon priest wearing checkerboard cloth (Mali): for the Dogon, the checkerboard is a fundamental pattern that represents a wide range of symbolic activities. (From Griaule [1948] 1965, pl. IVa)

the third and fourth verses of the Navajo "Beginning of the World Song," one hears: "The earth will be, from the very beginning I have thought it. The mountains will be, from the very beginning I have thought it. The earth will be, from ancient times I speak it. The mountains will be, from ancient times I speak it" (ibid., 19). The world, we see, is thought into existence, and consummated through what we would call "art."

Such egocentricity, we might argue, is not at all different from the proclamations of artists and art critics in the West; yet on at least one important level the Navajo view is completely different, and that is on the level of symbols and on the role that concrete symbols play in the Navajos' view of themselves.[10] For them, not only is all human activity

10. Indeed, one might even argue that the concept of egocentricity has no meaning here at all; for, within such a continuous symbolic framework, even the most grandiose personal statement can contain a shared symbolic vocabulary. When a Kwakiutl chief, for example, destroys his enormous wealth in order to intimidate an exchange partner in a potlatch, what we recognize as a supremely egotistical gesture may also be what

symbolic, but symbols even antedate the first human beings; thought
is not the originator of symbols, but symbols exist before thought.
They are primordial, since humans, according to the Navajo, cannot
think without symbols.[11] As a consequence of this relationship, nature
exists not as an intangible abstraction, but as a platform on which
preexisting symbols are given life through man—a process in which
form is given meaning by, and *only* by, the enactment and reenactment
of symbolically meaningful events: that is, of artistic creation. It is
here, precisely, that the Navajo view parts ways with a neoclassicism
in which all of the great ideas have already surfaced within a tradition
of which we are a part. Unlike the neoclassicist, who is constantly
struggling to recapture something distant, the Navajo would cease to
maintain a natural state of ongoing beauty[12] were they not to perpetuate the symbols that only they can give life to, that only they can make
surface through "artistic" creation. Art, in other words, is all around
man because the symbols can be realized only through him. Nature is
not exotic and nonhuman; it is symbolic and entirely of man. The Navajo, then, live closer to nature, as we say, but they do so because nature is in and of them. With respect to humans, nature is not defined
as antithetical to personhood, as a category so alien that humans—as
in so many "nature" photographs (Fig. 10)—are eliminated from our
conception of what is natural; likewise, art is, for the Navajo, not a way
to express individual unity so much as it is a vehicle for stressing the
unity of all things. Art, creation, is what holds the universe together,
not what distinguishes individuals within a culture.[13]

Mauss called a "total prestation"—i.e., a complete gesture of group identity. Like all
culture heroes, in other words, the chief is merely the focus for demonstrating the capacity for all members of the group that he literally "re-presents" to refrain from reciprocal activity, to resist making contact, by withholding those objects to which all members are "connected" and by which, therefore, they may be "known."

11. As Vernant points out in a yet-unpublished paper ("The Private Man inside the
City-State," 1986), the case was quite similar in Classical Greece. There, self-consciousness was not reflexive; for Greeks, existence was "prior to the consciousness of
existing." Thus, the assumption that reflexivity is necessarily universal, or even viable
as an anthropological technique for cross-cultural analysis, is at least methodologically
naive, if not thoroughly ethnocentric.

12. The idea of perpetuating a state of ongoing beauty is emphasized, Witherspoon
argues, by the Navajo focus on the notion that beauty is something that must be continually restored (1977, 13–46).

13. If art, as a symbolic integration, is "creative," yet the converse may also be argued—namely, that art, as a separating exercise, is destructive. The best proof of this
comes not from the exotic but from within Western tradition, and particularly in contemporary art's obsession with entropy.

FIG. 10.   Carleton E. Watkins, *Mirror View of El Capitan, Yosemite, No. 38* (ca. 1866): clear indication of the isolation of people from nature may be seen in the genre of "nature" photography, in which images of people rarely figure. (Courtesy Christian A. Johnson Gallery, Middlebury College)

What, then, happens to the individual? What is the role of the individual Navajo or Dogon artist? Certainly, this is a complicated question, for in the contemporary West we so much emphasize the
unique—even unusual—nature of artistic genius (or scientific genius,
or, for that matter, any kind of individual achievement) that we hardly
think of artists as people who reaffirm the basic ideas upon which our
society is based. Our focus is, moreover, so fixed on the individual that
we find it hard to disengage ourselves from questions concerning personal motives and goals. We see artists less as representatives of all of
us than as people out for themselves. Imagine artists as people who
reaffirm the basic ideas upon which our society is based: could contemporary Westerners sustain such a notion? For us, artists are extreme examples of the concept of the individual—individuals who are juxtaposed to a group. Here, the controversial exhibition on primitivism at
the Museum of Modern Art in 1984—where Western "affinities" were
signed and non-Western ones anonymous—provides us with our best
example of just how antithetical our notion of art is to those "analo-
gous" forms that are commonly called primitive.[14]

When we return, then, to the complex issue of why the avant-garde
has taken an interest in so-called primitive art, the answers that present
themselves are, in fact, not so complex. One might argue that the affinities between the modern and the primitive are primordial, based on
the understanding of common archetypal themes. But such an answer
would deprive modern art of the sense of unique invention upon which
it is predicated and upon which our definition of the avant-garde is
based; it would also particularly offend our commitment to seeing both
artists and artworks as unique (avulsed) entities. How disappointing to
think that all our assumptions about genius, originality, and uniqueness had actually not resulted in anything "new." Surely this view cannot be maintained. There is, however, another answer that seems far
more tenable, and it has to do with the collapse of the radical thesis
upon which the avant-garde is based.

The history of what occurred in the art world of the 1940s and 1950s

14. For the most deeply critical review of the Museum of Modern Art exhibition
from both an anthropological and a historical point of view, see McEvilley 1984. See also
Rubin's and Varnedoe's rejoinders, and McEvilley's counterresponse, in *Artforum* (23[6]
[1985], 42–51). For a sampling of reactions to the show, see Bibliography.

in the United States is well documented, but what the effects of that period were for the avant-garde is only partly understood. The idea that a picture was not a window onto another reality had been in the air for some time, but it took Clement Greenberg to reduce this notion to a commandment. A painting, according to Greenberg, was a flat surface that, if "true" unto itself, should not deny that fact by offering an illusion of space. Forget illusionism and forget the idea that art had anything to do with manipulating known images: an interesting thought, but a photograph is paper and emulsion; a radio, wires and plastic; and so on.[15] The question, therefore, that must be asked is not What does truth to materials mean? but Why this focus on the character of materials at all? Furthermore, what, in a metaphysical sense, is being suggested about who artists are in our culture by such a narrow and concrete focus on the material world?

The question of why one should focus on the character of materials is the easier one to address, for it surfaced repeatedly throughout the 1970s and 1980s. Part of the answer certainly resides in the consequences of reducing all objects to commodities—which, of course, the cultural rejection of connectedness necessitates: the idea that no specific "thing" can have inalienable content, that is, finally removes our ontological awareness from the realm of the potlatches and *kula* exchanges that defined for Mauss the total prestation.[16] If what we desire is a purity of that material commodity called art, then we should, as Husserl once said about phenomenology, get back to the things themselves.[17] For American artists at midcentury a concern with things themselves resulted in an obsession with "flatness" and ultimately the esthetics of minimalism—the object depersonalized, truly the "coolest" of all art forms. Donald Judd's elegant metal bins are cool, but

15. Fried employed Greenberg's observation that virtually anything may be readable as art—"a door, a table, or a blank sheet of paper"—to argue that the minimalists (or the objective "literalists," as he called them) had so much focused on context and human proportion that their works constituted a kind of covert, theatrical anthropomorphism (Fried 1967, 15ff.), precisely the thing that minimalists, like Judd, intended to work against (ibid., 12).

16. Mauss's notion of a "total prestation" refers to archaic forms of exchange involving a complete range of social activities. Total prestations are, as Cunnison observes, "at the same time economic, juridical, moral, aesthetic, religious, mythological, and socio-morphological phenomena" (in Mauss 1967, vii). For a discussion of how total prestations affect inalienable content, see Weiner 1983, 1985.

17. See, especially, Husserl's *Logische Untersuchungen* ([1900–1901] 1975).

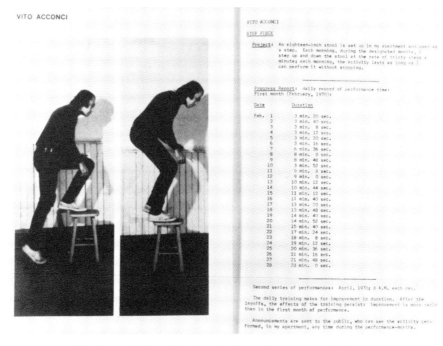

FIG. 11.   Vito Acconci, *Step Piece* (1970): Acconci steps up and down on a stool during a designated performance period. His audience is invited to view this performance art in his apartment. (By permission of Arthur H. Minters, Inc.; photo: Kathy Dillon)

actually not so cold as a single pencil line drawn around the circumference of a New York gallery, or a "performance" (Fig. 11) in which the artist purports to have entirely abandoned traditional art "objects." To warm ourselves up to these objective (or "deobjectifying") statements we need to know two things: first, that the works are being carried out in a legitimized context (art gallery or museum, or in an anonymous public space that becomes legitimized in the art-magazine article that will follow); and second, the name of the artist.[18] Normally, when attention is drawn to these two aspects of the modern art world,

18. "These days one might not be aware he was on artistic terrain without an artistic theory to tell him so" (Danto 1964, 572). And it is precisely this fabrication of artistic terrain—of context—that leads Fried to label minimalist sculpture "theatrical" (cf. n. 15, above).

it is done with the intention of discrediting the capacity of artists to live up to the bohemian ethic of antisocialism—to suggest that, after all, they are completely dependent upon an art establishment for contextualization. However, from an anthropological point of view, what is far more significant is the fact that both the legitimized context and the attention to self are structurally necessary if what one sets out to do is to make the strongest statement possible—the complete avulsion—concerning the radical opposition of self and other. A focus on the independent character of art, or on its objectivity (in the intellectual sense of being "other"), must involve an equally radical focus on the self and a context within which the radical categories of self and other can be explored either by conflating them or by opposing them.

Robert Smithson's mock "tour" of the monuments of Passaic, New Jersey (in which the artist visits and photographs storm drains and sandboxes), focuses specifically on this contextualizing process. But combine the dissolution of visual connectedness with the perpetuation of the idea that "art" has "meaning"—even of the most attenuated sort—and the result is not only a condition that moves from "creation" to "entropy," but one in which the deobjectified artwork moves from a concern with spaces that contextualize meaning either to meanings that occur in nonspaces or to artists as specific people. Smithson's nonsite, in which what can be "localized" occurs only at the periphery of an artistically designated "space," is the final statement in the dissolution of the object. All that remains is the dissolution of the artist himself.

III. "NAMING"; OR, DEATH BY ART

Of self and context, the latter, it seems, is more interesting anthropologically, because it functions as an indicator of how social institutions are utilized to define, establish, and renew socially sanctioned categories of thought. Yet the juxtaposition does not hold when the very relationship of these two categories is what is being questioned. Indeed, it is precisely in analyzing the category of "artist" that we run head-on into the real complexities of this problem and are confronted by its significance as commentary on contemporary culture. Here it is senseless to adopt a nostalgic attitude about the demise of an avant-

garde made up of unsocialized wildmen, for in fact obsolescence is
built into the category, if not an exactly planned part of it. What we
learn about affect in the modern context, perhaps, indicates most tell-
ingly the validity of this thesis; for the idea that one has to return two
or three or four or a dozen times to that gallery with its single line to
"understand" the magnitude of what is going on[19] is really only a natural extension of a problem that began when the nineteenth-century
French art-critical establishment took a leave of absence as the bastion
of public opinion. In so doing, it emphatically stated that affective experience, at least so far as art was concerned, would no longer be coextensive with other sorts of experience; rather, art would function only
as an independent category, a special domain into which the public
would venture like so many carousers participating in a Shrovetide
celebration. Here the artists become the wildmen who appear periodically from the bohemian wood to bring messages spoken in a language that reveals both nonsense and profound secret knowledge.
They are guides through what for all the world looks like a rite of passage, and their power prevails only within the affective domain of the
festival, within the walls of the gallery or the pages of a magazine. This
special focus for artistic meaning may, indeed, strike us as a radical
anticlassicism; but it also reinforces just how classically minded we are
outside the festival or the gallery door, and in so doing suggests to us
that meaning is offered only to those who consciously devote themselves to this new cult, who are willing to subject themselves to its ritual transformations.

Like the festival, the gallery controls affect. Affective experience occurring in a nonartistic realm lacks character and value; the contemporary performances that occur in so-called public spaces but are only
"realized" on the pages of an acceptable art magazine are covertly
preaching the gospel that affect experienced under "normal" circumstances is without meaning and for the simple-minded, or, worse yet,

19. This dilemma was, itself, elevated into an artistic experience through the notion
of Anti-Art, an art that, according to Battcock, "must not only be difficult to accept as
art, but . . . *must be unacceptable as art.* The assumption is that only the work that is unacceptable is capable of forcing a readjustment, a change, a disruption, a revolution of
the capacities and faculties that ultimately determine the meaning and effectiveness for
the individual of all information received" (Battcock 1969, 18). See Meyer 1973 for a
commentary; see also Kosuth 1969a.

that the translation of art's reflexivity and self-consciousness out of its own sphere gives rise to a variety of social psychoses. The individual who can truly not distinguish Donald Judd's artworks from shipping crates or dustbins is one, indeed, who is very much in trouble.

There is, of course, nothing prohibiting the artist from continuing to play the role of wildman or alien seer; the problem comes when society moves in the direction of civilizing this Tarzan of the Apes—when we try to merge the desire for individual discovery and the romantic passion for the socially disenfranchised with an art that is clearly and emphatically tamed and institutionalized, when the avant-garde moves out of the festival context and into one that looks suspiciously normative. What then is the artist to do?

Begin by trying to be a part of the establishment while simultaneously denying that what you are doing has anything to do with what has been done before. The natural result, of course, is a situation wherein one denies oneself while simultaneously propagating an "artistic" persona. "I am driven to create; it all happens spontaneously, subconsciously," artists used to say. And today, though the romanticism has been quelled, artists still call themselves such and band together in the interest of what passes for innovative thinking and the right to be called a creator. This is not egomania; quite the opposite. It is unintended self-sacrifice in the name of the cult of the individual. What is extraordinary, in other words, is not how radical artists can be, but how conservative is their sense of the artist's persona. Ultimately, it is this conservativism that kills the avant-garde, because it necessitates a position that, by definition, lacks the strength of its own conviction.

So strong is their devotion to individualism that artists have, in the name of body art, the objectively "truest" of all art,[20] committed suicide by treating their own bodies as so much modeling clay.[21] For all

20. After all, it is only the body of which we have both objective and subjective knowledge.

21. Rudolf Schwarzkogler cutting himself to pieces in 1969 is perhaps the most ghastly example, though there were other, equally troubling "performances," many of which became legitimized as "art" through their being either performed in galleries or shown to the public via the photo essays that legitimized them as art. Artists shot, stabbed, and bit themselves into fame, or had others hang them up on hooks. The self-abuse was certainly not new; but the fact that it became eagerly embraced by galleries and museums certainly was.

this radical behavior, what lives on is not the individual performer, but a name that is added to the long list of heroes of the institution appearing on a new kind of monument, one that glorifies the institution through self-sacrifice. Here rituals do not—as do rituals in the "primitive" cultures they emulate—result in a new name, a new change of status, a transition from "art" to something else, but a repetition of the same name by which they entered into what was meant to have been a transformational event. Worse yet is that, in participating in this new religion of sacrifice, artists have also robbed themselves of the capacity for avant-garde activity and for the changes it promises, since the precondition of ritual transformation is an acceptance of the fact that, in being transformed, one's identity—one's social role—must change irrevocably. In the end, the theories that govern their radical acts—the flatness, minimalism, performance, and the rest—are not their own inventions; rather, they come down to them as part of an institutional dogma. If one asks oneself how many artists of the past thirty years are willing to—or can—articulate that canon, or how many artists are interested in working anonymously, one readily senses how bohemia was born and died decades ago, how artists have sacrificed who they are for how they are known.[22] Art cannot be coextensive with creativity at large, because the single constant in what defines art in any postmodern sense is its capacity to make one aware of oneself, to be marked or named, to be made distinct. In fact, this process of naming or marking is so pervasive within the Western metaphysical framework that anonymity—a real option for the avant-garde—is per-

22. Popper points out how even the attempts to subvert artistic privilege and to deny art as a distinctive activity have resulted in yet more individualism and narcissism: "If we look closely at Non-art and, in particular, at Conceptual art in the most restricted sense of the term, we find that they represent the attempt to stress art's self-reflexive potentiality to the exclusion of the actual fabrication of the art work. . . . Since the art object is succeeded by the artistic event or in the last resort by the presence and body of the artist himself, it becomes possible for the art market to recuperate the new forms" (1975, 269). Even though artists such as Joseph Kosuth try to abolish all intermediaries, "making the art idea coincide with the creative process" (ibid.), the end result is the maintenance of traditional hierarchies and the individualism of the artists. Kosuth's continual self-reference as being the first to do such-and-such, as well as his "recuperation" (through naming) of the supposedly "anonymous" efforts of other artists, shows how inescapable is the art world's domain of reference. It is not art unless someone calls it art, artists such as Ad Reinhardt claim. Art is only art by the naming; not naming is not artistic.

ceived as not only improbable but undesirable.[23] And, even in those cases where anonymity is a specific focus for artistic endeavor,[24] the art world eventually recuperates through naming the individual and his or her work. Art, in other words, is not a part of anonymous individual action, and artists who work anonymously (or people who adopt anonymous roles) are dangerous confidence-men, who need to be rooted out of culture as we know it.

To get a sense of how great a challenge anonymity is to contemporary notions of performance and culture, one need only imagine an anonymous performance scenario. Imagine if you were to be told, for example, about a group of artists who, in a radical effort to dissolve tradition and escape established performance frameworks, have begun to work completely anonymously; perhaps they do not even share among themselves the actual identity of the creator of a particular artwork. After being sworn to secrecy, you are informed that the arrangement of furniture in the very room in which you are sitting—the books and magazines, the carpet, the lighting—is all part of an elaborate performance piece. This is not a performance piece in the sense, as described by Goffman, of putting on fronts for social events (stages, as it were), but a performance piece in which everything, down to the scratches on the furniture or the smudges on the walls, is part of a carefully orchestrated bit of conceptual art in which the avant-garde have sought the limits of experience by devoting extraordinary attention to the staging of this event without self-consciously interrupting the purity of the experience by demanding our recognition or applause. Then, let us suppose, these performance artists assume roles as, say, janitors, secretaries, students, administrators, and professors.[25] To

23. One need only consider how many non-Western works of art are created anonymously to see just how culture-specific this process is.

24. Daniel Buren's efforts to "avoid uniqueness" by being a "producer" rather than a "creator" are probably the best examples of working toward anonymity. However, his efforts are yet more markedly in the direction of a kind of affective neutrality and, furthermore, so anti-illusionistic that the inevitable result of being aware of his activities, or of participating in them, is more self-reflexive individuation, and ultimately more attention to Buren. Kosuth has a "secret exhibition," *15 People Present Their Favorite Book* (which he then later writes about). And On Kawara (whose work Kosuth calls "extremely private") travels around the world continuously, doing such things as mailing to a well-known critic daily postcards of the time he awakes each morning.

25. "Ah," you may say, "so everyone becomes an artist." Far from it. When the av-

most of us, performance carried to this point is absurd, if not quite mad—an imitation of mental illness, if not a confidence trick. However, what we have done is construct not just an absurd parody, but a natural extension of avant-garde activity, a means by which art returns from its intellectual atrophy to discover that transformation can have meaning only if we accept the possibility of an irrevocable change in identity. In primitivism we parody the attention to detail and to ritual meaning that anthropologists so often discover in other cultures, while we fear the connectedness that might lead us to be creatively transformed.

It should not appear strange, then, that the final agenda of the avant-garde less concerns anonymous, "connected" activity than it does an attempt to confiscate the artifacts of the exotic, to domesticate, define, and institutionalize them, to mark them with our names rather than let ourselves be transformed by them. The plan is a bit delicate, because the exotic must be shown to be legitimately connected to our social institutions and artistic concerns, yet also, somehow, external (if not inferior) to them. Just how pervasive are the canonizing tendencies by which we launder the primitive into "art," and how absolutely this canonizing is tied to the radical individualism of the cult of "art," is most clearly and blatantly seen in the comparison of so-called primitive art to an art that qualifies as "modern" (Fig. 12). For all the formal similarities so frequently attended to, there exists one absolute and unresolved opposition—that being, as I have indicated, that each and every one of our modern works of art bears the name of its creator, while virtually none of those so-called primitive works carries such a hallmark. Naturally, we can—if we look for them—find cases in which artists are individually recognized and rewarded as such within exotic cultural contexts; but the point is that these are not the cases that provide us with what we understand by the word "primitive."

One senses that it is precisely because of the resistance of so-called primitive art to the cult of the individual that it has—as did other proclivities in the 1960s, 1970s, and 1980s—become the focus of artistic

---

erage Hindu, for example, hands one a gift with the right hand rather than the left, he or she is not necessarily involved in a symbolic act. But if, in fact, one wishes the action to have a special meaning, it may carry as much symbolic or esthetic weight as one feels is appropriate to the intensity of the event.

FIG. 12. Cover of vol. 1 of *"Primitivism" in 20th Century Art*,
a two-volume work edited by William Rubin (1984) and published in conjunction with the exhibition so titled (New York,
The Museum of Modern Art, © 1984): this exhibition attempted to demonstrate affinities in spirit between so-called
primitive artists and major figures in twentieth-century art.
Much of the criticism of the show focused on the museum's
coopting of non-Western art in the interest of expanding the
domain of Western artistic genius.

concern. Perhaps this is so; but what is far more important is the question of just what kind of metaphysics has led to the radical individualization of artists that is also the bohemians' radical psychological isolation and, finally, their victimization. Surely, one cannot blame a handful of artists and critics for a crime belonging to society at large. Translated into metaphysics, "flatness"—the desymbolization of art—clearly is the standard of a post-Enlightenment Platonism, if not a radical monotheism. Like the Islamic prohibition against graven images, flatness is based upon the Platonic premise that illusions are not in any sense "real" and that imitators, as Emerson would have it, are doomed to mediocrity. The radical anti-illusionism of things falling flat, as it were, is also a radical individualism—one that has its origin in a monotheistic view of illusion. Illusions are false; they are superficial and, moreover, unnecessary to any all-seeing, omniscient deity. What we see in the antiobjectivism of modern art is traditional Judaeo-Christian metaphysics in the guise of avant-garde theory.

Imagine applying the criterion of "flatness" to a piece of checkered cloth made by the Dogon. No window onto anything, we say, just light and dark squares. Of course, we *can* appreciate it this way, especially so long as we are unwilling to entertain anything that we ourselves have not instigated or that we do not already know. However, for the Dogon, this simple pattern can stand for a complex matrix of images; it represents, according to Griaule ([1948] 1965, 111):

> the pall which covers the dead, with its eight strips of black and white squares representing the multiplication of the eight [ancestral] families; the facade of the large house with its eighty niches, home of the ancestors; the cultivated fields, patterned like the pall; the village with streets like seams, and more generally all regions inhabited, cleared or exploited by men.

"So what?" we might say. "It is still a checkered cloth that I appreciate as a work of art because of its unique features—formal or otherwise. I do not need to know a thing about its symbolic complexity in order to appreciate it as a work of art." This view is, of course, justifiable and adequate from an entirely egocentric—or ethnocentric—point of view; quite acceptable, also, if one is not troubled by photographs in the Museum of Modern Art of a man carving himself to bits

FIG. 13. Jackson Pollock at work in his studio: Pollock hoped that the participatory nature of his style would in some way echo the psychic participatory character of Navajo sandpainting. (Photo: Hans Namuth)

in the name of art, or of someone crucified upon a Volkswagen. If what one has in mind is a rather pedestrian glorification of our favorite Judaeo-Christian martyrs for personhood, then self-sacrifice to a traditional notion of identity will do very nicely indeed. In fact, one need go no farther than Pollock's first equation of his own work with the Navajo shaman's to see the incipient machinations of a self working hard at being its own worst enemy (Fig. 13).

IV. SO MANY MOTHERS
OF INVENTION

But "flatness" means nothing to those for whom a world populated by artworks that purport to be unlike anything else also means nothing. To those of us who find a checkerboard pattern by Carl Andre (Fig.

FIG. 14.   Carl Andre, *Copper-Aluminum Plain* (1969): by the late 1960s mini-malism had pushed its program of nonrepresentational art to the limits. Without the framework of a gallery with its lighting and labels, viewers were frequently incapable of isolating what constituted a particular work of art. One result was a further mystification of the artist's persona. (William J. Hokin collection)

14) unlike anything else "never done before, absolutely unique," the Dogon respond by affirming that a work of art can have meaning only with respect to images that are already known, that are primordial. Theirs is a visual metaphysics of identity and affirmation. Because symbols are the basis of shared categories, they have a life that is not only independent but necessary; and because they are necessary, there exists a natural proclivity on the part of humankind to find those sym-bols in every aspect of life. Theirs is a metaphysics of affirmation rather than one of negation, dissection, and separation. We need not belabor the point: what would give the Dogon pleasure in flatness would be its potential for affirming illusion, for establishing a complex identity, not its capacity to liberate itself from anything currently known or to state that flatness itself is all that can be known.

If what we want to do in looking at the art of another tradition is to isolate those cases where so-called primitive artists discriminate be-tween good and bad art on esthetic terms that are, in theory, much the same as the kind we might apply when we say that Mary is a better artist than John (or Mary is more creative than John, or Mary is more radical than John), then—if we look hard enough—we will find an example here and there in which the art of some exotic or alien culture appears to fit the notion we have about what art is. A good example of such a comparison occurs when one studies the material culture of the Yoruba of Nigeria.[26] Among the Yoruba it is not at all uncommon for people to praise or criticize a work on formal grounds and then decide that one piece is superior to another because it is better or more thought-provoking. Nor is it, moreover, uncommon for the Yoruba to call attention to the individual creator of the piece, the "artist." However, a closer look at Yoruba art provides examples that lead us to suspect that even this correlation is not as neat as it at first appears, and that, indeed, our desire for discovering "individuated" artists and "art" objects in other cultural contexts may be only the result of an effort to assimilate within our artistic canons what would otherwise be another unfamiliar mode of thought.

Take, for example, the class of objects known as *ibeji* ("twin" figures; see Fig. 15). A look at several of these figures provides us with a category of images coherent enough that an art historian, say, might feel quite comfortable in looking at them from a formal point of view and then deciding that one was better "art" than the other. However, a Yoruba discriminating among *ibeji* does not do so as the disinterested critic of this kind of Yoruba art. In fact, a woman extolling the qualities of her collection of *ibeji* most likely does so because she is their mother. They are for her the living incarnations of her dead twins: for the Yoruba, that is, twins, living or deceased, are a very powerful thing; because they are double, they have more—perhaps too much—of what makes each of the rest of us human. When any twin dies, it puts out of balance a necessary relationship that it shared with its other half; and in order to see that balance maintained, the mother will carry these *ibeji* with her, will honor them on feasts and birthdays, and will even offer little bits of food so that the dead twin, passed on to another level of existence, will not go hungry and become angered. Surely, this is not the stuff of "art" as we know it.

26. See, for example, the work of Thompson (1968, 1973).

FIG. 15.   Yoruba *ibeji* ("twin") figures: though qualitative considerations are central to Yoruba esthetics, these objects serve a specific cosmological function that subordinates their role as focal points for abstract contemplation or measures of good taste. (Photo: Eugene R. Prince, from Daniel B. Biebuyck, *Tradition and Creativity in Tribal Art* [Berkeley and Los Angeles, 1969; rpt. 1973], pl. 77)

To understand what the *ibeji* might mean, we must venture into the far more complex domain where art becomes part of religion and part of what makes a society. Such a directive is not intended to challenge the sense of freedom of expression and interpretation upon which our Western notions of "art" are based. Rather, it is a challenge directed toward our awareness of just how egocentric and unadventurous is our notion of "art," especially when what we do when we set out to look at the art of another culture is to reshape it into a category of thought with which we are comfortable. In this respect our interest in the art of other cultures ought rightly to result in an interest in other modes of thought—even when such modes of thought have the potential to undermine conceptual categories with which we are comfortable. What we should be asking ourselves is not what aspects of other cultures reaffirm all that we already know, but how different ways of dealing with the material world help to suggest to us new and different ways of seeing. If we cannot, in other words, entertain the idea that artists can reaffirm the basic ideas upon which a society—or, at least, social "connectedness"—is based, then we have little to gain that is new by looking at much of so-called primitive art.

Ironically, when we search out the exotic for formal affinities we are, in fact, using art to reaffirm certain basic metaphysical principles upon which our culture is based, even though we conduct our search under the auspices of individual achievement and unique invention, or, perhaps, precisely *because* we do so. Indeed, these *are* our principles. In a way, we are trying to achieve an intellectual balance that is not so different from the sort of metaphysical balance sought out by the Dogon or the Yoruba. The difference is that for us such balance is reflected symbolically not through art but rather in the radical juxtaposition of subject and object, of unique individuals and mass collectives, of artists as single-minded people rather than as communal representatives.

Odd it is that the artist at once reaffirms the metaphysical distinctions upon which our culture is based by declaring his exclusion from the masses. Strange that artists are charged to explore the imaginative capacities of our shared cultural categories but do so by placing their unique names in bold print at the base of each work or within the lines of a verbal description of the so-called nonobjective performance. This contradiction is clearly a terrible burden for artists to bear, but it becomes inevitable the moment we move from a metaphysics concerned with the necessary unity of human experience to one focused on the uniqueness of individual experience. Where other cultures don their funny faces only at certain predesignated times of the year, we wear ours full-time. Our "personhood," in other words, is less achieved through periodic rites of passage, in which the self is regularly redefined; rather, we live in a constant state of self-definition, in which *reflection*, for all that this word means, is not only a desirable state but a moral imperative. When we ask ourselves, therefore, why it is that modern life seems to have removed us from looking at the world from a vantage governed by a desire for symbolic balance, and why it is that we have exempted ourselves from the charge to render that balance visually, the answer is that unity is for us, as Whorf (1956) showed some time ago, a covert category, one that we do not emphasize even if it governs us all the same. Democratic though we may be, we cling to the cult of the individual because it is that cult precisely that assures the continuity of our objective metaphysics.

■   ■   ■

In this first chapter we have seen how the opposition between self and other in the arts is grounded not only in a pervasive Western metaphysical concern with Platonic individuation and "naming," but in the avulsion of individuals from objects in the environment that results from such thinking. Despite a supposed deobjectification of "art" and an attempt to escape the traditional confines of the art world's museums and galleries, the fundamental ontological categories of the fine arts have, it was argued, gone unchallenged and, indeed, largely uncriticized. The consequence of maintaining the traditional categories of "artist" and "artwork" is the perpetuation of the central notion of art as a commodity, not in the materialist sense of the word, but in the Maussian sense—that is, as something lacking symbolic connectedness.

The acute need to define and to understand categories of thought by literally separating them has resulted, moreover, in the isolation—and even the destruction—of individuals and of those ideas that are grounded in a world of familiar associations. Not only are artists being chopped up in this new religion, but the entire postmodern movement so much depends on traditional notions of the person that the process of naming, itself, has gained priority over the activities that define a person's connectedness and ontological status.

In the following chapter, we will see how our insistence on "art" as a distinct category has also contributed to our inability to entertain other modes of thought and, more troubling still, how that insistence has disenabled our efforts at gaining access to other unusual systems of thought that sometimes occur within our midst. In particular, the following chapter focuses on the role of symbolic connectedness in unfamiliar forms of remembering, and on the implications of such unfamiliarity for what might be termed "cultural ecology."

2

Environment for an
Animated Memory

This is a map that will take you somewhere, but when you get there
you won't really know where you are.

                                                    Robert Smithson

I. A POSTMODERN ECOLOGY?

In the autumn of 1971 an exhibition was held at the Hayward Gallery,
in London, of six tanks containing two dozen catfish, in addition to
oysters, lobsters, and shrimp. The artist, Newton Harrison, had
named this work *Portable Fish Farm: Survival Piece 3* (Fig. 16). His plan
was to electrocute and eat the two dozen catfish in public.

Predictably, Harrison's work met resistance from the Royal Society
for the Prevention of Cruelty to Animals and from animal lovers of all
varieties; the Arts Council, under pressure to cancel the killings, decided to censor the electrocution but not prevent it. In the end, the public was spared having to witness Harrison's demonstration of what pollution of the seas would one day necessitate, while some critics
wondered to what extent this demonstration could be called ecological,
let alone artistic. In a review subtitled "Big Fish in a Small Pool," Jonathan Benthall pointed out that while Harrison claimed to have been
concerned with a " 'cycle of production and consumption,' . . . there
was no hint in the presentation of his artefact that he was interested in
the central idea of ecology, which is that of continuity and interdependence of processes" (Benthall 1971, 230). Indeed, the idea of interdependence gave Benthall the opportunity to wonder about the role
played by "an elaborate support system of water-heaters, agitators, sy-
phons, etc., powered by electric current which presumably was generated at one of the big power stations in South London that belch

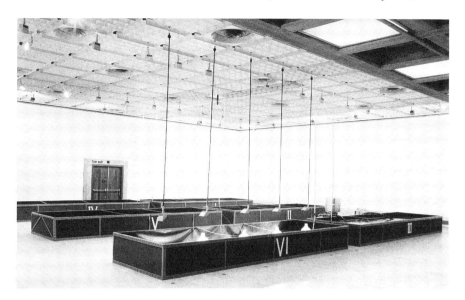

FIG. 16.   Newton Harrison, *Portable Fish Farm: Survival Piece 3* (London, 1971): in an effort to replicate a particular ecological condition, Newton Harrison nourished, electrocuted, and then ate the contents of his fish farm. This statement about what pollution of the seas might one day necessitate drew outcries from a number of humanitarian groups, including the RSPCA. (Photo: John Webb)

smoke into the air" (ibid.). Benthall stopped short of suggesting that Harrison collect and recycle the excrement of the members of the Contemporary Art Society, though he considered it. While finding Harrison's work quite thought-provoking, he wondered whether all the artist's talk of survival was more a reflection on American consumerism and "the economic jungle in which an American artist . . . has to compete" (ibid).

Though *Portable Fish Farm* was an unusual and self-conscious commentary on the relationship between the concerns of artists for art and for the environment, the circumstances surrounding Harrison's piece reflect the many contradictions embodied in what today is meant by the environment, and what a concern for ecology actually means. If Harrison's manner of killing fish is "more humane . . . than the normal techniques of suffocation or percussion, let alone the lingering tortures devised by gentlemen anglers" (ibid.), why should the RSPCA involve itself in such a "hopelessly self-contradictory position" (ibid.)? If Newton Harrison is preoccupied with the rhetoric of survival, why kill fish? And if this kind of art is meant to reflect an awareness of "cycles of production and consumption," why should the piece end at all, let alone at a banquet for other self-conscious performance wallahs?

While the British public and the press labeled the event cruel, the real issue, as Benthall suggests, is one of ritual. In a culture that openly sanctions many forms of violence, what is especially disturbing about such art is the fact that violence has been placed into a context that has more meaning; it has become an integral part of certain shared categories that cannot be limited or contained. Like finding out that one actor has actually hurt another in a staged performance, it is the shock of an event's lack of containment, rather than the facts of what actually occurs, that so unsettles us.

Surprising, then, that for all our abuses of the concept of ritual (as when it is used in biology as a metaphor for meaningless, repetitive behavior), we still desire to protect those things that strike us as ritualistic from the incursions of individuals whom we suspect of disrupting the boundaries between the sacred and the world as we otherwise know it.[1] What bothers us in Newton Harrison's performance, then, is not the fact of death, but its context; even in the face of the most profound kind of transformation, it is the affront to our sense of context that troubles us.

Death may be troubling, but crossing the categorical boundaries that separate normal activities from a ritually charged atmosphere—where even actions identical to those carried out in "normal" space can carry enormous significance—is more troubling still.[2] That we are frequently more disturbed by boundary disruption than by the fact of experience may readily be seen in a converse example, in which a public

----

1. Benthall points to the discomfort we experience with the use of the word "sacrifice" to describe the destruction of animal life in laboratory experiments (1969, 207).

2. I recall once having attended a lecture in which the question of human sacrifice among the Greeks was answered in the negative, since what, it was argued, the Greeks were up to was actually a kind of glorified murder. No one questioned, or in fact seemed much troubled by, the fact that individuals had actually been killed, or, indeed, that it might have been an unnecessary indulgence; what was bothersome was the idea of taking life in this way.

FIG. 17.   Vito Acconci, *Way Station* (Middlebury, Vt., 1983): here Acconci hoped to set up a place of rest for students; instead, the work became the target of vandalism. (Photo: Erik Borg)

becomes upset by learning that what it took unself-consciously to be part of everyday social space was actually part of a symbolic event.

Some years ago the performance artist Vito Acconci was invited to create a permanent structure (his first) for Middlebury College. For that commission he designed his *Way Station*, a decorated metal box somewhat larger than a telephone booth, which students might enter on their cross-campus excursions. Many, at first, thought that what was going up was simply some kind of utility building, an electrical service container or toolshed. But discovering that this was meant to be "art" resulted in an outcry that the landscape was being desecrated and that the natural beauty of the area had been destroyed. Advocates argued that the sidewalks, buildings, heating vents, and the like were even more offensive. Those detractors with a sense of civic duty raised a petition to have the work removed. Others, feeling that they had been duped, responded by using *Way Station* alternatively for golf practice, as a lavatory, and, finally, for firebombing (Fig. 17). While many members of the community were quite disturbed by events surrounding this piece, it became clear that the problem was entirely a categorical one, for so much of what we have come to call environmental art focuses on the boundaries, the connections, between cultural categories—on what we regularly term "ecology"; for, though ecology generally refers to a wide range of environmental relations, relations themselves can be specified only by reference to the boundaries that either connect or separate one thing from the next.

Though there are a great number of instances of environmental art that raise questions of an ecological nature, the social circumstances surrounding such works necessarily make them especially useful in analyzing the concerns of artists relative to those of ecologists, and for studying ontological issues that for us are culture-specific.

II. ONTOLOGY: A WOBBLING AXIS

In an article entitled "Environmental Art: Strategies for Reorientation in Nature" (1985), Nicholas Capasso argues that the common bond of all so-called environmental artists is their desire to reorient humankind within nature. Following arguments popularized in the 1960s and early 1970s,[3] Capasso focuses on the metaphysical displacement that originates in the Judaeo-Christian opposition of man to nature and that is exacerbated by the "constant novelty of experience" (1985, 73) characteristic of modern life. The result for many environmental artists is a situation in which either they attempt to raise an awareness of the ecosystem so as to reform technological society, or they become advocates of an absolute flight from that society, whereby "they strive to start from scratch and recreate the world, a reorientation with nature . . . on the most basic cosmic level" (ibid.). The former type of endeavor is, strictly speaking, the more obviously ecological, because it maintains some fundamental faith in the connectedness of experience, even if that experience is based on assumptions about the relationship between man and nature that are, literally, groundless—that is, that are

---

3. See, for example, Alvin Toffler's *Future Shock* (New York, 1970).

themselves based on a metaphysics of disjunction. But it is the latter type that most clearly states the very problematics of disjunction, because here we see a deliberate attempt to reconnect man and nature. Works such as Nancy Holt's *Sun Tunnels* (Pl. 7), in which a series of concrete cylinders set up in Utah's Great Salt Desert both display various constellations and frame the solstitial sunrises and sunsets,[4] clearly demonstrate how artists hark back to what they understand to have been the fixed axes, the immovable, unwavering points of orientation, that situated preindustrial societies. Here, Neolithic monuments become the focus for a mystification of the natural continuity of preindustrial life, and the work of the artist becomes a "primal gesture of creation, i.e., [of] orientation within chaos" (ibid., 74). Charles Ross's *Star Axis*, in progress since 1974 in the New Mexico desert south of Albuquerque, will one day enable its viewers to situate themselves cosmologically by experiencing the 26,000-year cycle of wobble produced by the earth's axis. Here, the paths of stars will orient us in a space that itself is variable.

Yet the question of whether reorientation is at all possible goes unchallenged. For when the cosmos (within which the individual artist *chooses* his or her new fixed point) is perceived as fundamentally chaotic, there can be no absolute cosmological continuum to make any given choice either inevitable or necessary—except, of course, for each *individual* who claims to find it thus. How many *groups* of people can be said to have been reoriented in a fundamental way by Holt's work will only one day be measured by how many subcultures will be shown to have been centered around this fixed—yet rather arbitrary—point. The archaic sites that many earth artists seek to imitate were, obviously, *shared* environmental points of reference that belonged to a particular set of common cultural categories. Conversely, while today's artists frequently work within the desert, or in a deserted landscape, it is never clear whether the choice of location works more in the interest of showing that the artwork is *theirs*, or whether the location itself stands as a commentary on the disconnectedness of humankind. Capasso says that the desert enables the artist more clearly

---

4. The images of constellations are created on the insides of the tunnels by holes in the cylinders.

FIG. 18*a*.   Christo, *Valley Curtain* (Rifle, Colo., 1970–72): the public success of Christo's work results largely from a carefully executed public relations campaign, including the placation of environmental groups. (Photo:
Harry Shunk; © Christo)

to establish "a fixed point in chaos," to create "gestural marks . . .
upon a uniformly featured, planar . . . landscape" (ibid., 73). But no
one who has actually studied desert ecology would call that landscape
"uniform" or "chaotic." One fears that, in escaping from the visible
distractions of daily life, these works become completely embedded
within the individual artist's experience of that life. In this respect,
Elizabeth Baker is perhaps taking a rocky path when she suggests that
"these works have a complete clarity of impact, unconfused by any

FIG. 18*b*.   *Valley Curtain* (construction). (Photo: Harry Shunk; © Christo)

accidental environmental factors" (1983, 73); for, even though the works have clarity, it is a clarity that coincides with notions of art with which we are already very comfortable: a photograph of *Sun Tunnels* has the same bounded and disconnected clarity as does a piece of sculpture or a color-field painting. There are no societies that have arisen around it in Utah, and the need to photograph it at all has already limited its scope in a way that is most discomforting.

Are we, then, to assume that artists who work "within technology" (whatever this might mean) are more intellectually honest? This view, too, is hardly viable; when Robert Smithson approached a number of strip-mining companies in an effort to transform their environmental wastelands into esthetically meaningful earthworks, his critics cried out that he had become the apologist for the very people who had desecrated the landscape, "hiring himself out to decorate an area of landscape the mining company had exploited" (Auping 1983, 97).

It is, finally, when we look to cases in which artists and environmentalists must coexist within the same landscape that the absurdities abound. Though Christo Javacheff, for example, has often expressed a concern for environmental issues, the proportions of his work and the synthetic materials he employs have consistently raised the ire of environmentalists. His controversial *Running Fence*—an eighteen-foot curtain that extended across twenty-four miles of California and into the sea—was brought to a halt by environmentalists who were concerned about the movements of animals and the extraordinary overuse of the landscape that would result from the work's builders and visiting tourists. After agreeing not to build the fence, as planned, into the sea, the artist did so anyway—a change of heart that resulted in demands that he be prosecuted (ibid., 92–93).

Probably one of Christo's greatest problems stems from his attempts to cooperate with environmentalists and his acceptance of their concerns. His press release prior to the raising of his *Valley Curtain* (Fig. 18a) informs the public that "no tree cutting or terrain clearing is foreseen. Passage of wildlife through the valley and the migratory movements of birds are under study with the objective of avoiding a disturbance of the location's natural ecology" (Javacheff 1973, n.p.). Yet any casual look at the same publication in which his letter is printed will make all too clear how much drilling, digging, pouring of concrete, and moving of earth were necessary to suspend his 200,000-square-foot curtain across a valley in Rifle, Colorado, for twenty-eight hours (Fig. 18b). And while plans called for a conscientious cleanup of the site, purists rightly felt that the area had been permanently transformed.

Though Christo's work may strike us as less than entirely ecological, it in no way compares with that of Michael Heizer, whose *Double Negative* of 1969–71 displaced 240,000 tons of earth with explosives in two Nevada cliffs. Heizer's solution to environmental complaints is much simpler: he buys the places where his work will be created. Indeed, transforming one's own private property is considerably easier than creating works in public places, as was readily seen when Richard Serra created his *Tilted Arc* (Fig. 19) in 1981 in the New York County Courthouse Plaza. In this instance a 73-ton, 120-foot-long, 12-foot-

FIG. 19.   Richard Serra, *Tilted Arc* (New York County Courthouse, 1981):
before its removal in 1989, Serra's work epitomized the ongoing battle between the artist's freedom to express himself and society's freedom of access
to public spaces. (By permission of the Leo Castelli Gallery)

high steel barrier cut through a favorite public place, considerably altering the movement of people within it.[5]

Works like Christo's *Surrounded Island*, in which the artist covered the sea near Miami with pink plastic, can easily cause anxiety among those who would have us keep our hands off nature; yet it is equally interesting to see just what sorts of work are actually promoted by institutions whose job it is to protect the environment. Michael Singer's subtle use of natural materials has brought him support from a number of environmentally focused organizations, including the U.S. Department of the Interior and the Smithsonian Institution (Auping 1983, 99). Under the aegis of an appropriate sponsor, the works of Singer tend to soften the traditional opposition of humans and nature, though other artists, such as Alan Sonfist, may unwittingly point out the absurdity of certain notions of the environment to which many subscribe.

Not far from Washington Square in downtown Manhattan one can see an area of fenced-off shrubs and trees: this is Sonfist's *Time Landscape* (Fig. 20), in which the artist reconstructs what Manhattan must have looked like some centuries ago. Like any other place in New York that is left unattended for more than a day, this fenced-in area regularly becomes a dustbin of paper and plastic waste, and the trees and bushes that are meant to indicate what Manhattan was like are little more than stunted transplants strewn with trash. Were one even able to find a first-growth tree to put within this miserable bit of cyclone fence, the technology does not exist for moving alive anything so majestic; one imagines this entire enclosure transplanted back in time to a primeval Manhattan and senses how pitiful a gesture indeed it is.

Singer's and Sonfist's concerns, therefore, may—despite their uncertainties—still be juxtaposed to Heizer's notion of the artist as a "defiler" (Smithson 1979, 173), where the ego of the artist excises envi-

---

5. According to "Atilt over *Tilting Arc*," a notice in *Artnews*, "A petition signed by nearly a thousand federal office workers accuses the sculpture of 'casting an ominous and threatening shadow not only on we [*sic*] who work here but on the public as well.' Calling the work 'unsuitable for its present location,' the petition states that *Tilted Arc* obstructs access . . . and 'brutally destroys the plaza's vistas and amenities.' A second petition, circulated by employees of the Environmental Protection Agency and containing 300 signatures, complains of disrupted pedestrian traffic and warns of the sculpture's potential as a 'graffiti catcher'" (*Artnews* 80[10] [Dec. 1981] 12).

ronmental concerns completely, where what makes something art is the artist's insisting it is, "when you can convince someone else that it is" (ibid., 178). The problem of self and the environment, like the essential contradictions that are realized in environmental art, has led either to a "revival of archaic sentiment," to quote Smithson (ibid., 175), or to a belief that "there is no need to refer to nature anymore" (ibid., 174) because the landscape is perceived as being coextensive with the gallery; Smithson's "nonsite," which (like language itself) has its center everywhere and its limits nowhere,[6] describes a periphery within which everything is potentially artistic, if only someone (an artist) marks it as such.

Lewis Carroll, as environmental artists realize, had arrived at a similar absurdity long ago, particularly with his *Sylvie and Bruno Concluded*, wherein a German professor describes how, in order to achieve greater accuracy, cartographers expanded their maps, making them larger and larger until they equaled the size of the countries themselves. Since such a map could not be spread out without reducing the world to darkness, the citizens "now use the country itself, as its own map" (Carroll 1939, 557). It is interesting to note that Smithson singles out this very passage as "a parable on the fate of painting since the '50s" (1979, 77). This comparison seems especially valid when one realizes that the other consequence of what Carroll describes is an inability of the actual to be reduced to anything but itself. Or, to view it another way, symbols—that is, reductive representations—become desymbolized by being made actual; there is no correspondence between symbols and the cosmos, because there *are* no symbols that reflect anything approaching an absolute correspondence between microcosmos and macrocosmos.[7] A Platonic representation is, by definition, an aberration, and anything that attempts to reduce something to something else—to make paint and canvas imitate what they are not—is necessarily defective. This is certainly the Judaeo-Christian naming itself the avant-garde.

Carrying this notion to its logical conclusion, one literally *is* reduced

6. On language as an infinite museum, see Smithson's "A Museum of Language in the Vicinity of Art" (1979, 67–78, esp. 67).

7. Indeed, symbols are not even possible in Carroll's construct, because there exist no correspondences upon which symbol making or symbol apprehending might rely.

FIG. 20*a*. Alan Sonfist, *Time Landscape* (New York, 1965–): this fenced-off area of Manhattan is meant to evoke a sense of what the island might have looked like before colonization. Good fencing keeps out some trash and most street people. (Photo: author)

FIG. 20*b*.   Alan Sonfist, *Time Landscape* (side view). (Photo: author)

to speechlessness, since any kind of relativity of things within the world is an assault on the distinctive character of any particular thing.[8] It is precisely this argument against connectedness that accounts for the popularity of entropy among postmodernists, the gradual atrophying of all things, and for the oddly cogent argument that one sign of a highly developed culture is its capacity to sustain "meaningless" activity.[9] Here, the codification of cultural canons leads to a tyranny of meaning, if not its complete absence; like the world of things all of which are irreducible, the sign of high culture is its capacity to be cosmopolitan, to realize that culture too is infinitely divisible. Every man is an island, and every island a separate nation.

A logical consequence of this view is that time is an illusion, that the past and future are the same, because they are imperfections of the map of the world in which we now find ourselves.[10] The past and the future have only a sentimental meaning, and our attachment to them is reflected in our obsession with science fiction or the ecological romance of a lost natural state. Likewise, the bland, almost catatonic, speech of the statesmen of the postmodern (like that of Andy Warhol) reflects their conscious attempt to disengage themselves from the sentimental, to disengage themselves from the vocabulary of past and future.

This catatonic condition, of course, itself gives rise to a sentiment that is entrenched within Judaeo-Christian metaphysics and within reactions to that metaphysics. As such, it does not, and cannot, reflect an absolute or inevitable view; rather, it merely reflects the condition of the culture of which we are a part and a kind of thinking that today is dominant. And if this metaphysics is recognized as culture-specific, its sentimentality (for even Warhol engaged in a special kind of sentimentality) can, likewise, be viewed as a manifestation of a particular cultural disposition. What the glib inevitability of the art world's acceptance of entropy suggests is more our unwillingness to consider other ways of thinking than our arrival at anything like an absolute objective statement.

8. A most absurd parody of this problem is described by Swift in *Gulliver's Travels* when language itself is replaced by *things* carried on one's back.

9. McFarland, for example, argues that "culture primarily witnesses the absence of meaning, not its presence" (1987, 113).

10. Smithson notes the similarity of future and past, and describes the activities of another artist as "transforming a terrestrial site into a map" (1979, 173). For him, a nonsite is "a three-dimensional map of the site" (ibid., 172).

If anything, a focusing on entropy indicates our unwillingness as a culture to accept the preconditions of other ways of thinking. Nor, therefore, are we likely to accept that our unwillingness to *imagine* other ways of thinking is the consequence of our Platonic obsession (despite the actual significance of *anamnēsis* for Platonic epistemology) with the inferiority of materialized *images*. Clearly, a disdain for images logically makes us suspicious of the vehicles of imagination, and especially of the memory systems through which connectedness may be realized. It is not surprising, therefore, that the domain of memory, and especially the modes of thought by which it might otherwise be manipulated, expose for us not just the xenophobias and solipsisms of postmodernism but, more important, how the idea of cosmopolitan culture and its canonical constraints function to limit the integration of human thinking in ways that are other than reflexive.

III. *AXIS MUNDI*

For Hindus throughout the world the universe is understood as emanating from a central mountain (*mahāmeru*). This high place is not only their *axis mundi*, but the auspicious domain of everything good. For Hindus on Bali it is, moreover, the home of their gods and deified ancestors. Against this high, auspicious place is juxtaposed the demonic sea, the place of witches and demons (and tourists). Imagine, therefore, every Balinese living in a worldly space that is, in itself, a microcosm of the shape of the universe. Now imagine that this framework is also governed by the universal distinction between right and left (Needham 1973). Right-handedness is auspicious; left-, inauspicious. Things done to the right, or with the right hand, are good; the left hand is reserved for insult, evil magic, defecation—indeed, everything that is vile or polluted.

Most people are quite capable of imagining such a world; where the difficulty comes is in attempting to grasp its behavioral consequences. For when one combines the symbolism of right and left with that of mountain and sea, one realizes that doing things with one's right hand in the direction of the mountain is good (keeping the sea to one's left), and that clockwise movement (i.e., doing things with the mountain to one's right) is auspicious; anticlockwise, the opposite. Every action that one performs, in other words, is potentially symbolic, because the symbolic and the real are one and the same. This is not to say that every microcosmic particle has to have meaning, but it does mean that such things *can* have meaning if one wishes them to. Every action, to use a Judaeo-Christian concept, can have the character of prayer. And because the whole universe is understood as a reflection of this structure, all things that we call "foreign" are, for the Balinese, part of their universalist view. There is, that is to say, no "outside" beyond this absolute structure.

All of the above is, again, quite comprehensible, but one also readily perceives how the implementation of such systems would, in cultures that do not maintain them, result in behavior that is aberrant. Imagine the average New Yorker entering a subway only from staircases on the Hudson side of the street, or always driving to and from work along a clockwise circuit: for the modern city dweller, such behavior falls into a category that we commonly label neurotic. Yet it is precisely this kind of ecological interrelatedness that should be experienced if what one wants to have is a sense of how connectedness is established and maintained. For the Balinese concerned with behaving gracefully, such behavioral systems can, at least in principle, be constant, and one's actions in the rice field may, thus, take on the character of prayer. The point that needs to be emphasized here is that we are not, as postmodernists would charge, promoting the mystification of the "other." Rather, we need to focus on how criticizing mystification itself becomes an excuse for not engaging ideas alien enough to produce even the mildest discomfort.

Oddly, postmodernists suffer from the same penchant for "alienation" as do dyed-in-the-wool mystics: though we regularly glamorize the connectedness to the land of exotic cultures or "primitive" tribes, in fact very few outsiders are willing actually to entertain the behavioral premises of such ontologies. In the following section we will consider a few of the ways in which altering one's ontological awareness might affect one's mode of thinking; however, there is yet an important point to be made about how the process of naming enables us to become romantic about other modes of thought without ever coming to terms with them. The ongoing emulation of the North American Indians' connection to the land is often a mere ruse for what is, in fact, an unwillingness to permit a group that we recognize as another culture to be adaptive;[11] here, cultural autonomy is a part of our attaching a name, a label, a "thingness" to others. Like the proliferation in the modern world of new nations and minority identities, social self-knowledge becomes part of being able to name, while naming itself erodes adaptivity. Thus, the sentimental historicism, or puritanical romanticism, of many ecologists actually contributes to the disintegration of other cultures by *fixing* them, by *arresting* them, with a name. In naming, we relieve ourselves of the burden of actually considering the implication of how a different way of thinking can completely transform the conditions that make for meaningful social relations.

IV. THE ANIMATED MEMORY

If this focus on spatial connectedness and the meaning of things sounds like a plea for rethinking animism, or a reconsideration of the science of the concrete, perhaps it is.[12] When Tylor said that animism is the result of "point-blank natural evidence" (1913, 1:500), or when Evans-Pritchard said that Zande witchcraft supplies the missing link in the

11. Probably the most compelling example of this problem can be seen in instances where so-called traditional cultures proffer conflicting claims about sacred prerogatives. The well-known dispute between the Hopi and the Navajo in Arizona—where both tribes claimed an ancient right to the same land—shows us just how wanting is the common juxtaposition between modern cultures that have no connection to the land and traditional ones that do. Both tribes, in this instance, qualify for romantic attention from outsiders, while the displaced Mexican-American (whose grandparents and great-grandparents may have farmed some of that same land) was silently forgotten. Especially interesting in the Hopi-Navajo case was the extent to which outsiders attempted to limit the adaptability of what could be called traditional. As one might have anticipated, the ecologically minded environmental movement sided with only a very particular lifestyle, which appeared to be "truly" Indian. However, as one Hopi Tribal Council member retorted, "I don't have to dress dirty and live in a hovel to prove that I'm traditional to white people" (Conason 1986, 26). Not surprisingly, it is the white advocates of the Native Americans who appear in the most absurd roles, since many whites, or at least non-Indians, become part of such disputes for ideological or personal motives. Many of these "motley pilgrims" get involved for their own reasons, one Indian leader points out: "We have lost generations in America, as the result of the breakup of the extended family. They are attracted to the extended family and clan systems among the Indians, and the security that provides" (ibid.). Indians, in this case, become living proof that another way of thinking about the world actually existed, and keeping them apart stands as a proof of that difference.

12. For all the anthropological discussions of fieldwork and participant observation, how many anthropologists studying, for example, Hindu views of sacred objects have ever attempted, experimentally, to enable a particular object to be the vehicle of some paranormal force?

coincidence of certain events (1937, 70), what was being suggested to us (in spite of Evans-Pritchard's criticisms of Tylor) was not so much an inferior or defective way of dealing with experience, but a way that was—and is—quite literally more empirical, more securely grounded in experience and observation. One may object by arguing that dreams (the basis of Tylor's views on animism) are not real, or even that dreams define, by opposition, what "reality" means. However, because dreams may be given an actual status in a culture studied, anthropologists may find themselves, as participant observers, compelled to consider them in ways that are not entirely comfortable. Moreover, to consider dreams in such a way, to offer them some kind of empirical status, is perhaps more informative than the notion of such play, such pretending, might suggest: since one-third of one's life in any cultural context is spent involved in one's dream world—and since, in addition, one "really" is dreaming—this activity involves a kind of point-blank natural evidence that is in some ways more faithful to experience than our modern-day heuristic substitutes. Who, after all, has ever seen a subconscious or an id? What exactly is meant when some of us say that they "exist"? Though we commonly assume that such concepts have "real" status in the sense of something that can be observed, or describe them with words that animate them, it is essential, particularly in anthropology, that we give way to indigenous categories whenever possible.

I am not suggesting here that we abandon—or that we even could abandon—what we have learned about, say, the differences between gifts and commodities, or the ideological shifts that may be commensurate with certain kinds of social development.[13] Rather, I am arguing that different modes of thought will, necessarily, treat signs and symbols in ways that are methodologically different, and that it is important for us to be aware of how frequently, even in the modern world, we rely on an inherently animistic vocabulary—when, for example, we say that language has a life of its own, or when we discuss the psychological "reality" of the phoneme, or when we conceptualize modes of discourse as "things." Perhaps this sounds like a case for methodolog-

13. See, for example, Chapter 3 for a discussion of the way in which a concept of national identity affects the development of a cultural canon, and how, in turn, modes of thought are also transformed.

ical pluralism—for the belief both that no theoretical construct can be comprehensive except within the cultural context that gives rise to it, and that such constructs are incommensurable cross-culturally. If so, it should not be surprising that the best evidence for such a plea for reenvisioning objective relations comes precisely from that arena of "point-blank natural evidence" to which Tylor refers, and not from any new-wave theorizing. Any number of examples could be cited of how sign systems evolve into landscapes so complex that we are incapable of reconstructing their etiologies.[14] Two examples, I feel, are especially cogent—the first because it comes from within the mysterious domain of the mentally retarded; the second because it is an elaboration of a cognitive technique to which any reasonably intelligent person ought to have access.

The first example is that of the twins, John and Michael, considered in Oliver Sacks's *The Man Who Mistook His Wife for a Hat* (1985). What is most interesting about the twins is not that they have a prodigious capacity for phenomenal mathematic feats—that they can conjure up twenty-figure primes and, like so many African twins, do certain things the rest of us do, only much better—but that, however extraordinary the performance, their system for so doing remains completely beyond our grasp. Incapable of doing accurate addition or subtraction, or, indeed, of even understanding what the concepts of multiplication and division mean, they rely, as Sacks puts it, on some kind of "prodigious panorama, a sort of landscape or physiognomy, of all they have ever heard, or seen, or thought, or done, . . . in the blink of an eye, externally obvious as a brief rolling and fixation of the eyes, they are able (with the 'mind's eye') to retrieve and 'see' nearly anything that lies in this vast landscape" (1985, 189). By "anything," Sacks means that they will, with their IQs of 60, "also tell you the date of Easter during [a] period of 80,000 years . . . as if they were unrolling, or scrutinising, an inner landscape, a mental calendar. They have the look of 'seeing,' of intense visualisation" (ibid., 187). Rather than calculate, in other words, they "see," as Sacks puts it, "a vast (or possibly infinite) landscape in which everything could be seen, either isolated or in re-

14. In fact, any polythetic class will exhibit this characteristic; see Needham 1975, 1983.

lation" (ibid., 190). Now how close, we might ask, is the process employed by the twins to our own notions of abstraction, to the recognition, say, of portraits through caricature? In discussing Dmitri Mendeleev's description of the numerical properties of elements as "familiar faces," Sacks remarks that he "saw the elements, iconically, physiognomically, as 'faces'—faces that related, like members of a family, and that made up, *in toto*, periodically arranged, the whole formal face of the universe" (ibid., 196). These so-called iconic minds see "all nature as faces and scenes" where numbers, or the numerical properties of elements, take on an anthropomorphic character that confirms on some fundamental level an absolute correspondence between persons and things, between persons and landscapes, or, as in the case of Hermann von Helmholtz, between certain musical tones, which become " 'faces' for the ear" (ibid., 198). More important, what the twins suggest to us—though we find it impossible to visualize *their* landscapes[15]—is that they abstract (or, rather, represent, make present, conjure) through specific family resemblances. Their landscapes unfold, in other words, as chain complexes (to use Vygotsky's metaphor), or polythetic classes (to use Needham's), or rope fibers (to use Wittgenstein's), or pony manes (to use Sacks's), or as smoke (to use Küchler's recent analogue). The disjunctions, in other words, between persons and things—and, thus, between one thing and the next—are so minimized as to make identical the symbolic and the real. We are not, as in semiotics, focusing on connections in a landscape of things; rather, things (if the word applies at all) are realized through a connected landscape.

One might argue that minimalist or performance art, with its focus on process, has moved in a similar vein. Tony Smith's well-known description of a late-night drive on the unfinished New Jersey Turnpike[16]

15. One might even define "individuality" as a notion stemming from the capacity for developing unique visions; for no one could ever expect to have total access to one's own memory landscape, yet all know—through its performance—the extent to which it has been "realized." To put it more simply, "individuality" in the case of the twins becomes "actualized" through performance; as the artist Nam June Paik says, "Art is what *artists* do" (Gardner 1985, 66). Perhaps the emphasis should be placed on "do" rather than on "artists."

16. Smith described this experience as a kind of reality that had no expression in art, even though the unreality of the event meant that what he experienced was purely artificial. For a discussion of Smith's description, see Fried 1967, 19.

and Daniel Buren's endless strips of paper signifying "a path of no return upon which thought must embark" (in Meyer 1972, 76)[17] are two
examples of how "thingness" gives way to "connectedness." However, as these demonstrations are called "art," or, at least, are considered artistically relevant, they can never replace experience as such, because they continue to return to the art world's categorical havens.
Because they are incapable of being transformed out of that categorical
domain, they are merely a mock-form of the twins' mental landscapes
and cannot, therefore, be fruitfully compared with them.

That the twins "can tell one the weather, and the events, of any day
in their lives—any day from about their fourth year on" (Sacks 1985,
180) would seem totally unbelievable were it not for another (and my
second) example, which somehow brings the twins' landscapes a bit
more within the domain of what we may readily conceptualize. This
second example is that of the memory palaces, and especially those
made famous by sixteenth-century missionaries who used the device
in order to record and store vast quantities of Christian doctrine—in
order to have, that is, complex tools for confronting the foreign. Spectacular though the twins' feats may be, they are not unrelated to those
of a missionary who could, as Spence describes it in *The Memory Palace
of Matteo Ricci* (1984), recall immediately a list of hundreds of Chinese
characters by establishing a mental landscape (in this case, rooms of a
palace filled with memory sculptures) from which information could
be retrieved, much as the twins' numerical landscapes apparently unfold under the scrutiny of their squinting eyes.

What Tylor meant by "point-blank natural evidence" was, of
course, his conviction of the absolute correspondence between the
concreteness of so-called reality and the concreteness of its reciprocal
inversion—that is, the "different" reality made known to us in the
world of dreams, the only world, after all, that those of us unfamiliar
with numerical landscapes and memory palaces can experience while
maintaining an affirmative sense of an unquestioned and known vision. For Sacks, the murky comparison of Lévi-Strauss's "savage
mind" with the thoughts of children or of the mentally impaired is

---

17. Though Buren was well aware of the need to remove his activities from the domain of art and to reestablish them in a different reality, the fact that the work was re-
cuperated as "art" essentially destroys the "rupture" he sought.

valid, at least on the level of how the concrete is apprehended. The comparison is, moreover, particularly fruitful if what we are seeing is *not a regression to the concrete*, but a preservation of it, "so that the essential personality and identity and humanity, the *being* [as it were] . . . is preserved" (Sacks 1985, 165). What makes the mnemonists, then— and the twins in particular—so interesting is that what appear to be the *calculations* of a left-hemisphere-dominant brain, the "computer tacked onto the basic creatural brain" (ibid., 2), are in fact "left-handed" (i.e., right-hemisphere-based) landscapes that restore, replace, compensate for, or preserve identity (ibid., 4). These landscapes, in other words, are imaginative constructions or reconstructions, holistic processes for rearranging the concrete. One must remember that such reconstructions may, equally, be entirely unsuccessful in arriving at an affectively translatable vision;[18] however, sometimes these reconstructions do indeed succeed in establishing a magic that has credence in a right-handed (i.e., left-hemisphere) world. When I say "right-handed" or "left-handed," I do not mean to oversimplify the biological complexity of the distinction by suggesting that so-called right and left ways of thinking may be perceived as absolute categories, or that the hemispherical analogy need be pushed too far; but I would argue that the degree to which the symbolic binary opposition of right and left parallels what are popularly taken to be features of modes of thought in which one or the other of the brain's hemispheres predominates suggests to us that the opposition will not readily be dispensed with either by intellectual maneuvering or by scientific discovery.[19] For example, though one might argue that a good memory for facts may more fruitfully be described as a function of the intellectual capabilities of the left hemisphere (i.e., more properly a "right-handed" activity), we fail to realize, as Frances Yates has pointed out, that we live in an era where printing and the prevalence of literacy have led to an impoverished notion of how information can be processed by a single properly trained

18. An example is a man from my childhood who spent every day recording and storing the numbers of trolley cars on bits of paper that filled his pockets.

19. In other words, despite how unfashionable a model the right/left distinction may be in the natural or social sciences, it is not an organizational principle that can be readily dismissed. See, for example, Needham's *Counterpoints* (1987).

individual,[20] that "whilst it is important to recognise that the classical art is based on workable mnemotechnic principles it may be misleading to dismiss it with the label 'mnemotechnics.' The classical sources seem to be describing inner techniques which depend on visual impressions of almost incredible intensity" (Yates 1966, 4). We are, in other words, dealing not only with the accumulation of bits of information, but with the intense visualization of an entire panorama—either a systematic superimposition of images for purposes of information storage, or a deliberate superimposition of unrelated forms for purposes of creative stimulation.

However, what makes the right/left distinction even more interesting and compelling than its apparently worldwide symbolic importance, and more relevant to the topic of "connectedness," is the argument from silence that arises from contemporary research on the human brain. If we are to accept as fact the assertion that "we will find a thousand descriptions of left-hemisphere syndromes in the neurological and neuropsychological literature for every description of a right-hemisphere syndrome" (Sacks 1985, 3), then we must equally accept the concomitant probability that the study of other modes of thought will only rarely result in a successful appreciation of the methodology by which one might otherwise manipulate the concrete.[21] We know about as much of what the twins "see" as we do of what "seers" visualize in other cultures;[22] indeed, we may even know much less, particularly if what qualifies as "knowing" is only those things that can be, quite literally, *distinguished*, in the sense of being separated abso-

20. In view of the fact that the average American child spends six thousand hours in front of a television before ever entering a classroom, one must ask whether such visual training precludes the possibility of gaining access to other modes of visualization, especially if those modes do not readily submit to having their "chain complexes" categorically unpacked.

21. Witness our failure to perceive how a memory palace actually functions. While we can readily imagine how such a palace might look, we are probably incapable of understanding how, for example, someone like Matteo Ricci might be so adept at utilizing his visual design that he could be given a random list of hundreds of Chinese characters and, without rehearsal, spontaneously retrieve them in any order requested. We are not, in other words, dealing with a mere elaboration of the techniques employed by students "cramming" for exams.

22. One thinks here of Castaneda's compelling questioning of whether or not the sensation of flying experienced under the influence of hallucinogens actually resulted in flight. Don Juan, that is, must deal with the persistent question "Did I fly?"

lutely from the imaginative landscape in which they may be embedded. What the pioneer neuropsychologist A. R. Luria called "a realm
of great wonder" (Sacks 1985, 6), or what Roland Barthes described
as the catharsis of the spectacle (1957, 13–24), may be but an intimation
of the processual or associative focus of those who explore imaginative
landscapes as a means of restoring and resocializing the self. By this,
as it were, left-handed view, the autistic child is involved less in a mistaken view of objects than in, perhaps, an indifference about establishing a process—a developmental focus—that binds the concrete to a
landscape of associations that are socially shared.[23]

How is it possible for the concrete to be absorbed into a landscape
that is both processual and comprehensive? The Navajo, as Witherspoon demonstrates, say that beauty must be maintained by an ongoing process that is expressed only in and through man (1977, 151).
In this case, language does not have so much a life of its own that it
devolves into a disconnected and independent Saussurean agent; nor
does self-consciousness become reflexive, folding in on itself and, thus,
becoming contained. Though for the Navajo, symbols antedate humankind (and, in this sense, are independent), they enter the landscape
only in and through man. As Cacciari argues in an article on Arcimboldo's *trompe-l'oeil* painting (Pl. 8), "rather than the abstract exaltation
of any single element . . . it is the harmonic system to which the figure
conforms that is the goal of the work. . . . For Arcimboldo, the disquieting, the *Unheimliches*, lies in representing not so much the extraordinary or the unprecedented as the extraordinariness, the 'mirac-
ulousness,' of the ordinary, of what commonly is, or can be, the object
of direct, precise experience. The disquieting lies in *hallucinating* the

---

23. An example of just such a disjunction (and of its resolution) may be seen in the
responses of my Balinese neighbors to a quite mad member of the community who
made a habit of delivering lectures in tongues from the promontory in front of his home.
When I asked how this performance was considered by them, I was told that the man
had been possessed by demons and that they had yet to figure out the appropriate way
of exorcising them. It was the process of ridding him of the demons that was important;
once the binding developmental focus had been ascertained, he could be cured—and
cured, moreover, without any stain to his character. Anyone, after all, could find oneself
in a weak moment the victim of such an inauspicious circumstance. His view of the
world, that is, was not wrong; it was simply out of line. His train, to use a common
modern metaphor, had jumped the tracks.

experience that normally ties us to things as they are, as they appear" (1987, 70). Though the particular elements in the work may pique our curiosity, it is "the harmonic system to which the [apparently disassembled] figure conforms that is the goal of the work" (ibid.). As with the Navajo who becomes the vehicle for realization, "here, man is a prodigy, worthy of veneration and honor, for his character *summarizes* all creation" (ibid., 73). Like the Navajo performer who brings to beauty preexisting (but unrealized) symbols, "people are absorbed in the metaphors that indicate them, and in metaphor alone are they celebrated" (ibid., 77). The resulting "monsters," as Cacciari calls them,[24] renounce the "unique, unrepeatable character of the sitter" to the extent that they are not, and cannot be, part of any "inquiry into *inwardness*" (ibid.). In rejecting inwardness, Arcimboldo also asserts the portrait's "infinite distance from any 'psychology'" (ibid., 77). For us, of course, these monsters *are* hallucinated and, therefore, not credible—as is Dali's *Face of Mae West Which Can Be Used as an Apartment* or his *Paranoiac Face* (Fig. 21), to which Cacciari compares Arcimboldo's work. As with Edgar Rubin's famous figure-vase reversal or the so-called devil's tuning fork (Fig. 22), we cannot admit the contradiction that will enable us to see both worlds as legitimate. Our methodological monsters' horror resides in the realization that in admitting to them we also admit to the paranoia that, for us, is the consequence of letting them be realized in our landscape, our event horizon.

How, therefore, do we apprehend another mode of thought wherein the world is only realized, as the Navajo say, in and through man? Lévy-Bruhl, perhaps, came closest to a solution with his notion of participation ([1949] 1975)—a notion at the foundation of the entire fieldwork enterprise. Yet Lévy-Bruhl, and all anthropologists who follow him in this endeavor, could not escape his awareness that new modes of description (and especially new modes that insist upon giving authority to neologisms) will, as he said, fatigue and repel us by constantly undermining traditional categories ([1949] 1975, 64–65)—that is, *our* categories of thought—to which new meanings have been

24. That they are "monstrous" at all is relevant, as we will see, to the conclusion of this chapter.

FIG. 21*a*.   Salvador Dali, *Paranoiac Face* (1931; © 1990 Demart Pro Arte /
ARS New York): Dali understood paranoia as a creative means for perceiving the superficial overlap of imagery; here and in figure 21*b* we see two of
his more famous examples.

attached; while, on the other hand, traditional modes of description are
the very problem that compelled the search for new categories in the
first place. His answer to this dilemma was participation. Yet Lévy-
Bruhl was also quite aware that participation (at least of the pure kind
that anthropologists dream of) is not possible in cosmopolitan contexts, for one cannot abandon self-consciousness—at least not self-
consciously. Among modern-day Igbo, for example, a new persona
has appeared in a sequence of traditional festive dancing. This is the
white man as anthropologist, or district officer, or both (Fig. 23), iden-
tifiable not just by the pinkish pallor of his mask and by the pith helmet
he wears, but by the fact that, rather than dance, this persona stands
rigidly at the periphery of the performance recording events on a note-

FIG. 21*b.*   Salvador Dali, *Face of Mae West Which Can Be Used as an Apartment* (Figueras, hall from the Teatro-Museo Dali, 1943; based upon gouache with collage *Mae West*, 1934–35).

pad.[25] If this be participation, it is of a very peculiar sort; but still it is more participatory—in the sense of evoking some kind of reciprocity in a landscape of indigenous categories—than the armchair philoso-

25. The vitality of this highly adaptive notion of tradition contrasts markedly with revived traditions in cosmopolitan or pluralistic societies, where what is considered "traditional" rests in a quite static vision of the past. In the former, we honor Christ, to use the Roman example, by offering him a place in the pantheon; in the latter, we honor him by categorically distinguishing him from anything Roman. Similarly, our critical awareness of the vitality of tradition rarely enables us to be fully aware of how discussing cultural heritage, in a way, reinvents it; while this book was in press, for example, a

FIG. 22.   *Above*, Edgar Rubin, figure-vase reversal; *below*, devil's tuning fork: the difficulty of employing Dali's visual methodology is epitomized when one tries to envision simultaneously all of the realities in which these *trompe-l'oeil* images make sense.

phizing that results, if not in neologisms, then at least in unwieldy analytic categories.[26]

One cannot, of course, dismiss the deployment of such new categories *tout court*, for they help those who construct them make better sense of their own worlds. One often enough hears the name of Edmund Husserl in discussions that endeavor to reevaluate the "phenomenal" nature of objects, of their relations and relatedness, that it is important to remind ourselves that Husserl's attempt at an absolute

modified version of the image provided in Figure 23a appeared on a collection of essays about cultural history (Clifford 1988). No doubt the fact that the image already has a "history" predisposes us to reinterpret it in new and different ways.

26. Anyone who has tried to read much postmodern art theory will immediately sense the degree to which its often mysterious character stems specifically from unwieldy analytical categories, if not from a simple failure to make itself clear.

FIG. 23. *a*) "White man," *Onyeocha* (Igbo masker at Amagu Izzi, Nigeria, 1982): participation carries an unusual meaning when the involvement of outsiders is imitated in their habitual observing and recording of native life. *b*) White man emerging from ground; sculpture in the *mbari* house for Ala in Umuedi Ofekelem. (Photos: Herbert Cole)

distinction between people and things—an attempt that characterized his early efforts to "get back to the things themselves," as he put it— resulted not, as was his hope, in a fresh start for objectivity, but in a radical reenvisioning of the materiality of objects. Yet getting back to the things themselves, especially by way of the neologistic reinterpretation of the material world, can reinvent boundaries between humans and things as much as it can reverse them. It does not undermine Husserl's brilliance or genuine contribution to the history of ideas to point out that in the realm of intellectual history we too have many descriptions of left-hemisphere syndromes in the literature for every left-handed (i.e., right-hemisphere) one. What is significant for the present consideration, in other words, is not the extent to which Husserl was, in any strict sense, right or not, but rather the fact that he felt *at all* that he needed to get back to the things themselves, as if we had once been there and could only now reflect melancholically, as Panofsky (1955) said, upon how things were in Arcadia long ago. The "thing," that is, is understood as having accumulated so much cultural baggage that its original identity has been interiorized, obscured, even masked.

By this view, the decoding of inner meaning is a concomitant of the notion that there in fact *is* an inner meaning, some interiorized thing, that exists as an independent entity—one requiring an expert in artificial intelligence to approach, through a code, its "real" source.[27] I am not challenging here the potential significance and deep complexity of the categories of thought that define "culture" as such, or, for example, necessarily taking issue with the notion of a cultural unit as "anything that is culturally defined and distinguished as an entity" (Eco 1976, 67). What does, however, interest me is the extent to which entities are meant to be absolutely distinguished (that is, distinctive, individuated), how even (and especially) the most radical theories can become strongholds of an alarmingly traditional materialist perspective, whether we are talking about art objects or performance artists as objects themselves. *The interpretant is not the interpreter*, Eco emphasizes (ibid., 68). A sign, he says (quoting Pierce), is "anything which determines something else (its *interpretant*) to refer to an object to which itself refers (its *object*) in the same way, the interpretant becoming in turn a sign, and so on *ad infinitum*" (ibid., 69). Aside from the obvious syntactical ambiguity of this statement, what we may observe here is a process wherein objects become mystified. To such objects is, at once,

27. It is worth noting that, despite the efforts of Judd and Morris to arrive at a Platonic "wholeness" (where wholeness means specifically a singleness of shape that has no parts), Fried still accuses them of an implied connectedness, a social theatricality that has its basis in assumptions about "inner" meaning. According to Fried, "the apparent hollowness of most [of their] work—the quality of having an *inside*—is almost blatantly anthropomorphic" (1967, 19).

attributed a kind of animistic volition (even a desire to be connected), while, simultaneously, they are meant to constitute a radical, even inaccessible, otherness.

Objects thus molded are, despite the radical rhetoric, still the stronghold of materialism, in that, to adhere to the system of thought in which they have a function, we must also willingly become participants in an environment in which we are forever distinguished from them.[28] Put another way, we are compelled to hysteria in that we are invited to be interred in an atmosphere of independent agents from which we have ourselves been cut off.[29] My argument, in other words, is that *the desire to animate "things," or to create "things" out of abstractions that seem to have life, is a natural proclivity; it is the avulsion of symbols that is culture-specific.* Despite the focus of semiotics on connectedness, it, like phenomenology, can also invite us to apologize for a materialist perspective by suggesting, somewhat melancholically, that we *could* understand the connectedness of things *if only* we were intelligent or natively perceptive enough to understand the deeper (read "invisible") interrelations to which things adhere. Meaning is not, and cannot be, superficial—that is, *on the surface*. Nor, therefore, can it be part of any mental landscape that may be visualized. We seek to hunt down objects, to accumulate and confiscate by categorizing, unitizing, and controlling them. We argue that our focus is on relations and connectedness, while simultaneously arguing for independence. The focus here is on self-control, not on self-evidence.[30] Like good Calvinists (for whom gain *per se* is good), we contain our desires and control our objects not by animating them in a self-evident landscape where the symbolic and real may be one and the same, but by hunting them down and accumulating them, by commodifying, and by distinguishing

28. One of the main difficulties with the major philosophical attempts to focus on relations rather than on the things being related (e.g., phenomenology, semiotics, deconstruction, reflexivity) is that one must also have a sense of the "thing" in order to consider the neglected relation. The result of such enterprises is not only a heightened self-consciousness, but the misperception that relations—rather than *certain kinds of relations*—have been neglected. As Simmel pointed out some time ago, "Objectivity is by no means non-participation (which is altogether outside both subjective and objective interaction), but a positive and specific kind of participation" (1950, 404).

29. In this sense both deconstructionism and reflexivity invite a kind of disconnected intellectual excitement.

30. As Morris says, "the concerns now are for more control of . . . the entire situation"; see Fried 1967, 16.

symbolic exchanges as "unreal," as transactions in which something unreal stands in for a thing having real or actual status.

Like the swinging-singles tour of one of our major museums entitled "Why Hate Modern Art?" the cult of the objectified self cannot, in fact, accommodate a landscape of self-evidence, because the self is realized not through the ultimate connectedness of things, but through its ultimate distinction from them. Because of their capacity to disengage themselves from the object of desire, the best Calvinists do not focus on the self-evidence of things that can be genealogically related; they do not, as it were, overpopulate the world with associative ideas, even if, in not doing so, they exhibit a discomforting self-presence with respect to those objects. We cannot, in other words, perceive a more flexible body-image boundary, one that makes us less self-conscious about our status with respect to the objects that surround us. My comparison here is Christo and Acconci—the former artist successful through a baroquely complex program of social relations that enables his public to accept his creations;[31] the latter, as we have seen, sometimes unsuccessful (or successful in a more combative way) because of the insecurities he engenders in his (often unwilling or ignorant) participant-viewer. Especially telling in this respect as Acconci's *Following Piece* of 1969 (Fig. 24). In that peculiarly anthropological work the artist spent twenty-three days involved in a kind of fieldwork parody in which he randomly followed strangers around New York City. While we follow Acconci following someone unaware of being followed, we begin to sense how art has led us toward, but then backed away from, the reenvisioning, reconstructing, the putting back together—the literal re-membering—of our cognitive horizons, and how the artist, in so doing, has lost the power to engender our trust or to demonstrate anything like a new kind of magic.

V. WHAT IS LEFT?

Of course the question Why hate modern art? has as its natural corollary the question Why hate modern artists? First of all, I do not think

31. A survey of the publications dealing with Christo's major works provides a sense of the extent to which his projects are legitimized through protracted and often mundane legal interactions.

FIG. 24. Vito Acconci, *Following Piece* (activity, "Street Works IV," Architectural League of New York, October 1–31, 1969): Acconci's random following of strangers in New York survives as an unintended parody of fieldwork in the social sciences; that it is "art" rather than (or in addition to) one of the perverse forms of harassment endemic to modern life is only evidenced by the context in which it takes place—namely, an "exhibition" sponsored by the Architectural League of New York. (By permission of Arthur H. Minters, Inc.; photo: Betsy Jackson)

that we will get anywhere by lamenting, as artists often do, the fact that they do not have—or have lost—an ability to produce magic, or that they have lost that social role. However, I do think that it is important to recognize the extreme pattern of avoidance that has characterized our attempt as a culture—or, rather, our unwillingness—to confront the "point-blank natural evidence." The cultural analogue to the claim that "we will find a thousand descriptions of left-hemisphere syndromes in the neurological and neuropsychological literature for every description of a right-hemisphere syndrome" (Sacks 1985, 3) must surely be that in certain cultures—in Bali, for example—we have so much demonstrable scholarly interest of a quite general sort; yet how many psychoanalysts, for example, have been willing to submit their analytic categories to the intellectual challenges offered by the Balinese case? I would even go so far as to argue that it is precisely because the Balinese notion of the performative landscape is so "left-handed" that it has eluded, or has been largely ignored by, psychologists and psychoanalysts. What I mean here is not that there has been no psychological interest (indeed, the fascination is abundant), but that the more dogmatic forms of psychoanalysis have steered clear of damning other cultures outright, while those who have had a "psychological" interest in things Balinese (e.g., Bateson, Belo, Mead, Roheim) have largely declined to confront the perverse consequences of what on the surface at least appear to be some extraordinarily bizarre forms of ritual conduct. The probability that this apparent analytic avoidance has some foundation in fact comes, as it must, not from analysis itself, but from the point-blank natural evidence of visually rendered indigenous categories. The ritual context in which performative events take place, I would argue, is specifically associated with the left; and, moreover, it is also meant to be capable of elaborating an infinite, yet explicit, landscape, a structure that is both self-evident and all-encompassing. In fact, as I have elsewhere argued, the *karang bhoma*, the monstrous antefix that marks the point of transition between the world of men and the inner temple in which the three worlds meet (viz. the worlds of gods and ancestors, of men, and of demons), is, quite literally, a left-handed image, reflecting, on the one hand, a straightforward graphic depiction of the sensory capacities of the right hemisphere of the cerebral cortex (Napier 1986, 199–206), and, on the other, a structural landscape in which oppositions are conflated into harmonic, holistic, restorative ritual events that seek to rearrange the concrete through iconic manipulation. This parallel of the neurophysiological and the symbolic is not, on my part, an analytical trick; for the face itself is particularly associated in the Balinese mind with the merging of the right- and left-handed paths, with the more or less Tantric domain that focuses on its own magical landscape, presenting *in toto* a summary of all Creation. In so doing, I would argue, the ritual enactments that take place within the walls of the temple—and the Tantric reciprocity that is central to the conflict of Rangda and Barong, which pits a demonic and threatening witch against an equally demonic "protector" of social order—are paradoxical events that resolutely defy decoding. It is, in other words, no accident that the Balinese have constructed a notion of performative behavior that becomes so embedded in magic that the totality of the event strives toward the obfuscation of meaning in any explicable sense. Not that these events are not and cannot be interpreted; rather, paradoxes are constructed that make us more aware of the poverty of *any* conclusive remark we might wish to make about the nature of any particular event. Thus, while we may observe that a given trance performance is addressing a specific social condition, or that the same people seem to be going into trance, or that someone stands to lose or gain by a ritual's outcome, we also note that those who proffer the swords that the trancers turn against themselves are often those who take them away (Fig. 25), and that the many hands that contain someone in trance are also the hands that encourage such trances.[32] Possession, in other words, is truly an avant-garde activity, in that those in trance are empowered to go to the periphery of what is and can be known, to explore the boundaries,[33] and to return unharmed without drawing so much attention to themselves that they endanger (to recall Marcel Mauss) the ability of the event to stand as a total social phenomenon. People in trance do not—as performance artists in the West sometimes do—leave wounded bodies in the human world. Only

32. That we are able, that is, to arrive at a heteroglot description does not necessarily indicate that we are also willing to accept the social cohesiveness of the performance or the inseparability of its parts.

33. The military origin of the term "avant-garde," of course, suggests just this type of activity.

FIG. 25.   Balinese trance: here we see, paradoxically, both the protection of individuals in trance by fellow villagers and the encouragement to engage in trance by those same individuals. Observers commonly focus on the individual involved in the trance itself, though an awareness of how the entire group performs is essential to an understanding of trance as an avant-garde activity. (Photo: Claire Barron)

those improperly prepared, and impostors (those whose notion of the avant-garde is contained in the material person), risk hurting themselves while raving chaotically with their daggers.[34]

At the level of analysis, this left-handed construct—which cannot be divided without losing its meaning—laughs in the face of all would-be interpreters of Balinese culture. Based upon a sacred and secret language to which few Balinese even have access (putting aside the an-

34. According to the Balinese, those who are truly entranced do not hurt themselves; only impostors run the risk of losing a god's protection.

FIG. 26. Balinese monsters devouring a cassette tape: the horrific face that normally appears as a temple guardian may also take on an entirely humorous meaning. (Photo: author)

thropologist vain enough to attempt to describe what it all means),[35] these rituals are, paradoxically, open to all and yet highly esoteric. Indeed, the strength and resilience of the monstrous images evoked in such contexts are *attested* by their liberal use in unconsecrated situations: on the grille of a car, evoking the casual jokes of beachside hooligans, or on the reels of a cassette tape (Fig. 26). Here, the monstrous face survives what in less confident hands would be perceived as sacrilegious profanation, and it does so by devouring all, including our attempts to attach any precise limitations to the domain within which the face may function. Perhaps this statement actually reflects a belief

35. Just where the highest and most complex Balinese linguistic forms merge with a private, magic language is a point that escapes nearly all but those ritual officiants who are directly responsible for such contrivances. On the general issue of magic writing, see Tambiah 1968.

that this awareness of the diversity and relative character of modes of thought cannot be undermined by the Balinese themselves or by the intellectual bounty hunters who shoot, if not from the hip, with a camera or a scholarly monograph. The belief that religion is adaptive and incapable of fragmentation, analysis, and objectification is, thus, clearly stated inasmuch as its paradoxical and often contradictory character is held out defiantly to those foolhardy enough to think that they are capable of interpreting it.[36]

This adaptability is seen not only in the context of ritual innovation; it is also seen in the contemporary arts, where tourists are contextualized in painting or in spontaneous mask performances. It is also seen in the ways that Balinese assimilate the foreign—both as a basis for new technology and on the level of intellectual enterprise. One of the more startling realizations I have had to come to terms with since becoming interested in Balinese masks and performative behavior has resulted from experiencing just how much the Balinese actually *like* anthropologists. If, that is, the task of the Balinese is to summarize Creation—indeed, to maintain an absolute correspondence between microcosmic and macrocosmic—then anthropologists too must be included, and a male and a female one will do even better. What is more, if artists of the West can put our artifacts on exhibition, and even assimilate them into new Western artifacts, so too can we—must we—absorb the categories of art history and anthropology into our performative domain. If, that is, Westerners can permit themselves to absorb the artifacts of other cultures into their cultural domain (Fig. 27), so too can the Balinese, as did the Igbo with their personification of the anthropologist, decide to make a traditionally black pig-mask white because it is destined for an art market in a country (Australia) where, the artist believes, there are only white pigs—so too can we be assured in the self-confidence that if there is even such a category as "art," then we, the Balinese, must be the greatest artists on earth; for why else, I have been rhetorically asked, do so many people come to Bali to buy paintings? And if the Western response to the so-called primitive world is to accumulate its artifacts in museums, or surreal collections, or cults

36. Anthropologists, for example, are enough at odds with how to fix the morality of Balinese magical practices that some even feel that the *pedanda* priest, the Brahmana who is meant to be the purveyor of all that is "white," is as often purveying its opposite.

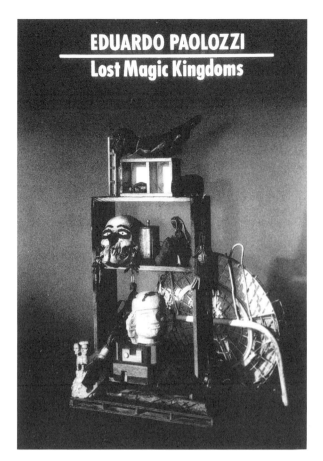

FIG. 27.   Catalog cover for the exhibition *Eduardo Paolozzi: Lost Magic Kingdoms and Six Paper Moons from Nahuatl* (London, Museum of Mankind, 1985): in this exhibition at England's leading ethnographic museum, artist Eduardo Paolozzi appropriated anonymous ethnographic artifacts in the interest of creating his own collages and assemblages. (By permission of the Museum of Mankind)

FIG. 28.   Signs of cultural adaptation among Solomon Islanders (*left*, the traditional ear ornament; *center and right*, postcolonial transformations): the seriousness with which we consider the Western artistic appropriation of the "primitive" is oddly out of keeping with the humor that we regularly resort to when viewing the "primitive" appropriation of the West. (By permission of the Rautenstrauch-Joest Museum)

of the antique, then should we not consider having Maori, in addition to performing rituals on the steps of the Metropolitan Museum, re-arrange our Van Goghs, hang them helter-skelter, or use them as offerings to *their* gods? No, if we are certain that art and anthropology cannot tell us things we do not already know. Yes, if we have the courage to see our sacred cows assimilated by another tradition, to watch the Balinese pitting the comprehensive adaptability of their own tradition against all comers.

How complete, finally, can this incorporation ever be, particularly when adaptation is so frequently eroded through the laughter of outsiders? (Imagine, for example, the average Westerner's reaction to the images provided in Figure 28.) How can a culture exercise its adaptive vitality without exciting the curiosity, the sarcasm, or even the anger of those who recognize that which is adapted as part of a different kind of cultural category? This question, of course, can never be conclusively answered; but it is interesting to see, in an age in which both anthropologists and artists occasionally complain about the often disenfranchised and statusless positions they are burdened with, just how holistic and encompassing—how resilient—adaptation *can* be. One very minor experience typified for me this agglomerative capacity of Balinese culture. One day, while riding in a bus through the heart of the Balinese tourist center of Sanur, I made out a flashing multicolored bumper sticker on the back of a pickup truck we were following. As we caught up with it, the moiré effect caused it to change into a rainbow of lurid colors that sparked my curiosity. I strained to see its message, which, once in focus, simply read: Anthropology, The Study Of Man.

.   .   .

In the first two chapters I argued that our peculiar notion of the human body and the human body-image has disenabled us from experiencing certain sorts of symbolic activity, and in particular that, while the desire to animate may be universal, the proclivity to expel the "symbolic" from the "actual" is culture-specific. I also argued that self-consciousness may be perceived as the denial of surface realities and that our notion of psychology as a describer of inner realities limits our capacity for perceiving modes of thought that depend upon the visualizing of landscapes of family resemblances.

In the next two chapters I argue that each time we relinquish as a culture our Platonic sense of how meaning is internalized, we pursue the natural tendency to equate the symbolic and the actual through systems of thought that equate micro- and macrocosmic structures. I choose two great moments in history—the rise of Greek culture and the revision of cultural history in seventeenth-century Rome—to illustrate, first, how the birth of culture as we know it is specifically tied to a thesis of personhood that deemphasizes superficiality by internalizing the monstrous that is represented in the foreign; and second, how the same tendencies reemerge whenever we relax the regulations that govern cultural boundaries. Whereas the Greeks, in other words, used the foreign to define personhood, to proceed from a notion of performance characterized by surface meaning to one in which the foreign becomes part of a complex individual psychology, certain Roman Catholics of the seventeenth century usurped the foreign by placing the Church at the apex of microcosmic/macrocosmic relations, and, in particular, by making the "foreign body" in its most meaningful sense into a system of relations that would enable the devout Catholic to visualize the symbolic and real as part of the same experience.

In Chapter 5 I will suggest specific ways in which these unifying tendencies are countered in contemporary culture with the goal of achieving a less demanding concept of the foreign. For the moment—and before venturing into the next chapter—bear in mind that it is not coincidental that the Classics not only are one of the most interesting areas in which to investigate concepts of foreignness, but are also the domain in which our ways of seeing (what is "western" about Western civilization) are rooted. Arguments in and about the Classics are, therefore, necessarily more heavily laden with meaning for us as a culture, but also more thoroughly immersed in our cultural prejudices. My choice of subject matter for these chapters is, therefore, not arbitrary, but governed by the thesis that there reemerge new ways of dealing with the role played by the foreign in symbolic relations whenever we are capable as a culture of addressing the problem of the delicate balance demanded by the natural tendency to equate microcosmic and macrocosmic images.

3

Greek Art and Greek Anthropology:
Orienting the Perseus-Gorgon Myth

What do we actually understand by "greatness"? The word is used in so many different ways that one might despair of ever attaching a clear meaning to it. What is there that has not been called "great"? Side by side with achievements without which no existence worthy of men can be imagined we find the ludicrous and the monstrous. It is precisely in this confusion that the concept of greatness represents something men cannot live without.

Elias Canetti, Crowds and Power

I. RECONNAISSANCE

Archetypes discoverable in the comparison of collective representations act as primary factors of experience.

Rodney Needham, Reconnaissances

The story of Perseus and the Gorgon head reflects a crisis both in the notion of the Greek person and in the definition of Greek culture. As a foundation myth, it must be adaptive; it must be capable of defining and redefining notions of personhood and, specifically, a transformation in cultural identity over time. As a vital part of cultural redefinition, the myth functions, therefore, not so much to reiterate the plot of some ritual event, though it may provide cryptic evidence for such activity;[1] the function of a foundation myth is, rather, to describe a transformation in meaning, to enable future symbolic acts to achieve definitions that are new and different. Thus, while a foundation myth may or may not embody the plot of a real cultic practice, its focus is

---

1. For a discussion of the probable connection between Gorgons and specific ritual events, see Napier 1986, 20–21, 83–91.

on becoming, on providing a groundwork for the new by offering a foundation that is archetypal yet adaptive enough to accommodate changes in meaning that are both public and private. While it may be necessary, therefore, to ask about the relationship between the Perseus-Gorgon legend and actual historical events, of equal importance is an inquiry into the changes of cultural and individual identity; we must consider, in other words, not only the significance of Perseus as a founding Mycenaean king, but his role as an agent for redefining Greek culture and the personal meaning of what it could mean to be Greek.

If Perseus is moved to be great through a compulsive egocentrism, we must put the question of the Gorgon conflict in terms of another question—namely, Could there be any prospect more terrible than someone with my (his) promise being defeated by a monster?[2] But if, on the other hand, he is a more or less average person upon whom has been thrust the role of ritual performer or king—the anonymous individual made great by the demands of his social role—then our reading of the myth's meaning is, indeed, quite different. That our addressing this problem is essential to our understanding of the myth—to its implications for Greek cultural consciousness, political awareness, canon formation, and notions of the person—is made clear by an examination of Perseus's ideas of himself before he pursues the Gorgon Medusa. If Perseus's response to Polydectes' demand (that he bring as wedding gift the Gorgon head) was to ask himself whether there could be any prospect more horrifying for someone so naturally gifted as he, then he is indeed a symbol of the paranoiac view that petrifaction would quite literally arrest the progress of his deserved greatness. Such a self-concept is suggested, as one would suspect, in the classical view of the megalomaniacal tyrant. Pherecydes presents in the fifth century B.C. the view of just such a king; his Perseus makes a contract with the king of Seriphus after the hero utters what sounds like an insult or curse. Asked by Polydectes to bring a horse as gift to his wedding (Polydectes is to marry Perseus's mother), Perseus scoffs at the idea of presenting a gift that would be both appropriate and traditional. Perseus's suggestion that he bring the Gorgon head instead is not so much a

---

2. See Canetti 1978, especially his discussions of rulers, paranoiacs, and notions of greatness.

boast of his prowess as it is probably an ill-tempered threat; for later, according to Pherecydes, Perseus does in fact bring a horse as originally requested, but is held to his arrogant rejoinder by the king, who defies him to make the curse hold good. If, on the other hand, we regard Perseus as the deindividualized person—like the Etruscan *phersu*, the *Ur*-person who was, if we are to believe Altheim (1929), a kind of deindividuated manager of a masked funerary performance—then the apprehension associated with his ascent to kingship is not so much worsened by the fear that his heroic role may be abruptly stopped by the Gorgon's petrifying gaze as it is mitigated by his acceptance of the symbolic power embodied in the office itself. Here, Perseus becomes an administrator of the divine, not a divine ego.

In fact, the myth reflects both of these perspectives. Perseus, in other words, is both the deindividualized ritual performer of one type of social order and the ego-oriented tyrant of another. Like the Gorgon face, which is a composite image, a nexus of opposing emotions,[3] the myth also epitomizes the paradox of self-evidence: whatever is self-evident requires no elaboration; yet nothing is known in itself (as Aristotle well knew) unless it can be known in its parts, or unless it can be compared by family resemblance with other things that are known or contrasted with things that are not. Part of the expansiveness of the myth, therefore, rests in its capacity to reflect and externalize, to project what is self-evident and primordial, and to define what is meant by the new person or the new social order through specifying and encompassing either the ancient or the exotic. It is, indeed, the myth's attention to the "foreign"—to the Greek examination of "otherness"—that has sensitized classical studies to the consideration of foreign elements within the myth while simultaneously making foreignness itself the legend's most singularly important thematic focus.

Who was Perseus? And what might have been his knowledge of the foreign? If the calculations of Mylonas (1957, 15–16) are correct, the Mycenaean king Perseus most likely ruled, if he lived at all, in the mid-fourteenth century B.C., probably half a millennium before Homer and Hesiod and a full thousand years before most of the testimonies and fragments that are regularly cited in reconstructing what his legend is

---

3. Napier 1986, esp. 199–206.

about. Tiryns is the kingdom that Perseus offers to rule after accidentally killing his grandfather, an act that fulfills the prophecy that gave
rise to the hero's adventures in the first place. It has been widely considered the oldest of the sites that have come to be called Mycenaean:
"I perfectly agree," wrote Schliemann, "with the common opinion
that the Cyclopean walls of Tiryns are the most ancient monuments
in Greece" (1878, 9). When Perseus came to found Mycenae, if it was
he who did so, Tiryns was already well established, having been in-
habited since Late Neolithic times. Clearly, with such historical obstacles, the prospect of learning anything about the Mycenaean Perseus
from Classical and Hellenistic evidence seems slim indeed. All the
more reason for asking why the legend of a Mycenaean king should
become so important in sixth-century Greece.

Yet we do know that in the mid-fifteenth century B.C. the eastern
Aegean was undergoing great cultural change. Tiryns had entered into
three successive phases of building—the last structures having been
erected in the thirteenth century B.C. but brought down already by that
century's end: its ruined Cyclopean battlements greet modern visitors
to the site. Who destroyed Tiryns remains unknown. It would be four
hundred years before the Greek temple destroyed by the Argives in the
fifth century would be built on this site. We do not know what the
word *Tiryns* means,[4] only that its walls were put up by the Cyclopes,
those monsters with the single eye, and that it was ruled by Perseus,
the founder of Mycenae.

II. INSIDE THE ELBOW ROOM

That the Perseus-Gorgon myth is about the establishment of a new
kind of order—real or imagined—is incontrovertible; that is what the
Greeks said it was about. Perseus was not only the mythical founder
of Mycenae, but the first of the four generations of Perseid kings who,
followed by four Pelopids, constituted the traditional lines of Mycenaean descent. The story of his slaying the monster is like many others
wherein the defeated is represented by a mask that becomes the signal
for the opening of a new and radically different era (see, e.g., Lévi-

---

4. A contested etymology is offered by Georgiev (1973, 250; 1981).

Strauss [1975] 1982, 220). Far more complicated than the change itself is the question of what kind of system this new social order replaced; for, indeed, when radical social change takes place, one's own ancestors may become outsiders, achieving the status of diachronic foreigners. To establish, therefore, what kind of order was given up, what to Greeks of the Classical period would seem super-alien (i.e., foreign), we must first summarize the complex genealogy preserved by the classical structure of the story—that is, the version that has come down to us. Here, I will not focus on the wealth of magical images and the psychological significance of the legend; rather, I will summarize its genealogical complexity.

Acrisius and Proetus were the twin sons of Abas, the son of Lynceus and maternal grandson of Danaus. It was Danaus who, aside from being the eponymous ancestor of the Danaans, was remembered for having had his daughters marry his enemy's (Aegyptus's) sons only to kill all of them (except, of course, Lynceus) on their wedding night. Upholding the familial predisposition for conflict, Acrisius and Proetus quarreled with each other, like Esau and Jacob, while still in the womb. When grown, they fought for control of the Argive kingdom and, in so doing, invented the shield. Acrisius won their dispute, driving Proetus to Lycia, where he married the daughter of King Iobates.[5] With the help of his new father-in-law, Proetus returned to Argive territory and occupied Tiryns, a place fortified for him by the Cyclopes. In the end, the brothers divided the kingdom, Acrisius ruling from Argos and Proetus from Tiryns. The dissension of these twins, then, brought about the primordial division of the Argive kingdom. Proetus had three daughters, who went mad, and later a son, Megapenthes; but Acrisius had only a daughter, Danaë. Acrisius learned from an oracle that his grandson would kill him; to prevent such a fate he locked up

5. That Lycia was for the Greeks equated with things "Oriental" and that it was symbolic of the "foreign" in general may be deduced from a number of episodes and individuals connected with it. Worth noting, for example, is the relationship between the mythology of Proetus and that of Melampus, the prophet of Dionysus. Given the king's name, it is curious that what this "*Wundermann* par excellence" (Burkert [1962] 1972, 211) does is madden the daughters of Proetus to the degree that they think themselves cows. The fact would seem insignificant were it not for the sacred significance of cows outside of Greek culture and the fact that Melampus is the figure most frequently turned to when considering the possible existence of a kind of Eastern "shamanism" in pre-Classical Greece. See nn. 13 and 16, below.

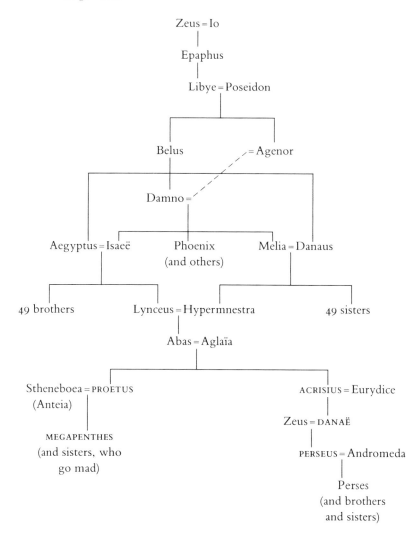

Danaë, but Zeus managed, nonetheless, to impregnate her. Perseus was thus born, and Acrisius, in an effort to rid himself of his potential slayer, set mother and son adrift in a wooden coffer. Eventually they were pulled in by the net of the fisherman Dictys on the island of Seriphus. It was Dictys's brother, Polydectes, who wished to marry Danaë and who sent Perseus off in pursuit of the Gorgon Medusa. Having decapitated the monster through magical contrivances and divine intervention, Perseus returned to Seriphus by way of Ethiopia, where he rescued Andromeda, who was being sacrificed to the sea monster Cetus, by her father, Cepheus, the king of Ethiopia. Perseus had a son by Andromeda named Perses, who stayed behind to become the ancestor of the Persians. (Perseus later had five other sons and a daughter, Gorgophonê.) On Seriphus, the hero petrified Polydectes and handed over the kingdom to his brother, the friendlier Dictys (who had also descended from Danaus). Perseus, Andromeda, and Danaë returned to Argos to find that Acrisius had fled to the land of the Pelasgians. Perseus, wishing to reconcile himself to his grandfather, went there and, at the funeral games in honor of the king of Larissa, accidentally killed Acrisius with a discus. Ashamed to return to Argos, he effected an exchange of kingdoms with Megapenthes, son of Proetus. Perseus thereafter ruled Tiryns, leaving Argos to Megapenthes.

This account, though greatly abbreviated, gives at least a sense of the genealogical complexity of the social relations that govern the story. Striking, first of all, is the presence of a descent system characterized by dualities and opposition, a system emphasizing the corrupting power of twins (Acrisius and Proetus), competing brothers (Dictys and Polydectes), and exchange partners (Perseus and Megapenthes). Each relationship, moreover, is effected by some kind of direct exchange: a battle over Argos, a petrifaction on Seriphus, an exchange of Argos for Tiryns. What, we must ask, necessitates these exchanges, and why, in particular, are they so associated with conditions of social unrest and individual strife?

Part of the problem is certainly that Acrisius, by not having a male heir, did not have a proper kingship or kingly marriage. He is, in other words, without a sexual and social role—a fact that lends support to Hesychius's contention that Kronos was known by the Phrygians as Acrisius,[6] a form of the monster Agdistis (Kronos having also been told that his offspring would displace him). Acrisius, as he is inquiring about how he can get a male child, receives word from the oracle that his grandson will kill him. When he learns his fate, in an effort to avoid it he locks his daughter in a "brazen" tower so that she may not bear children, but Zeus visits her as a shower of gold (Apollodorus 2.4.1).[7] The idea that this tower was in fact a decorated tholos tomb has been

---

6. See Barnett 1956, 225.
7. Cf. Sophocles, *Ant.* 944ff.; Pausanias 2.23.7; Horace, *Odes* 3.16.1–8.

often enough repeated to warrant consideration. For Danaë to be inseminated in a tomb may not be altogether *outré* in a culture one of whose persistent beliefs was that death and rebirth are natural corollaries. Zeus's loss of seed into a womb that is tomblike—or rather, a tomb that is womblike (for the similarity in the shape of the tholos tomb could not have escaped a culture so knowledgeable in the ways of divination and dissection)—was certainly an idea understood by Greeks. Greeks of the Archaic period, indeed, so equated marriage and death that the same vessel—namely the loutrophoros—served both for the wedding bath and for decorating the graves of those who died unwed, providing the deceased, as it were, with the accoutrements of the marriage that was not realized in the present life.[8] Since Danaë cannot comply with her father's wishes and bear a son, Acrisius attempts to force her into its complementary opposite—that of dying unwed in a tholos tomb. Perseus, as would be expected of a hero, triumphs anyhow, if not through any strength of his own, then at least so that he may fulfill the oracle. In so doing, he both defies and strengthens the traditional connection between birth and dying by the very act of decapitating Medusa, for here more than anywhere else in the myth death and parturition are sealed in the disturbing violence that yields yet one more pair of twins, Pegasus and Chrysaor, from the monster's neck. Fate cannot be changed by the machinations of the likes of Acrisius. What, then, makes Perseus different? What makes him capable of influencing his own heroic destiny?

That Perseus is frequently depicted unbearded before taking the monster-maiden's head and bearded after doing so provides some clue, as does the fact that he straightaway proceeds to find a wife who does no less than bear him the ancestor of all Persia. The difference between Acrisius and Perseus is that the latter does, indeed, slay or destroy another kind of order, or otherwise symbolically transform it, by bringing the Gorgon to life again as an aegis or mask—an apotropaic device

8. For a provocative discussion of the Greek connection between tomb and marriage chamber, see Seaford 1987 (especially 107–8, 113, 121). Commenting on the likeness of Greek ritual laments for the dead and those for brides, Alexiou writes that "the similarities are due not to lack of originality, but to the sustained parallel in the ritual of the two ceremonies of wedding and funeral" (1974, 120). See also Danforth and Tsiaras 1982. Note, finally, the metaphoric use of dying as a traditional poetic convention for representing sexual intercourse.

that he uses to establish the social order upon which Mycenae will be based. He transforms that other order, rather than trying to escape it entirely; he sacrifices not Danaë or Andromeda—the two women in his life both turned upon by their kingly fathers—but the source of another order itself. He kills death, as it were, to recreate life.

At least two important themes need to be isolated at this juncture. The first is the deliberate conflation of various rites of transition in the Greek imagination. The second is the symbolic correspondence between rites of transition and changes in social order, between rites of passage and the birth of a nation-state. That the myth concerns a change of order cannot be doubted; but one also cannot dismiss the possibility that the myth may, as Croon (1955) has argued, be modeled on an actual rite of passage.[9] This idea is worth considering not only because of the arguments offered by Croon. As we shall see, mirror images, for the Greeks as for so many of us, symbolize not only an awareness of self and other, but an awareness of self as Greek.[10] In urging this avenue of interpretation, I wish to draw attention, in other words, to the parallel birth of individual psychology and that of cultural identity; I wish, also, to suggest that the pattern through which these two awarenesses are realized is precisely that of a rite of passage. One need only experience the haunting acoustics of a tholos tomb to realize that the entire structure must have functioned as an elaborate transitional "stage" for ritual activity;[11] odd, then, that this environment should also become, as it were, a birthing room of Greek culture.

Lest all this sound contrived, we must endeavor to ascertain just what kind of order is being changed. And it is here that myth-theory and concepts of the foreign—of other cultures, of other modes of thought—become relevant, since a culture, like an individual, may be

9. On the possible impersonation of Gorgons in pre-Classical Greece, see Napier 1986, 83–86, 181ff. The discovery of Gorgonesque helmets at Tiryns, indeed, lends credibility to the thesis that the Perseus-Gorgon legend proffered in the Classical period represents a revision of an earlier tradition in which Gorgons were impersonated.

10. Here, specifically, Perseus's use of Athena's shield is relevant, though Richard Seaford has called my attention to the importance of mirrors, generally, in Greek rites of passage.

11. Indeed, the connection between places of birth—both literal and symbolic—and the theatrical stage is not just metaphoric. It is striking, moreover, to note that one of the acoustically perfect architectural images that was evoked in the Renaissance to describe theater in the round was none other than the tholos tomb (Bernheimer 1956, 232).

defined in the caricature that a mirror image provides: the less onto-logically "oriented" the individual, the more disjunct and unassimila-ble is that "other"; the more ontology and microcosmic/macrocosmic correspondences are emphasized, the more symbolically rich and meaningful that "other" aspect of "self" becomes.

III. APPROPRIATE DEMONS

The ancient history of Tiryns and its Cyclopean battlements is shrouded in mystery despite an architectural correspondence between this fortification and certain Hittite structures. Relevant though the factual history of Tiryns may be, what is significant to the Perseus leg-end is the fact that these walls—which Pausanias (9.36) thought more remarkable than the Pyramids of Egypt—were in the Greek popular imagination considered to be the handiwork of demons (whatever, at any given historical moment, the demonic may be understood to en-tail). For the Archaic Greek mind, these demons were the Cyclopes: lawless savages in Homer (*Od.* 9), amorous wooers in Theocritus (*Id.* 11), thunderbolt fashioners in Hesiod (*Theog.* 149)—three separate tra-ditions perhaps, though perhaps also variations of a more complex idea.[12]

As is clear in Aristophanes' *Acharnians*, in the episode of the Persian envoy whose mask was said to consist of nothing but a huge eye and a Persian beard (*Ach.* 92), it is not difficult to see how one makes parody (or myth) out of an abstract idea by making concrete what is symbolic. The business of establishing radical categories, especially, thrives on taking the fabulous and exotic at face value, letting the exotic speak for itself in a strange way, providing implicitly a definition of what "we" are as a social category by letting the foreign present itself in the oddest terms possible. In other words, the way one might envision foreigners who maintain that they have some kind of eye in their foreheads is actually to put one there, making them either Cyclopean or panoptic. That the Perseus-Gorgon story may be responding to a real awareness

---

12. Their paradoxical nature connects them with other mythological figures such as the Satyrs and Centaurs (Napier 1986, 45–82). According to Seaford, "The satyr is an ambiguous creature, cruder than a man and yet somehow wiser, combining mischief with wisdom and animality with divinity" (1984, 7). See also Seaford 1976.

of some bizarre—perhaps foreign—notion of seeing (in every sense of the word)[13] is suggested both by the presence of forehead "eyes" in the mythology of the Argive Perseus, and more significantly by the consistency with which these images may be associated with the order that Perseus rejects.

This other order is based not only on eyes that involve other "ways of seeing" but on a system that is triadic rather than dualistic. The Graiae are exemplary in this respect. Like the Cyclopean triad in Hesiod (*Theog.* 149: Brontes, Steropes, Arges), the Graiae also come in threes (Pemphredo, Dino, Enyo: ibid., 270–73). These gray old ladies share a single eye in their foreheads and a single tooth; these Perseus must steal in order to discover from them the way to the Gorgons. Again another trinity, the most important of all, appears; its members are the Gorgons themselves, sisters of the Graiae—including Medusa, the one who gives birth to yet another pair of twins (Pegasus and Chrysaor) when decapitated by Perseus. It was Poseidon, god of the sea and of horses, who sired the twins, and he, too, is a member of a ruling trinity. Poseidon rules the ocean while Zeus above rules the skies and Hades below the underworld.

We have here something of a tyranny of trinities: Gorgons, Graiae, Cyclopes, the daughters of Proetus, and the brothers Zeus, Poseidon, and Hades. Two sets (Graiae, Cyclopes) have an eye in their forehead with which they see (or are seers in some particular way). The other sets have no single forehead eye but may have a third eye similarly positioned; for the Gorgons, as sisters of the Graiae, were also sometimes thought to have a third eye, and, according to Pausanias (2.24.2–4), an ancient idol of Zeus from Argos—the so-called Zeus of the East—had three eyes, two in their normal places and a third in the forehead. This emphasis on foreheads becomes increasingly interesting when, as we shall see, the forehead eventually becomes the focus of a complex iconography. Though no pre-Classical image of Zeus (or for that matter of any other pre-Classical figure) has been found to date that pos-

13. Note that it is the three-, four-, or hundred-eyed monster Argos, the eponymous giant of the city of Argos, who is made the guardian of Io, "the wanderer" who roams to the farthest reaches of the foreign world. Compare my remarks about Lycia (above, n. 5). Note, also, that it is Argos Panoptes, the "all-seeing" Argos, who is decapitated by Hermes at the behest of Zeus. According to Moschus (2.58ff.; schol. Ar. *Av.* 102), Argos turns into a peacock, the "Oriental" bird *par excellence* (see n. 15, below).

sesses such a third eye, we have countless numbers of Gorgons on whose foreheads some particular kind of marking occurs (see Fig. 30). What are these marks? What do they mean, and what is their origin?

On the whole this question has been avoided. Most art historians attribute them to some kind of stylistic filling-in. Of those who have approached the problem more directly, Beazley likened the marks to charms employed by Sicilians to ward off the evil eye, and, more recently, Jackson has proposed their connection to a Chalcidian-Egyptian iconographic scheme based most probably on the lotus motif. Referring to their appearance on eye cups, however, he concludes, "but these eyes were above all a *design*, an iconographical conglomerate, a happy accident. No attempt to find a meaning in them should be taken too seriously" (Jackson 1976, 68). Yet it is clear that these designs, with minor exceptions, occur *only* on Gorgons and related eye cups,[14] and, more important, that they do not occur on all examples, a fact that suggests that these marks were neither capricious nor universally understood. One must conclude, then, either that the marks were important but not essential, or that the Greeks considered them as a feature of the Gorgon but were not exactly certain of *why* they were important. The fact that these marks are not explained by any Greek writer suggests that either of these hypotheses may be valid. The stylistic "filling-in" argument is unpersuasive, for, if it were true, we would find these marks on other *en face* images (which we do not). And if the *horror vacui* was really so much in the minds of Greek potters, why are not the marks present on all Gorgons, and, more significant, why are the marks used on even the smallest of faces, some of which occur on an otherwise open field? (See Fig. 32.)

The only conclusion that satisfies all the above questions is that the marks are an innovation introduced in response to an exotic, perhaps imperfectly understood, idea—that they either derive from a foreign image adopted by the Greeks or else are part of a Greek notion of the

---

14. The rare exceptions to this rule include a trefoil pattern on the forehead of a Corinthian helmet in the Delphi Museum (no. 8409), suggesting a design that is apotropaic rather than simply decorative. There is also an eye cup in the Louvre (*CVA* 17, pl. 95, no. 6 [F 130], Louvre III He, 1951) on the forehead of which is a Satyr on whose forehead are two dots. See also Napier 1986, 236 n. 20.

foreign. I will try to show that this hypothesis is supported icono-graphically and historically as well as by internal evidence from within the Perseus-Gorgon legend. I will not argue that the Gorgon is of for-eign origin, but—insofar as such distinctions may be drawn—that she represents in the Greek mind a concept of the foreign. My major ar-gument will, therefore, be iconographic. But there is a second, histor-ical, argument that needs to be posed repeatedly; it concerns the ques-tion of why the Perseus-Gorgon legend becomes so popular at this time—why, that is, the story of a fourteenth-century Mycenaean king should be a prominent, if not the predominant, myth of a sixth-century culture striving to achieve a national identity.

IV. A MARKED DIFFERENCE

Every investigator who has sought out possible foreign influences on the Greek Gorgon has focused on one of Greece's close neighbors—either on places such as Asia Minor (where there were Greek colonies) or on cultures (such as Egypt) that might have exerted, through con-tinuous trade, some kind of cultural influence. Critics of the idea of a foreign influence on the Greek Gorgon are, however, quite right in say-ing that, while certain connections may be drawn, none of the hy-potheses put forward to date is entirely convincing. Part of the diffi-culty surrounding this issue concerns not archaeological fact, but the way the issue itself is construed. There is, for example, absolutely no reason that the Greeks would have had to have regular contact with a certain foreign culture in order for that culture to become a focus of Greek imaginative thought; indeed, if the focus of their concern with another culture had to do with defining the foreign or exotic—or de-fining themselves with reference to the exotic—then all the more rea-son for reaching imaginatively for the limits of the then-known world. Looking from this vantage, we must consider not only the immediate neighbors of the Greeks, but also those cultures about which their im-mediate neighbors might themselves have conveyed a knowledge of such fabulous things as make for a definition of the exotic or barba-rous. Once the Perseus-Gorgon story is approached from this point of view, there is no reason to restrict ourselves either to Asia Minor or to

North Africa in looking for notions that, albeit in some less than canonical version, might have stimulated the Greeks to enrich one of
their prized legends. Any Egyptian or Near Easterner could have provided the Greeks with tales of places more remote and yet more exotic
still. Especially given the exploits of Cyrus the Great, several distant
lands become eligible candidates for comparison, and one—namely,
India—provides some unusually rich evidence.[15] Here, one must remember that the connection between Achaemenid Persia and India is
coextensive with the reign of Cyrus—that is, much older than Herodotus's descriptions of Indian warriors (7.60–88)—and that such connections could, therefore, function for Athenians in their attempts
symbolically to upstage Persian cosmopolitanism.[16] If, that is, Indians
were known to be the "exotic" element in the Assyrian armies and
slave hordes, it would be natural for sixth-century Athenians to want
to state *their* superiority over such exotic peoples too.

Strange though it may seem that the Gorgon becomes the focus for
an involved superciliary iconography, far stranger is the fact that each
and every one of these emblems is explicable in Indian terms, and that
the Sanskrit word for "thunderbolt" (*vajra*) also signifies the tridentate
mark that underlies the idea of the third eye—an inner power that is
also an outward devastating force, an ambivalence that may either kill

15. According to Rawlinson, "we have direct evidence of early trade by sea between
the Phoenicians of the Levant and western India as early as 975 B.C., when Hiram, King
of Tyre, sent his fleet . . . to fetch 'ivory, apes, and peacocks' from the port of Ophir to
decorate the palaces of the Temple of King Solomon. . . . There is no doubt that the
objects imported came from India" (1975, 425). While Ophir is now thought to have
been an Arabian rather than an Indian port, it was, in any case, a place where Indians
and Phoenicians met to engage in trade. Though Achaemenid expansion under Cyrus
brought India under Persian control, "the earliest contact between Greece and India was
made about 510 B.C., when Darius the Great, having advanced as far as the head-waters
of the Indus, sent a Greek mercenary named Scylax of Caryanda to sail down the river
to its mouth, and make his way home by the Red Sea. Scylax took the old route followed
by the Phoenicians, and, after a voyage lasting two and a half years, duly arrived at [the
site of the later] Arsinoë, the modern Suez. His account of his adventures was probably
utilized by Herodotus, who was born at Halicarnassus, not far from Caryanda, in 484
B.C., about the same time as the death of Gautama Buddha" (ibid., 426).

16. Though some examples of Athenian confiscation of Persian symbolic property
are discussed below, here it is important to reiterate how the Perseus-Gorgon legend is
revised to make the hero's son, Perses, the ancestor of the entire Persian civilization. One
need only recall Cyrus's own title, "King of the World," to sense the dimensions of pre-
tense resorted to by tyrants (such as Pisistratus) who would compare themselves to Persian rulers. In other words, it would be perfectly natural, given the subjugation of India
by Persia, to think of the former in the context of comparing oneself to the latter.

FIG. 29. Attic black-figure eye cup signed by Nikosthenes as potter (ca. 520 B.C.: Virginia Museum of Fine Arts, Museum Purchase, the Adolph D. and Wilkins C. Williams Fund; no. 62.1.11): androgynous Gorgon with three-pointed forehead mark from the tondo of an eye cup. Emptying the cup means also confronting the petrifying face; losing one's head, thus, is cleverly equated with being "out of it."

or cure.[17] As I have elsewhere, and at some length, discussed these forehead marks (1986, esp. chaps. 4, 5), I will not here consider them in any detail. But the facts that the Greeks say nothing about them, and, moreover, that they are *all* explicable by reference to an Indian iconographic canon deserve more than passing notice. Figures 29–31 give a sample of the markings that are found on black-figure vases and eye cups from the mid-sixth century B.C. onwards. These marks commonly occur as a single point (Fig. 30a), or a configuration of two (Fig.

17. Though the tradition of the third eye is generally thought to antedate the display of sectarian marks on the forehead, actual archaeological evidence suggests that the display of the mark is equally ancient.

FIG. 30.   Gorgons with various forehead marks: a selection of the hundreds of mostly sixth-century Gorgons that appear with some kind of forehead sign. That these marks occur exclusively on Gorgons and eye cups is especially curious, given their use throughout Indian tradition to make sectarian distinctions. *a*) detail from Attic vase (Louvre, CP10357, Cliché des Musées Nationaux, Paris); *b*) Gorgoneion by Lydos, ca. 560 B.C. (Attic black-figure plate, Munich, Staatliche Antikensammlungen und Glyptothek, no. 8760); *c*) fragment of Attic vase (Fitzwilliam Museum, Cambridge, GR. 205-1894); *d*) detail from kylix by Nikosthenes (Cabinet des Médailles, Vase 319, photo: Bibliothèque Nationale, Paris); *e*) detail from Attic vase (Fitzwilliam Museum, Cambridge, GR. 13-1937); *f*) Panathenaic red-figure amphora by the Berlin Painter, late 6th c. B.C. (Munich, Staatliche Antikensammlungen und Glyptothek, no. 2312); *g*) Attic black-figure amphora by the Amasis Painter, 6th c. B.C. (courtesy Museum of Fine Arts, Boston, no. 01.8026, Pierce Fund, purchased of E. P. Warren).

30b) or three (Figs. 29; 30f, g) points on the forehead. Four points (Fig. 30c) and line-and-point configurations (Figs. 30d, e; 31) also exist. Three is the most prevalent number, the points forming either an upright or an inverted triangle. And this triadic theme is reiterated in the tridentate and trefoil shapes that are also common on both Gorgons and eye cups.

In the Indian iconographic canon a meaning is provided for these marks that is both comprehensive and coherent. One is the symbol of unity. Its emblems are the *bindu*, the circle or point to which the universe may be ultimately reduced, a mark signifying both sexuality and procreation; *bhasma*, ash, what is reduced by fire (*bhasmaséséh* being, according to Hindus in Bali, the ash mark on the forehead that unites the living and the dead—i.e., both death and parturition); and *nāman*, name, appellation, the forehead mark that also gives identity. Each of these ideas attempts to present a total image in as reduced a form as possible. A variation on the symbolism of one itself, of unity, commences with the introduction of a vertical line, implying the unity of binary opposites such as right and left, male and female, and so on (Figs. 30d; 31b). The image of line and point (Fig. 31a; cf. Fig. 34) also forms the basis for the sacred syllable *oṃ*, the Indic word of words, the graphic depiction of the sound that unites the universe. This mark, therefore, signifies a single unifying sound, and its place on the forehead is legitimized by the yogic notion of the third eye, the eye that opens either as a meditative force or as an externalized power. Two points (Fig. 30b), again, symbolize duality, as do four-pointed configurations divisible by two (Fig. 30c, e). More complex still is the symbolism of three. Its meaning is that of the unity of opposites, of their resolution, of two reduced to one. On Gorgons it occurs either as three points (Fig. 32), as a trefoil (Fig. 33), or as the upright or inverted three points of a triangle (Figs. 29; 30f, g). It is the most common of all the forehead marks, and the most interesting.[18]

For Indians, the three-pointed mark represents a complex set of ideas that can only be summarized here, but it is important at the outset to recognize that the exact meaning of any mark need not have been

18. Note here the Pythagorean refutation "of the concept of participation and 'separation'" (Burkert [1962] 1972, 53) and the consequent perfect (unifying) character of odd numbers.

FIG. 31. *a*) Mastos (ca. 510 B.C., courtesy of the Trustees of the British Museum, B376); *b*) Attic black-figure eye cup signed by Nikosthenes as potter (ca. 520 B.C.: Virginia Museum of Fine Arts [see Fig. 29]): that superciliary marks occur exclusively on eye cups as well as Gorgons and that Greeks used (as we use) body terms to designate parts of the cup suggest that the entire cup was understood both as a container and as a symbolic head.

FIG. 32. Attic black-figure kylix (Cambridge, Fitzwilliam Museum, no. 11085): the argument that the marks on the Gorgon's forehead result from the Greek artist's *horror vacui* is clearly undermined by the need to present the marks even in an otherwise open field. Here also we see the graphic association of eyes, drinking cups, and Gorgons.

understood for it to have achieved a certain significance. Even among Hindus themselves, the exact meaning of any given mark may not always be known. As Moor pointed out long ago, the common person is often disinclined to understand fully the meaning of these marks, so that "the less comprehended, the more such things are admired. . . . Everything mysterious is profound, and repeated accordingly" (1810, 400). This said, however, it is necessary to consider further these three-pointed marks, because in India they have much to do with androgyny and ambivalence, features characteristic of the Gorgon (Napier 1986, 89–90, 129), and because the Indian iconography of the forehead fits rather remarkably the peculiarities of the Greek case: that Zeus wields the thunderbolt, and that the Argive Zeus of the East was said to have

FIG. 33a.   Laconian black-figure cup from Etruria (Paris, Louvre, Cliché des Musées Nationaux, E.669): as in India, the sectarian mark may also be signified by a trefoil, particularly when a god, goddess, or androgynous deity may manifest itself in three forms or as a member of a trinity.

had a third eye; that Poseidon wields the trident, and that the *vajra* is both the trident and the thunderbolt in Indian legend; that the one-eyed Cyclopes fashioned thunderbolts; that the Graiae have a seeing eye in their foreheads; and, above all, that the androgynous Gorgon Medusa (ibid., 89–90), their sister and Poseidon's mate, displays a very complex forehead iconography.

In Indian tradition, it is a horrific androgyne—such as the modern-day Śiva—who carries the three-pronged spear. His androgyny means that he is literally ambivalent, and his feminine manifestations, such as Kālī, bear an astonishing resemblance to the bearded Gorgon—includ-

FIG. 33*b*.   Laconian black-figure hydria. (Courtesy Museum of Fine Arts, Boston, Frederick Brown Fund, 68.698)

ing not only glaring eyes, gnashing teeth, and a protruding tongue, but also a snake-entwined head and the sectarian mark that distinguishes her worshippers. These Hindu deities are also, above all, possessors of the third eye—the inner eye of enlightenment that is also an outward terrific force. In Indian mythology, the complex iconography of the third eye and the forehead finds its elaboration in the mark of the trident—the ambivalent eye is marked, literally, by the striking of the forehead with the trident, the thunderbolt. This three-pointed mark, the *triveṇī*, is so much connected with both the horrific and the erotic that the ideas of death and parturition are, as they are with the Gorgon, central to it. As with many triadic figures, the number 3 indicates ambivalence, and the forehead marked in any three-pointed configuration indicates ambivalence as well. Two marks indicate the opposition that makes ambivalence work—an ambivalence that Apollodorus tells us the Gorgon also possessed (3.10.3): "What flowed from her left side [Asclepius] used for the perdition of mankind; while what flowed from her right he used for their salvation, and by that means [Asclepius] raised the dead." One mark, the eye itself, is the resolution of ambivalence—that is, the resolution of paradox or contradiction. What is astonishing is the fact that each and every set of Gorgon marks is explicable by reference to the Indian iconographic canon, and that all the Gorgon's attributes—her arresting face, her snakes, her caduceus (Napier 1986, 169–70), her petrifying stare—are aspects of a refined and coherent Indian iconographic tradition.

What is the evidence for the antiquity of this symbolism in India? Though we have no comparable images from India for the period between the seventh and fifth centuries B.C.—indeed, we have few artifacts of any sort—reference to the *tripuṇḍra*, the three marks that would evolve into the Śaivite sectarian mark, occurs already in the *Upaniṣads* (*Bṛhajjābālaopaniṣad* 3.25ff.).[19] There both the rituals relating to the marks and the application of them are given.[20] The *tripuṇḍra* is said to

19. Cf. *Brāhmaṇa* 4.32–41. For example, "One should make the celebrated Tripuṇḍra mark over the forehead, ever keeping before his mind the three-eyed Śiva, the basis of the three Guṇas, the generator of the three worlds and the omnipotent overlord, uttering the five-syllabled Mūlamantra, 'Namaḥ Śivāya' [Salutation unto Śiva]"; and later, "when the Tripuṇḍra marks are worn in the prescribed manner with Vibhūti by any one, by him is worn the Trinity composed of Brahmā, Viṣṇu, and Maheśa, the three fires [Dakṣiṇa, Gārhapatya, Āhavanīya], the three Guṇas [Sattva, Rajas, Tamas] and the three worlds [Bhūr, Bhuvaḥ, Suvaḥ]."

20. Like all such religious texts, the *Upaniṣads* have been much altered over time, but in general they may be dated to before 600 B.C., though some date the group of which the *Bṛhajjābālaopaniṣad* is a part to the fourth century B.C. However, the continued use and emendation of many of India's sacred texts have made their dating highly problematic. In general, the traditional methods of dating define as "early" those *Upaniṣads* whose major focus is Brahmanical ritual, while *Upaniṣads* that refer regularly to the gods of the Śaivite pantheon (the later Hindu gods and goddesses) are considered "medieval." While the *Bṛhajjābālaopaniṣad* is connected by others with this later group, we have no way of knowing whether it is a spontaneous "medieval" creation, or an emendation of an earlier text. One can argue that a later vocabulary indicates a later date; one can equally

represent three eyes, the three *guṇa*s (the qualities of lightness, activity, and heaviness), three Vedas, three gods, three fires, and three worlds (*Bṛhajjābālaopaniṣad*, ibid.), just as the three-eyed Zeus of the East was said to symbolize (along with Poseidon and Hades) heaven, earth, and underworld. Likewise, the *ūrdhvapuṇḍra*, the Vaishnavite sectarian mark, occurs in the *Purāṇa*s (after 200 A.D.) but is popularly attributed to the *Yajurveda* (ca. 900 B.C.).

It is important to note that each of the various sectarian marks need not imitate exactly the marks of the Gorgon that have come down to us; for, indeed, the Indian texts describing these marks refer alternatively to three vertical or horizontal lines, single dots, three points, lines and dots, or triangles. Moreover, the very purpose of the sectarian marks demands that they be distinctive and that, therefore, they be altered over time. For this reason, the marks described in modern recensions of ancient texts are unlikely to imitate precisely their original versions. That the three lines of the Śaivites—to use the least Gorgonesque variety—are horizontal rather than trefoil-shaped or triangular is, for example, less significant than the fact that they are intentional variations on a basic triadic iconographic theme; what *is* significant is the formal idea (the number symbolism: the three gods, three eyes, three worlds, etc.), for the fundamental principles are what permeate all sectarian traditions. This said, it is interesting to note that exact parallels do exist (Fig. 34), especially within those traditions less susceptible to redactors and recensions: in folk art and iconography, in tribal and sectarian tattoos, and more pervasively (and more important) in the worship of the female principle in India—all of which antedate the modern sectarian marks, and probably also the ancient texts that are at their foundation and from which they receive justification. In modern as well as ancient yogic practice,[21] the three points at the forehead and the triangle they form are, significantly (for an androgynous Gorgon),

---

argue that a more modern vocabulary indicates an early, fundamental set of ideas that has been continually transformed. Clearly, this problem also plagues linguists studying any epic tradition.

21. Though descriptive materials outlining the details of yoga, tantra, and the "left-hand" path do not occur before the time of Christ, all the major elements are already present during the Indus Valley Civilization (ca. 2500–1500 B.C.). See Marshall 1931, I.78; Werner 1977, chap. 5. That Greeks were probably, in some vague way, aware of the "left-hand" path in India may be surmised from such traditional notions as Alexander the Great's supposed knowledge of the preeminence of the "left" among the Brahmans.

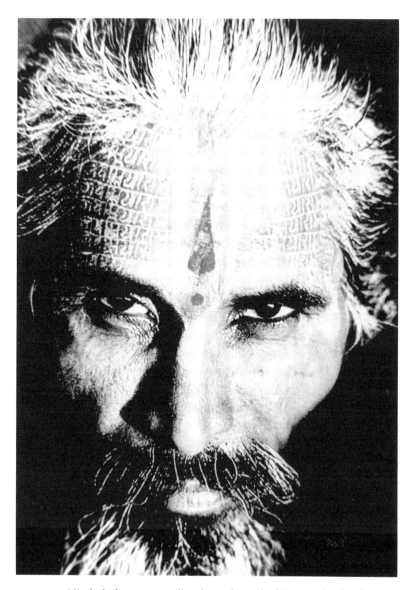

FIG. 34. Hindu holy man or *sadhu*: throughout the history of India the forehead has played an important role in distinguishing members of various sects as well as in designating the physiological locus of exceptional esoteric power. Though the iconographic permutations of such marks are nearly infinite, most have their source in the graphic representation of the sacred sound *oṃ*. Note how similar this mark is to the Greek mark depicted on the mastos in Figure 31. (Photo: Henry Wilson)

the symbol of the unity of masculine and feminine—their comple-
mentarity, their coexistence, even their potential androgyny.[22] "Of all
of the linear graphic symbols," wrote Zimmer ([1926] 1984, 148),

> it is the triangle (or, more accurately, "three-point") that plays the dom-
> inant role. It is also often called *yoni* (womb), rather than *trikona* or
> *tryasra*, the geometric term for "three-point." *Yoni* as womb is used gen-
> erally as a term for the *fons et origo*, but in its graphic, pictorial form as
> a triangle, it is a symbol of the Feminine as well. In the symbolic lan-
> guage of the tantras [indeed, the marks themselves are often called *tan-
> tra*], the feminine element represents the energy (*sakti*) of the Divine
> through which the Divine in play unfolds and manifests its essence. *Yoni*
> is *sakti*.[23]

Some years ago, Avalon (1959, 418) described these three points in
much the same way, arguing that the male and female powers must
necessarily be represented on equal yet opposite terms, the male being
signified by the triangle (the "three points") on its base, the female by
the same figure inverted (cf. Figs. 29; 30f, g). One might object that
the symbolism of primary numbers is universal; however, the way this
symbolism manifests itself in India and Greece certainly is not. Moreover, one need only look at the number of sexually oriented or blatantly erotic images that take the place of these marks in the "forehead"
areas of Greek eye cups to realize that they are somewhere in the same
semantic field as the yogic *bindu*, the mark that explicitly and implicitly
indicates sexuality as well as cosmic union.[24]

As I have already indicated, I am not intent here on arguing that the
Gorgon is an Indian concept or of Indian origin. I merely wish to suggest that the Greeks might have seen her as embodying the foreign, so
much so that they not only Orientalized but Indianized her as their
knowledge of the East developed. There are, moreover, other indica-
tions to suggest that the Greeks would have perceived the merits of an
Orientalization that was also an "orientation." Perseus kills the Gorgon
Medusa—*medousa*, the female leader; we naturally ask, "The leader of

22. The *Upaniṣads*, for instance, tell us that the combining of male and female, of
Śiva and Śakti, is a "triangular seat of fire" (*mūlādhāra*: *Bṛhajjābālaopaniṣad* 3.25ff.).
23. Note the correspondence between the Gorgon maiden's head and the Gorgon's
maidenhead—her giving birth to Pegasus and Chrysaor following her decapitation.
24. See, e.g., Korshak 1987.

what?" And how was it that the so-called leader of the three Gorgons was the only one who was mortal? Strange, it seems, unless she was made mortal in order for Perseus to overcome her, or unless she was a cult figure that personified the process of death and rebirth.[25] That the Gorgon is as old as anything Greek may well be true; however, her possible Greek antiquity in no way diminishes her "foreign" focus, for in a more restricted tribal context, for example, the foreign may begin on the other side of the river or, indeed, at the very edges of the village. Not only the name *medousa*, but also *Gorgō*, suggests things not entirely, or at least not only, Greek.

The Greek *Gorgō* has frequently been connected to the Sanskrit *garj*, "to (emit a) growl, roar." *Gorgō* also has as cognates such words as "gorge," "gorgeous," and "Gargantua." Its sound value in itself is also worth considering. *Gargaphia*, for instance, is the name of a sacred spring near Mount Kithairon (Burkert [1972] 1983, 113). The root **gharga*, R. L. Turner tells us in *A Comparative Dictionary of Indo-Aryan Languages* (1969), refers to the "gurgling sound of water," while *gárgara* is a whirlpool itself. This notion of not only the "gargling" growl that the Gorgon is named for, but also the "gurgling" sound of water, is striking when applied to the Greek conception of Poseidon as god of the ocean, and of the Gorgons as living on the shores of Oceanus. This aquatic connection is reaffirmed by the fact that as apotropaia the Gorgons function as do the eyes on boat prows and, in folk mythology, are related to other sea monsters, Nereids, and mermaids. The mirror, moreover, in which Perseus safely (that is, properly) shows the Gorgon head to his wife, Andromeda, was thought to be a mirror reflection in the waters of a well, a reflective opening to the underworld.

Here we begin to see how the fundamental categories upon which the Gorgon is based may be understood as being at the foundation of the pyramid of family resemblances, the organizational maelstrom, that structures the myth. This funneling process of progressive simplification, of revealing its salient features, is seen, in particular, in the iconography of the kylix, the drinking cup, and especially in the so-called eye cups (Figs. 29, 31, 32). These drinking vessels are identified

25. See, e.g., L. R. Palmer's contribution in *Transactions of the Philological Society* for 1958, "New Religious Texts from Pylos (1955)."

by the large eyes depicted on them, between which are usually found some erotic image—Satyrs, mask of Dionysus, copulation—or the same marks that are otherwise found only on the Gorgon's forehead. These marks indicate not only that the vessel for "gargling" wine depicts what is most significant in identifying a Gorgon, but that this iconography is distinctly ambivalent in the erotic/horrific sense. That the erotic and the horrific are part of the same iconographic structure proves better than any single testimony that ambivalence is at the basis of the Gorgon, and the fact that Gorgons are frequently shown in the tondo of the eye cup points to a specific correspondence between losing one's head and being out of it—that is, inebriated. That the Greeks were aware of the eye-cup Gorgon as an irreducible iconographic structure is apparent in their equal awareness of the vessel as an instrument, a kind of ethological homunculus—an indicator, that is, of human sensory capacities.[26] Like the enormous head with diminutive body that modern science tells us is the graphic illustration of the sensory capacities of the right hemisphere of the cerebral cortex, the eye cup is the instrument for presenting us with the image of a vessel that embodies a specific anthropomorphic idea. For the Greeks, the vocabulary of cup parts was as it is for us: eyes, ears, lips, body, and so on (Boardman 1976, Bron and Lissarrague 1984); the eye cup is, Boardman adds, itself a mask, or, we might argue, a homunculus—an enormous assemblage of facial parts. The eye cup that is a wine vessel gives us, in other words, the structural image at the base of the maelstrom, the face in the well, the simplest ensemble of signs by which a Gorgon may be known. This reflection is the objective figure of the subject. As Vernant (1980, 458) and Frontisi-Ducroux (1984, 147–60) point out, the reflection is more than the reality. It is the face of the extreme other—that is, the *foreign*—that enables one to become another while staying oneself; what is the same is two, and vice versa. In a mirror what one sees is oneself seeing oneself.

As for the "foreignness" of the Gorgon, certainly the worship of

26. See Napier 1986, 167–82, 199–206. Also interesting is the way that the Gorgon head represents the sympathetic component of the autonomic nervous system, and especially the so-called fight/flight syndrome. In Indian thought, the parasympathetic antithesis to this syndrome is epitomized in the restorative power of yoga, a fact most relevant here given the relationship between yogic powers and the iconography of the forehead.

ambivalent monsters was not, after Homer's time, to Greek taste, or at least to the taste of Greek intellectuals.[27] To Greeks of the Classical era, as to modern critics of the ritual theory of myth, denying the former order of things is accomplished in one of two ways: either by defining ritual so narrowly that it becomes atrophied into something meaningless, by petrifying it; or by simply denying that the older ways could have had anything at all to do with the refinements with which we now surround ourselves. In either case, the campaign is the same: to protest or propagandize—to purvey one's own objectives through a particular intellectual stance—and in so doing to isolate in a radical way, to use as one's measure what stands in opposition to the ideal toward which one currently aspires. In this respect, the highly emotional cast of modern critical rejections—that ritual could have nothing to do with the fine arts in Classical Greece (cf. Napier 1986, 30–44)—is itself a function of a canonical process wherein the older ways are recognized as such by protesting that artistic awareness can have little to do with ritual, while at the same time offering a definition of ritual that is so inflexible that it is meaningful only in providing a foil for a particular critical view. What is often overlooked is the extent to which our views have to be different, or at least represented as different, in order to be ours (and not "theirs"). Thus, the dichotomy between "us" and "them" is part of both a developmental change over time (in which we protest, often falsely, that we owe nothing to the old ways that is substantial—"Nothing to do with Dionysus" was the adage for the Greeks) and a recognition of difference at a given moment (in which concepts of the foreign enable us to identify what is "theirs" and not ours). In the Perseus-Gorgon story, the evidence is everywhere that an older order is being overturned and that the visual vocabulary of the foreign is the medium for making social change permanent.[28]

27. It is not the object of this discussion to venture into the complex history of the Greek fascination with the foreign; however, it should be noted that "representations of barbaric rites need *themselves* no more be barbaric than representations of any *x* whatever need have the properties of *x*-hood. By *imitating* practices it was *horrifying* to engage in (Nietzsche), the Greeks spontaneously put such practices at a distance and invented civilization in the process" (Danto 1973, 2).

28. The literature on the supposed foreignness of Dionysus is enormous; and this is not the place, in any case, to consider the accuracy of the many and varied indigenous Greek ideas about the Orient. However, the dubious character of much of what Greeks

V. THE CULT OF CULTURE

The mirror image is the perfect symbol of alienation.

Gérard Genette, *Figures*

To ask, finally, whether the Gorgon had a foreign origin is, I think, to put the question wrongly. What is relevant to an understanding of the myth is the way that the Gorgon reflects the *dernier cri* in exotica at any period in Greek history, for a case can be made for arguing that what to Greeks was the most foreign of places was that same place that provides so many striking analogies to the Gorgon's iconography—that is, India.

Though it is beyond the scope of this chapter to elaborate in any detail all the correspondences between Greek and Indian iconographic conceptualizations that may apply to a study of the Gorgon, I would like to return for a moment to the myth itself. There we are told that Perseus spied Andromeda while flying over Ethiopia on his return from Oceanus with the Gorgon head. Now it is well known that Greeks throughout antiquity were of the belief that Ethiopia and India were one and the same place. This view (expressed, for example, by Aeschylus, *Suppl.* 284–86) is often thought by modern scholars to be a naive confusion; but there is at least one excellent reason that these countries should have been equated in the Greek mind. Already in the third millennium B.C., Babylonian records prove the existence of trade between India, the Persian Gulf, and the East African coast (Casson 1971, 23–24). Cinnamon[29] and cassia[30] were transported from India and Southeast Asia, via Madagascar and Somalia, to the Mediterranean,[31] and cassia was known in Egypt by the fifteenth century B.C. Again, my

---

said and thought about the foreign in no way diminishes the anthropological significance of such statements. See, for example, Momigliano [1958] 1966, or Hartog's venturesome and more recent study (1980).

29. The word "cinnamon," deriving from the Malay *kayu manis* ("sweet wood"), was introduced into the Mediterranean by the Phoenicians, "adopted in Hebrew literature as *Qinnamon*, . . . which the Greeks easily adapted to *kinnamōmon*" (Miller 1969, 46; see also 154ff.).

30. The bark of *Cinnamomum cassia* Blume. The tree is found in India, China, and Southeast Asia (Casson 1984, 225).

31. See, e.g., Miller 1969, 42–47, 153–72; Detienne [1972] 1977, 16; Casson 1959, 179, and 1984, 225–46.

concern here is not to show that the Gorgon is Ethiopian or Indian, despite what the Greeks may or may not have thought the monster to be, and despite what "Oriental" motifs they may have utilized, consciously or otherwise, in describing the exotic.[32] Nor need it be fact that Indians were a part of the exotica of Persia from the time of Cyrus, or, from the standpoint of popular mythology, that an Ethiopian or Indian became the mythical queen of a Mycenaean founding father, for us to see that the Greeks were looking as far afield as possible to make the legend seem fabulous but credible. That the earliest Gorgon masks are the eighth-century terra-cotta helmets from Tiryns, however, does suggest the historical character of the myth, as does the later legend that the Gorgon head was buried beneath the marketplace at Argos (Pausanias 2.21.5)—that the head became, as it were, the foundation for a foundation myth as well as a foundation for a real place. What seems more to the point is that the myth provides a mirror of the foreign that is also a boundary marker of who and what the Greeks were. Relevant to the present discussion, therefore, is the extent to which cultural identity is understood to be a function of some type of cross-cultural symbolic exchange. It is not, that is, important whether Greeks had any firsthand knowledge of India. What is important is that, in achieving cultural identity, they perceived themselves as having entered into some kind of symbolic transfer. They took the Gorgon

---

32. Even in the midst of Homeric epic, one finds some very curious "Orientalizing" employed in designating the foreign. It is very odd, for example, that there should be 108 suitors in the *Odyssey*, 108 "foreigners" each trying to woo Penelope. Not only is 108 the most sacred number in India, but it has specifically to do with the numerical aspects of ritual performance, designating as it does the number of prayer beads prayed with by Brahmanas, the number of names of certain gods and goddesses, the number of yogic postures, the number of *pitha*s or pilgrimage sites sacred to Vishnu, the number of times the name of a deity is repeated each day by a high-caste boy once he has received the sacred thread. Though in the East itself there is no agreed-upon origin for the symbolic importance of the number, for Hindus on Bali it represents the 4 phases of the moon, times the 27 lunar mansions (Lansing 1983, 20–21). Another answer is suggested by the Orphic "Orientalizing" preserved in Pythagoras. According to Burkert ([1962] 1972, 23), 9 is (or so Aristotle claims of Pythagoras) the idealization of space, since it is the sum of 2 (the line), 3 (the plane [the triangle being the simplest plane]), and 4 (the solid [tetrahedron]). The number 12 is, for Hindus and Pythagoreans (or for that matter anyone who cares to look into the night sky), representative of the lunar year (i.e., time), so that 108 is "space" times "time," the framework, in other words, in which microcosmic/macrocosmic continuity is affirmed. Surely 108 is the numerical sign of space and time and, therefore, of microcosmic and macrocosmic stability. If ever there were a "foreign" number for the Greeks, it would have to be 108.

head as a trophy, as the symbol of both the conquering and the assimilation of the alien; in turn they offered Perses, the son of Perseus, as the invented ancestor of the Persians. They gave, through their hero Perseus, freedom to an Ethiopian princess while taking her to become Perseus's queen—that is, queen of Mycenae, and queen, therefore, of Greece.

How much, actually, does the Perseus-Gorgon legend have to do with Greek cultural identity? Or, to put the question another way, is it accidental that the Perseus-Gorgon legend rose in popularity during the birth of the Classical period in the sixth century B.C.,[33] and that we generally assign the birth of Greek drama to the precise moment at which a tyrant was able to organize competitions in which regional performances were hierarchically ordered (i.e., in which there were winners and losers)? That the tyrant Pisistratus organized the Great Dionysia in Athens, at which in 534 B.C. Thespis (the individual "father" of Greek drama) won his first victory in public competition, is surely not coincidental.[34] Whether or not one perceives a connection to exist in sixth-century Greece between ritual and drama, it is important to recognize that it was in the era of Pisistratus that the division between mystic ritual and public celebration was dissolved (Seaford 1984, 9–10, 30–31).[35]

What is more, it could not have escaped Athenian notice that the return of the exiled Pisistratus was mirrored—even legitimated—by his support of Dionysus, the "outsider" who embraced the common man. The connection between Pisistratus's exile and Dionysus's identity as a "god of the East" surely had great significance for Athenian commoners who saw in Dionysus an alternative to the aristocratic cults. In supporting Dionysus either directly or through supporting a

---

33. See Napier 1986, 85ff. Howe, for example, notes that evidence for the legend is infrequent before the second half of the seventh century, after which it appears virtually everywhere (1952, 81).

34. See Pickard-Cambridge 1927, 76ff. For a description of the way that ritual may be "rethought" in drama, see my general discussion of the origins of drama and the paradoxical nature of Satyrs and Centaurs (1986, 45ff.) and Seaford's (1984) essay on satyric drama in his introduction to Euripides' *Cyclops.*

35. What Seaford describes as the need to "make an effort of informed imagination" (1984, 1) is as much a challenge to the culture-specific modes of thought through which we express our critical categories as it is a simple challenge to an orthodox view of the birth of "art" in Greece.

festival given in his honor, Pisistratus not only brought "outsiders" (e.g., the people of Eleutherae) into the arena of Athenian social relations, but, in so doing, signaled a new kind of social identity, which did not depend on the inherited status implicit in the aristocratic cults.[36] Contrary to much modern academic opinion, cultural identity appears to be codified not through the supposed radical opposition of self and other (this being more the intellectual property of historical "explanation" and of various forms of academic discourse),[37] but through the assimilation of what one takes to be foreign into one's cultural sphere. What we are talking about here is not foreign "influence," but (and this is what matters anthropologically) the tactical use of the foreign in manipulating cultural canons[38]—or, to be specific, the appropriation of exotic cultural property by Pisistratus.

The argument, then, is not about "Orientalization" (which, by definition, depends upon a number of academic straw men), but about "orientation." It is not historical; for history itself functions to organize events and to codify them. Nor is it archaeological or linguistic. It is entirely anthropological: when one reaches out to find an image through which to define one's culture, one reaches to the limits of the known world—indeed, one systematically stretches those limits far beyond what may be factually known. Like the anthropologists or travelers whose worldliness depends upon a list of countries with which they can claim familiarity or an inventory of years spent in such places, identity depends upon the codification, the assimilation, of other places that may in reality be less wholly known than the hazy recollection of past experience frequently permits. It is, one might argue, *precisely* because Greeks could have had no complex knowledge of things Indian—though they could have, in the Near East or North Af-

---

36. As Parke points out, this was not the only such incorporation, it being "the period where there was a tendency to introduce into the city the prominent cults of local districts. [One may] see another such example in the admission of Artemis of Brauron to the Athenian acropolis. This was all part of the broadening of the basis of the Athenian state which was typical of the policy of Peisistratus and it is likely that he took positive steps to introduce and develop the cult of Dionysus—a deity of popular appeal whose festivals were the kind which tyrants encouraged in their movement away from the rites and privileges of the aristocracy" (Parke 1977, 128–29).

37. Note, for example, the frequent "alienation" by contemporary Classical scholars of arguments about Greece that focus on the "foreign."

38. See, for example, Stocking 1985 on the strategic use of cultural artifacts in the invention of tradition.

rica, *seen* them—that India becomes a real candidate for explaining an image that, in a sense, is also entirely Greek. By the sixth century, the Gorgon, in other words, becomes commonplace; but it does so as a striking and novel image of the exotic.

To be sure, much of what Pisistratus did appears to have focused on deploying the exotic in the interest of codifying Greek identity. His use of dramatic events to arrive at a cultural canon through the assimilation of diverse regional performances was a most striking example, as were his efforts to "stabilize" the text of Homer for recitation in the same context.[39] In this latter case, particularly, we see evidence of a conscious attempt to equate a new political authority and a new notion of culture with the political stability, the very legitimacy, of the nation-state. Pisistratus's interest in fixing Homeric form, or, for that matter, his affinity for Dionysus, or Athena, or Heracles, or Perseus, is, in other words, a way of demonstrating his rootedness in things Greek, while also demonstrating how assimilation and control of the outside could

---

39. Though Pisistratus's role as a "stabilizer" of Homer is controversial, the fact that the name Pisistratus appears repeatedly in Homer (and in the capacity of "leader of men") reminds us that the regular use of Homer in defining "early" Greek culture must be tempered by an awareness of how epic poetry in any culture—and particularly an epic that is popular—will be constantly employed to reflect the contemporary concerns of those who utilize it. That Athenians were well aware of the political ramifications of epic canon formation is attested by a number of literary traditions. According to Markoe (1989, 102), "one . . . tradition records that the Homeric poems were introduced as part of rhapsodic competitions instituted in sixth-century Athens. Diogenes Laertius (1.57) dates the introduction of the Homeric recitations to the time of Solon. A fourth-century tradition (pseudo-Plato, *Hipparch.* 228c) assigns its introduction to Peisistratus' eldest son Hipparchus, who required rhapsodists at the Greater Panathenaia to adhere to a fixed order in reciting the episodes of the Homeric poems. A separate tradition, attested in Cicero (*De Or.* 3.137) and many later authors, credits Peisistratus with a recension of Homer, stating that it was the tyrant who first arranged the episodes in a fixed order. Yet another tradition preserved in Plutarch (*Sol.* 10.1) records that Solon made an interpolation in Homer when reciting a passage of the *Iliad* on the occasion of the Spartan arbitration over the island of Salamis. Diogenes Laertius (1.57) ascribes this Athenian insertion (*Il.* 2.558) to Peisistratus. A reference to the same incident may perhaps be found in a fourth-century tradition preserved in Aristotle (*Rhet.* 1.1375B30) that refers to the Athenians' citation of Homer as witness about Salamis. All of these traditions attest to both an interest in and a familiarity with Homeric poetry in sixth-century Athens." As far as the evidence for Homer the individual author is concerned, it is important to remember not only that the earliest complete texts come from our own era, but that "there is no Ionian inscriptional evidence earlier than the seventh century B.C. and no knowledge of the text of Homer until the sixth century" (Emlyn-Jones 1980, 88). Pisistratus's part in the "tidying-up" of oral tradition involves, thus, a question not so much of determining whether or not a personal Homer was responsible for the *Iliad* and *Odyssey*, but of making sure that, by Pisistratus's time, texts and individuals could be absolutely connected.

lead to a newer, more cosmopolitan, more powerful social order, in which rank could be established through *individual* achievement rather than inherited through any aristocratic ancestral cult. As a tyrant, he was not alone in this awareness, though he undoubtedly capitalized on the general interest of sixth-century Athenians in things "eastern."[40] But his use, for example, of lions and Gorgons on the tetradrachm (a coin found in foreign hoards and believed, because of its high value, to have been used particularly for foreign trade: see, e.g., Bailey 1940; Kraay 1976; Kroll 1981; Markoe 1989, 107–9), or his monopoly on black-figure vases,[41] was not only a method of advertising his cosmopolitan ability to compete with and to outwit things foreign, but a way of establishing, through his own efforts and heroic pretensions, a stabilization of visual, verbal, and performance activities, a codification of the Greek artistic canon. The birth of acquired status and the appearance of Homer as an individual identity are, in other words, coextensive; the stabilizing and codifying of an epic or heroic tradition is, indeed, the most common way of establishing a cultural canon— that is, a nation-state and a culturally determined concept of the person. For, like that of a nation-state or an individuated author (or, for

40. This interest may be seen on many more fronts than have thus far been mentioned. As Andrewes puts it, "No one doubts that the prosperity of Athens greatly increased during the sixth century, and many historians have been sure that Peisistratus' encouragement of trade and industry had a large share in this. Their evidence is pottery, sculpture and buildings, to which it can be added that his ventures overseas stimulated trade" (1982, 408). In architecture we have the pronounced East Greek influence in the Old Athena temple. Later Attic *korai*, for example, demonstrate a close connection between Ionia and the Athens of Pisistratus. Markoe has recently argued that lions—and Gorgons, insofar as they are leonine—were employed in the shrines of Athenian aristocrats in an effort either to demonstrate their own heroic pretensions or to illustrate their cosmopolitanism, or both. In sculptural attire the chiton replaces the peplos. More specifically, "Athenian involvement in commercial exchange with the East is commonly seen as the primary motive behind Peisistratus' establishment of his son Hegisistratus as tyrant of Sigieon, an East Greek city under Oriental (Achaemenid) suzerainty (Hdt. 5.94.1; Thuc. 6.59.4)" (Markoe 1989, 104–5).

41. This well-documented monopoly is evident from the wide distribution of Athenian black-figure ware, but even more compelling is the local dominance of Attic vases and Homeric themes on the mainland. Referring to the overseas prosperity of Athenian trade, Andrewes remarks that "the certain fact in all this is the spectacular development of Attic black-figure vase-painting, and the virtual obliteration of its rivals in Corinth and elsewhere" (1982, 408). Controlling pottery production, of course, meant that the market was also flooded with visual images and epic themes that were to Athenian taste. The popularity in particular of Heracles, Dionysus, and Perseus, and the superabundance of Gorgons on all forms of pottery, illustrate how trade functioned to propagate the Athenian canon.

that matter, an academic discipline), the legitimacy of a canonical form rests in its capacity to delineate a bounded domain of experience.

No doubt the respect exhibited in classical times for Bronze Age tombs (Kurtz and Boardman 1971, 297) was, likewise, part of an attempt to revive—in the interest of Greek identity—the Mycenaean heroes, to legitimate contemporary seventh- and sixth-century political authority by connecting those recently deceased with past leaders and cultural heroes who were believed to have been divinely ordained. Surely it cannot be accidental that from the mid-seventh century onwards the legend of the Mycenaean king Perseus—slayer and assimilator of the exotic—should have become so popular on Greek vase painting, or that Pisistratus should at once have associated himself with specific symbols of the foreign so as to define, authoritatively, Greek culture as a bounded domain, Greek art as a bounded domain of images, and the Greek personality as the bounded focus of individuation. Perseus, as his name suggests,[42] is a heroic *Ur*-individual of Greek culture. When he slays the monstrous Medusa, he looks not only to the ends of the then-known world; when Perseus looks in the mirror of Athena's shield, we must realize that he is not only looking into the magical land of the foreign, but that, in so doing, he is also looking directly at himself.

42. Napier 1986, 130, 187.

4

Bernini's Anthropology:
A Key to the Piazza San Pietro

Nothing may be undertaken in honor of the Mother of God unless it be something great.

Alexander VII

I. A GRAND *CONCETTO*

In March of 1657 Pope Alexander VII presented, after private discussion with Gian Lorenzo Bernini, a revised plan for the soon to be constructed piazza in front of Saint Peter's Basilica. The idea was to replace the rejected trapezoidal plan with an oval one—a shape that the piazza retains, with some modifications, to the present day.[1] Over three hundred years have passed since the first oval plan was introduced, and we are still uncertain about the symbolic origins of the newer shape. Bernini's famous *concetto* for the Piazza Obliqua—that the colonnades symbolized the arms of the Mother Church—was only expressed well after the form of the piazza was conceived.[2] Moreover, these arms resemble more the piazza as we know it today than they do, as we shall see, the first oval plans (Fig. 35);[3] the earlier models included an additional colonnade, which enclosed the piazza and emphasized what Bernini felt to be the beauty and perfection of the circle (Kitao 1974, 14).

But the enclosed circle was not the only relevant motif. With such

---

1. For the most detailed study of the various transformations in the plans for the Piazza Obliqua, see Kitao 1974.
2. This explanation, by far the best known to the present day, began to gain ascendancy in the winter of 1658–59.
3. See several illustrations in Kitao 1974.

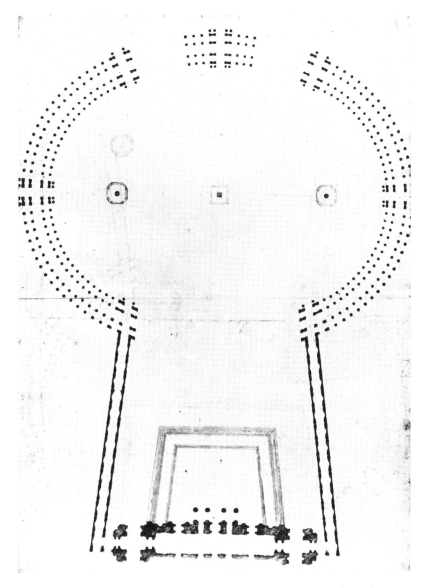

FIG. 35. Piazza Obliqua, "Vatican Plan" (ca. 1659): a view from the Church's perspective (i.e., inverted) of the earlier oval plan with third colonnade. (Courtesy Biblioteca Apostolica Vaticana)

an image in mind, we may turn to another *concetto* that, as Kitao (1974) has argued at some length, influenced the piazza's design. The image is that of an amphitheater, not only a space that emphasizes enclosure, but one that functions as a stage, as it were, for the performance of God's worship. Indeed, the word *teatro* was frequently employed to refer to the piazza in contemporary accounts (ibid., 20), and theatrical comparisons are readily made between the Piazza Obliqua and earlier works by Bernini.[4] But is the amphitheater, in fact, the fundamental image upon which the Piazza Obliqua is based? Could there be another image that more closely mirrors the shape of the piazza in the first oval plans? The answer to these questions involves consideration of the humanistic concerns of both Bernini the artist and Alexander VII, a man whose patronage of scholarship was legendary (von Pastor [1940] 1957, 269–77). In examining and comparing their respective interests, I hope to show that there is a yet more fundamental and simpler *concetto* upon which the oval plan for the Piazza Obliqua is based. The image is that of the uterus, the womb of the world inverted on the altar of God, an image that was known in the Renaissance to those familiar with Gnostic thought.

It is well known that Gnosticism was an important topic in seventeenth-century Italy. Though ultimately deemed heretical, the Gnostics were understood originally to have been "the intellectual party in the Church," a group whose object it was "to resolve the Christian message into a philosophy acceptable to cultivated minds" (Hastings 1914, 231). Engaged in what Harnack has called "the acute . . . hellenising of Christianity" (1958, 1.226)—that is, its agglomeration of various religious traditions—the central purpose of Christian Gnosticism paralleled precisely the intended function of the Piazza Obliqua. For Bernini, the agglomerative role of the Catholic Church as the Mother of all other churches was explicitly stated in his *giustificazione* for the Piazza Obliqua (Kitao 1974, 14), and Alexander VII's desire to redefine pagan archetypes in a Catholic context cannot be doubted. The dramatic discovery at the very entrance to Saint Peter's in 1609 of a Roman sanctuary to Cybele, the Mother Earth from

---

4. In 1665, Bernini himself would describe his *Due Teatri* as occurring in front of Saint Peter's (de Chantelou [1877–84] 1985, 82–83); see footnotes below, esp. nn. 13, 25, 31, 34, 38, 41.

whose womb emerges all life, provided a true catalyst for such think-ing (Vermaseren 1977, 45–51), but the entire process of reformulating pagan archetypes was crucial to the program and spirit of the Counter Reformation.

The pope's ardent devotion to "the pursuit of the arcana of Egyptian wisdom" (Heckscher 1947, 180) during a period of history when "minds were so well attuned to the inherent harmony between pagan prefigurations and their Christian fulfillment" (ibid., 156)[5] is a fact that, more than any other, makes possible a Gnostic influence on the Piazza's design.[6] Alexander VII not only commissioned Bernini to create a grand context for displaying the Egyptian obelisk that had been found at the monastery of Santa Maria sopra Minerva (the result was Ber-nini's famous "equestrian" elephant, Fig. 36),[7] but actually had the hi-eroglyphs on the obelisk translated by the Jesuit Athanasius Kircher. Kircher, one of the most admired intellectuals of his day, was the pope's chief confidant in matters scientific, historic, and esoteric.[8] His *Oedipus Aegyptiacus*, the work that was meant to explain these pagan prefigurations, was produced at vast expense, since special type had to

5. According to Dempsey, an interest in such theorizing reaches its height in the seventeenth century; "this interest is particularly evident in Rome, and more particularly within the entourage of Cardinal Francesco Barberini" (1966, 234).

6. "Despite the wide range of their interests and the diversity of their origins this group of antiquarians and collectors was a tightly-knit one, and the figured monuments which most caught their fancy were really of a fairly limited kind. The Vigne Carpi and Cesi, for example, were filled with religious and funerary monuments of a distinctly esoteric cast, the great majority of which were the products of the late antiquity and mystery cults and were profoundly infused with the syncretistic doctrines of that pe-riod" (Dempsey 1966, 234–35).

7. That the elephant itself was thought to be sexually symbolic is clearly shown in a somewhat earlier etching by Rembrandt. When one looks closely at his *Adam and Eve* of 1638, one sees that in the background there is an elephant—certainly a curious ad-dition to a scene describing the Fall of Man, until, that is, we remember something of Rembrandt's sympathy for the Jews and the fact that the most popular (and also the old-est) of medieval elephant accounts is a Jewish one that found its way into the *Physiologus* around the fifth century. The story of "the elephant's notorious sluggishness in sexual matters, has," according to Heckscher (1947, 173), "from the very beginning been in-terpreted as an allegory of the Fall of Man." Legend has it that the female elephant cannot conceive "unless she proceeds to the Gates of Paradise, in order to pluck the mandrake, eat of it, and also give it to her husband to awaken his otherwise dormant sexual de-sires. . . . Implicitly, the eating of the [psychoactive] mandrake, the *sine qua non* in the elephant's marital life, was understood to signify that the elephant—both male and fe-male—is the prototype of the ideal Christian spouse who will mate without sexual ap-petite, solely for the sake of offspring" (ibid.).

8. The fact that most of Kircher's ideas have not withstood the test of time should not keep us from admitting the enormous influence he had upon Alexander VII.

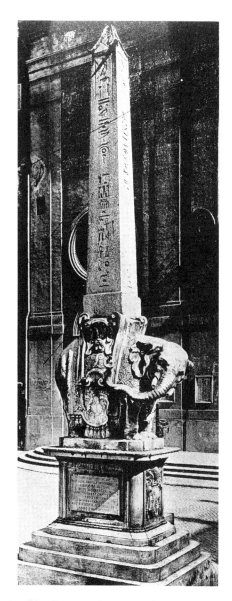

FIG. 36. Gian Lorenzo Bernini, *Elephant and Obelisk*
(Rome, Piazza della Minerva, 1667): this Egyptian obelisk, dating from the sixth century B.C., was excavated
in Rome and reborn on the back of Bernini's elephant.
Among the hieroglyphs depicted on it is the *ankh*,
which was interpreted by the Jesuit Athanasius Kircher
as the symbol of the all-embracing "World Spirit."
(Courtesy College Art Association)

be cast for Hebrew, Chaldaic, Arabic, Coptic, Samaritan, and even Chinese (von Pastor [1940] 1957, 272).[9] Alexander VII so admired this polymath that he put Kircher in charge of "a collection of curious and rare objects of every kind," which had been left to the Roman College (ibid., 276);[10] such was this pope's commitment to humanism. In fact, the pope's acute interest in both scientific and humanistic issues resulted in his reputation as one of the most worldly individuals ever to hold that office, a man capable of being "erudite in a distinctly secular sense" (Heckscher 1947, 181).[11] As for his specific role in redefining pagan archetypes, we can be sure that it was quite carefully thought out and deliberate. Instead of devaluing pagan images by denying or minimizing their specific origins, Alexander VII pointed out their rich Christian meaning by emphasizing their evolution from an earlier heretical and idolatrous form to their present one (ibid., esp. 158, 179); in this way, ancient knowledge was subsumed into a Catholic context. Specifically, the relating of such images was made possible through exorcism—through the cleansing of a pagan monument by the pope "as the expression of his desire to see man's eternal hope for a share in the gifts of Divine Wisdom glorified through himself" (ibid., 158).[12] Most

9. It is important to realize that this interest in prefigurations was intensely shared by the group of humanists surrounding the papal court in the second quarter of the seventeenth century. Girolamo Aleandro, secretary, adviser, and friend to Francesco Barberini, argued in the 1620s that paganism and Christianity were neither in opposition nor even very far apart. Rather, they could be seen, according to Dempsey (1966, 240–41), "as part of a long continuum, moving from a lesser to a fuller understanding of God, beginning with his first revelation to the Egyptians, who, according to antiquarians, 'invented' religion." Likewise, the Paduan humanist Lorenzo Pignoria, whose services had also been secured by Cardinal Barberini, had interests that "were not focused merely on the reduction of all the gods to a common principle, but were also absorbed in the theory that all religion was sprung from one spot, one historical moment in Egypt, from which beginning grew the whole bewildering variety of pagan divinities" (ibid., 236).

10. These objects formed the basis of the Kircher Museum, a collection that remained intact at the Roman College until 1870.

11. It should be pointed out that Alexander VII bought the library of the Dukes of Urbino and transported it to Rome, set up a new chair in Church history at the University, and in general did everything in his power to further both scientific and humanistic knowledge. It is said that Alexander VII would even forego the Italian siesta in order to converse about theological matters with his friends and acquaintances.

12. According to Heckscher (1947, 179), the obelisks "had to be exorcised before they could be erected 'under the cross.'" This act of exorcism "by no means cleansed them of memories of previous idolatrous functions. On the contrary, the very persistence of those memories links the obelisks with that particular wisdom of the Egyptian priests', which Kircher had in mind when he said that they were dedicated to the 'World Spirit'" (ibid.).

important in the present context was the way this reworking of ancient images applied to the Virgin Mary. On the obelisk project for the Piazza Minerva, Alexander VII, Bernini, and Kircher specified her archaic lineage;[13] to them, it afforded a context for certifying what they understood to be "a clear perception of the three archaeological strata of the Piazza Minerva site, matronized as it were by Isis, Minerva, and Mary, who are seen as a triad under the common denominator of Divine Wisdom. At first Divine Wisdom was incarnated in the Egyptian Isis, then in the Graeco-Roman Minerva, and ultimately, in its purest exponent, the Mother of the Lord Herself" (ibid., 180).[14]

On the popular level, a fascination with the esoteric elements of Gnosticism was no less pervasive.[15] Interest was great enough to support an active market in faked intaglios; speculation about the meaning of various Gnostic gems was common, and collectors delighted in their interpretation.[16] One such intaglio, given to the painter Rubens by the French statesman, scientist, and antiquarian N. F. C. de Peiresc (Bonner 1950, 80–82; Barb 1953, 194; Heckscher 1947, 177), and cherished by the artist, depicts a womb with a key placed upon an altar.[17] It is a type of intaglio for which we have other examples, and one that, I would like to suggest, provided the formal symbolic design upon which the Piazza Obliqua may have been based. Bearing in mind the

13. With respect to the microcosmic/macrocosmic significance of these piazza projects, one should remember that the Piazza Navona became the focus of the spectacular by being regularly flooded and, thus, bringing the four great rivers of the world onto the Catholic stage.

14. Here we see the perfect example of the Renaissance doctrine of *numen mixtum*. Referring, again, to the fascination with pagan monuments so prevalent at this time, Dempsey remarks that "unexpected combinations of attributes and deities, *numina mixta*, solar and seasonal imagery pertinent to the cults of Attis, Cybele, Isis and Osiris, Mithras and Hercules are the rule rather than the exception on these monuments. And the point cannot be too heavily stressed that it was precisely the cult aspect of these monuments which most absorbed both artists and antiquarians of the period" (1966, 235).

15. "From the early sixteenth century there developed a fashionable craze for emblem books, rebuses, and similar riddles" (Hall 1983, 295). This craze was precipitated on the intellectual level by the Neoplatonic belief in the occult language of symbols.

16. Kircher's interest in "applied hieroglyphics" already had many popular antecedents; the *Hieroglyphica* of Horapollo Nilous, for example, had been well known since its discovery in the fifteenth century (Heckscher 1947, 176). Nor was the interest in the seventeenth century restricted to Italy; in France, particularly, the antiquarian rage had led to considerable speculation about the meanings of occult and pagan images. See, e.g., Bonner 1950, Barb 1953.

17. For a complete interpretation of these images, see, in addition to sources cited in this chapter, Frankfort 1944.

FIG. 37. Four hematite gems symbolizing a uterus and an altar or key: the Gnostic image of a womb on an altar is coextensive with the notion of the feminine womb being protected by a masculine key. (Courtesy of the Trustees of the British Museum; after Barb 1953)

general popularity of occult imagery among seventeenth-century humanists, as well as the pope's keen interest in the understanding of pagan prefigurations generally, and, most important, his dedication to the glorification of the Virgin Mary, I would like to suggest that what Alexander VII and Bernini privately discussed before submitting their revised, oval design for the Piazza to the Congregazione in March 1657 was the idea of employing a symbol that, though originally pagan, nonetheless represented the most refined example of the Divine stage brought to life through the proportions of the human body. With this possibility in mind, we can now compare the aforementioned type of Gnostic intaglio with Bernini's addition to Saint Peter's.

II. AN IMAGE REBORN

Figure 37 shows a series of Gnostic intaglios, the meaning of which is discussed in detail by both Bonner and Barb (Bonner 1950, 79–94; Barb 1953). They depict an altar upon which stands a womb with a key. From the top of the womb project two winding appendages representing the Fallopian tubes. The meaning—which was known in the seventeenth century—is that of a charm for safe pregnancy, birth, and infancy. Here, the uterus with a key symbolizes the masculine control and protection of the womb and, hence, of the birth process generally. Compared with a view of the Piazza Obliqua (below, Fig. 43), the

FIG. 38.   Piazza Obliqua, Foundation Medal III (inverted): this foundation medal clearly depicts the important features of the oval piazza design, including the full oval with two main entrances, the obelisk and two fountains, and the Church (altar) of Saint Peter. (Photo: Fototeca Unione; courtesy College Art Association)

Gnostic icon seems of tangential relevance at best, until we consider the piazza design as it would have been viewed from Saint Peter's itself, or in any of the early representations illustrating the shape originally intended by Alexander VII after his and Bernini's private deliberations (e.g., Fig. 38). At once we recognize the superficial similarity of the two shapes (cf. Figs. 37–39). The question, then, must be asked whether or not, or to what extent, the meaning of the piazza corresponds to the Gnostic image. To my mind, there is no doubt that the analogy is direct and complete.

Figure 39 illustrates the fundamental elements of the uterine form along with the relevant Gnostic and Catholic identifications. At the base, both traditions depict an altar. The connections between Saint Peter, his chair, and the altar of God are among the most basic images of the Catholic world, but in the Gnostic context one is reminded also of Saint Peter's Basilica as a *petra genetrix*: "Upon this rock I shall build my Church." In Gnostic thought, the altar of God is related to the conception of Sophia, which, like the prefigurations of Mary on the obelisk, "is related in many of its features to that of the Mother (Ishtar, Isis, Atargatis, Cybele) who in the Babylonian myth descends into the abyss, where she is held prisoner" (Hastings 1914, 236). Here we see not only the "tremendous effort to incorporate myths of every kind" (Grant 1966, 11) that is characteristic of later Gnostic thought, but a deliberate attempt to equate, as Alexander VII one day would, Great Mother figures from different traditions. Like, therefore, the rock of the Mother Church that is Saint Peter's, it is the impregnation of the *petra genetrix* that gives life; the androgynous Agdistis, according to Pausanias (7.17) and Arnobius (*Adv. Nat.* 5.5–7), was born of the impregnated rock, and in Mithraism, a monstrous time-god (the so-called lion-headed personage) possesses the keys to the underworld.[18] In this capacity, the androgyne is, like Saint Peter himself, the figure responsible for man's fate—for holding the keys (Fig. 40), for loosing and binding the doors of salvation—while androgyny itself is a kind of primordial anarchy out of whose *conjunctio* arises, through divine intervention, some form of supernatural order. The keys to the underworld thus correspond to the keys of Saint Peter, which open the gates of Heaven and symbolize the pope's role as transformer. While a visitor to Saint Peter's might be hard put to see how Maderno's portico could function as a "key," once we review any of the attempts at rendering the piazza in two dimensions (e.g., Fig. 38) or representing

18. See especially Vermaseren 1977; for illustrations of Mithraic lion-headed figures, see Vermaseren 1956–60. On ambivalent leonine deities, see Napier 1986; on the relationship between Christianity and the subterranean in the seventeenth century, and Alexander VII and Kircher in particular, see Kircher's *Mundus Subterraneus* (1665). Kircher, in fact, was said to have been so intrigued by the details of the subterranean that he had himself lowered into Vesuvius in order to obtain empirical evidence for his study.

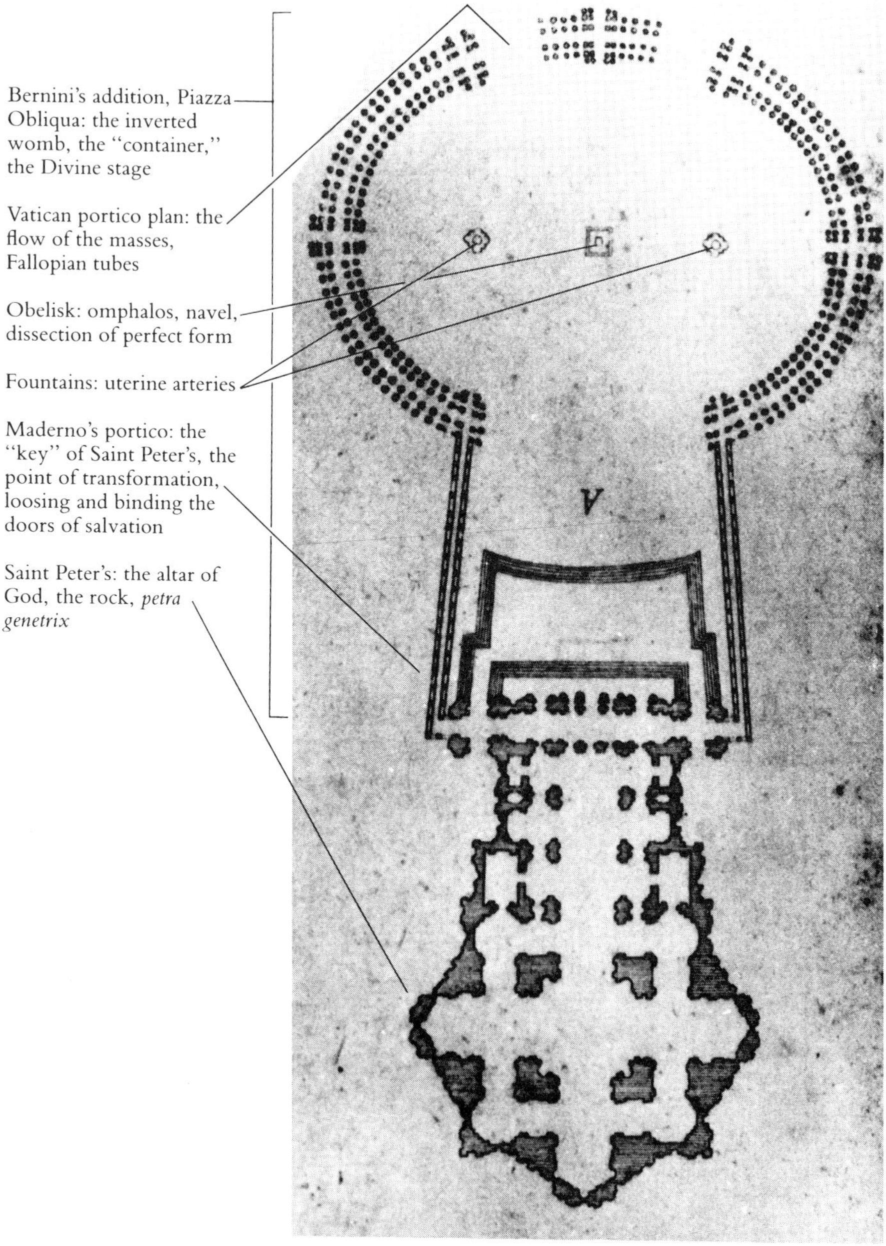

Bernini's addition, Piazza Obliqua: the inverted womb, the "container," the Divine stage

Vatican portico plan: the flow of the masses, Fallopian tubes

Obelisk: omphalos, navel, dissection of perfect form

Fountains: uterine arteries

Maderno's portico: the "key" of Saint Peter's, the point of transformation, loosing and binding the doors of salvation

Saint Peter's: the altar of God, the rock, *petra genetrix*

FIG. 39. A "Gnostic" view of the Piazza Obliqua, in which each major element of the design is interpreted as a macrocosmic rendering of an early Christian womb intaglio. (Inverted detail of an engraving by G. B. Bonacina, 1659; courtesy Biblioteca Apostolica Vaticana)

FIG. 40.   Bronze statue of Saint Peter from within Saint Peter's Basilica: like the Gnostic keys that open and close, so too do Peter's keys loose and bind, opening and closing the sacred space of the basilica and, by extension, the doors of salvation. (Arnolfo di Cambio, ca. 1296; courtesy Anton Schroll & Co.)

it in a plan (Fig. 39), the image of a uterine key becomes clear. What is more, the analogy also works on the symbolic level of the portico as a door, since it is the entrance to the house of God that marks the point of transformation, the controlled transition from a physical space to a metaphysical one—the very place, moreover, before which the followers of Cybele had periodically buried the *vires* of a bull in honor of the Great Mother.

As for the colonnade, Bernini's own specific contribution to this remarkable *concetto*, it can only be called the most brilliant piece of architectural symbolism anywhere in the Western world; for here we have the perfect "incorporation" into a Christian context of an idea that is more universal than specifically Gnostic—namely, that of the Divine womb conjoined with the altar of God. In the early plan, with its additional colonnade, we see how the idea of a full oval becomes dominant, being split into two openings through which the masses would throng onto the Divine world-stage (e.g., Fig. 38). Even the fountains have a physical correlate that was known among Gnostics, for they are positioned on the axis of the two lateral gateways into the piazza and correspond to the uterine arteries, which bring life-giving fluid into the womb.

Like the Gnostic womb, the Piazza Obliqua also has its center—the navel, the *omphalos*—marked by the obelisk (in this case not the Roman obelisk but the Vatican one). According to Saint Hippolytus, it was "the Sethian heresy which asserted that 'from the first grand intercourse of the three original principles' . . . light, darkness and spirit . . . 'there originates some grand form of seal [*sphragis*], Heaven and Earth. Now the shape of heaven and earth is similar to a womb [*mētra*] with the navel in the middle; and if anybody wants to demonstrate visibly this shape, let him skillfully dissect the pregnant womb of any animal and he will find a model of heaven and earth and of everything which lies in their midst unchangeable' " (Barb 1953, 198). Not only is the conjunction of light and darkness a theme central to those members of the cult of Attis and Cybele (whose rituals, according to the discoveries of 1609, had once been performed in the Piazza space), but the image of the *omphalos* itself was clearly suggested by Hippolytus; moreover, the connection between the Gnostic image and religious performance is suggested through the way that the obelisk, like the *omphalos*, functions as the axis for the turning of the key: ♇. The obelisk, already moved by Sixtus V to its present location at the entrance of Saint Peter's, needed only Bernini's broken colonnade of Tuscan columns crowned by an Ionic frieze (which the artist felt were masculine and feminine, respectively [Hibbard 1965, 155]) to make the image complete. It is the superb manner in which what was preexisting is reinterpreted, as much as the addition itself, that makes the Piazza Obliqua such an incredible work. This is a fact with which Bernini would no doubt have agreed; for him, genius meant being able to overcome every obstacle in making a beautiful work of art out of something already given. A truly great artist should be able to make something sublime even out of an imperfection, "to make use of a defect in such a way that if it had not existed one would have [had] to invent it" (Baldinucci [1682] 1966, 80).

As for whether or not the pope was likely to have known something of the heritage of the Gnostic image, we can say that at least he was keenly aware of a variety of related concepts. Not only can such an awareness be deduced from his concern with the prefigurations of Mary and the justifications necessitated by the discovery of Cybele's shrine, but certain Egyptian hieroglyphs sharing their symbolic heritage with the womb intaglios were the subject of both his and Kircher's scrutiny.[19] The Egyptian *ankh*, ♀ (the *crux ansata*)—the hieroglyph that represents a womb sealed off by a masculine cross or "key"—appeared on several monuments, including the Elephant Obelisk interpreted by Kircher for the pope, and the similarly shaped hieroglyph *sa*, ♀ , carries the specific meaning "protection." Here, it is important to realize that Kircher believed hieroglyphs to be mystical ideographs rather than a written language with specific phonetic values.[20] It would, in other words, be most appropriate for Kircher to suggest to the pope that the Church attempt to appropriate, through architectural form, the power inherent in this image (Reilly 1974, 57).[21] Further, even more important in interpreting the imagery of the Piazza Obli-

19. On the relationship between specific hieroglyphs and the Gnostic womb intaglios, see Barb 1953, esp. 199ff.

20. See, e.g., Reilly 1974, 56.

21. Kircher had, for instance, already worked with Bernini on the fountain project, sponsored by Innocent X, for the Piazza Navona. There he had been most enthusiastic not only about the symbolism of the Obelisk of Domitian (Kircher was charged with "restoring" the obelisk's hieroglyphs), but also about the overall symbolism of the construction of the fountain itself.

qua is the fact that the *crux ansata* (the "handled cross") was both the most significant of all symbols in Kircher's writing and the form that best represented the stated role of the Piazza Obliqua: *Crux ansata vehiculum spiritus Mundi significat . . . in omnia Mundi membra diffusam* (*sic*: Kircher 1676, 42, 47).

What, however, transforms this interpretation from speculation to probable truth is one important historical fact—namely, that N. F. C. de Peiresc, the "interpreter" of the Rubens intaglio, was not only a crucial figure in the progress of Athanasius Kircher's career, but the main supporter of Kircher's hieroglyphic studies in the years before Kircher went to Rome. Peiresc provided him with both encouragement and a number of rare manuscripts, sharing the knowledge of hieroglyphs that he himself had arrived at through his own enthusiastic research. When Kircher was ordered to go to Vienna to take up the former post of Johann Kepler, it was Peiresc who wrote to Cardinal Barberini with the hope that Kircher would instead be sent to Rome.[22] What is more, it was Peiresc who gave Kircher the many "curious and rare" objects—like the *vulva deificata*[23] given by Peiresc to Rubens—out of which Kircher would begin his famous museum in Rome. That Peiresc, moreover, could have had such an influence on the papacy and on the application of an intaglio to an architectural scheme is seen in his influence on Bernini's design for the baldachin at the crossing of Saint Peter's. For there, already, an early medal (now lost) had provided Bernini with a basis for a major architectural and sculptural program devoted to symbolic activity—a program of even more obvious religious significance than the Piazza Obliqua (Fig. 41). The medal in question had been given to Cardinal Francesco Barberini in 1636 by Claude Ménétrier, a French antiquarian then living in Rome. And it was none other than Peiresc to whom Ménétrier had sent a casting of the medal for his interpretation (Lavin 1968a, 13–14 and refs.)

22. Cardinal Barberini had himself been introduced to Peiresc by Girolamo Aleandro during the cardinal's diplomatic mission to France in 1625–26. "An enthusiastic student of archaeology and philology himself, [Aleandro] was the personal and respected friend of many of the most important scholars in Europe, with whom he engaged in a voluminous correspondence. Not the least of these was the great Peiresc" (Dempsey 1966, 238).

23. This is Peiresc's own description of the intaglio he gave to Rubens; see Barb 1953, 194.

FIG. 41. Lost medal employed by Bernini as a model for the baldachin at the crossing of Saint Peter's: here we have evidence that Bernini was predisposed to utilize an early Christian medallion as a symbolic model for a major architectural program prior to designing the Piazza Obliqua. (From Lavin 1968a, fig. 38, after de Rossi; courtesy Biblioteca Apostolica Vaticana)

The point that the above exegesis makes clear is that even if Alexander VII and his entourage had not seen the Gnostic image in the Christian one (and it is very difficult to imagine their not having done so), the idea would certainly have been of more than passing interest to them. And whether or not we one day uncover some correspondence that would prove irrefutably the symbolic parallel outlined here, far more interesting is the fact that the connection is valid from the perspective of Baroque metaphysics. Like the Tantric systems of India and Southeast Asia, what most characterizes the agglomerative interests of Baroque humanism is a desire to make the microcosmic reflect the macrocosmic and vice versa—or, in Alexander VII's case, to make the primordial images that occur throughout history coincide with his devotion to the Mother Church and to Mary as the Mother of God. Such a focus on symbolic unity is based on the belief that the human body is a microcosm of the universe, a belief rooted in the conviction that a correspondence between microcosmic and macrocosmic originated in scientific fact and that art could, therefore, mirror the universe.[24]

One need not, in other words, turn to psychological arguments about primordiality, or to comparisons with non-Western cultures in which there is a strong focus on symbolic unity. The impetus for a concern with symbolic unity in the Baroque era comes from within the period itself and need not, therefore, be inferred or superimposed. The argument for symbolic unity in seventeenth-century Italy arises from within the system it helps explain. This system, in turn, demands that the forms comprising the human body be the same forms that control great architecture. Looked at from this perspective, whether or not Bernini and Alexander VII's decision can be proved to have been a conscious one matters less than does the self-evident character of the symbols involved. What is important—and this is my argument—is that even if in their planning such a view were not known to them, upon learning of it thereafter they would have delighted in how closely their plan echoed the ancient image of divine maternity. But, having said this, the image itself was so well known at the time as to make their ignorance of it virtually inconceivable: to imagine, that is, that they could have looked at Kircher's collection of intaglios, or considered their revised plan as a symbol, and not have seen the analogy, is to do them an intellectual disservice.

---

24. See Hall 1983, 252. This focus is also founded upon the Renaissance conviction that seals are symbolically charged microcosmic entities (Yates 1966, 246ff.). Any feeling that the baldachin of Saint Peter's or the Piazza Obliqua could not be derived from something so minuscule or insignificant is probably a product more of our own cultural proclivities than of those of a period very much concerned with such correspondences.

III. CREATION AS SPIRITUAL EXERCISE

While it is clear how certain pagan ideas of the Divine womb could be understood by an intellectual pope as prefigurations of Mary, and while we now can easily see how Peiresc's and Kircher's interpretation of Gnostic womb imagery could have been relayed to both Alexander VII and Bernini, we have yet to consider the possible appeal of this ideogram for Bernini—a man so admired for his own intellectual powers by Alexander VII that he was invited to converse with the pope on a daily basis; a man whose point of view was so respected that, supposedly, the pope "was astounded at how Bernini, by the sole force of his genius, could arrive at a point in the discussions that the others had scarcely attained with long study" (Baldinucci [1682] 1966, 42). What meaning could such an image have had for Bernini, the artist? And if the inspiration for the Piazza Obliqua was the idea of the Divine womb, why is the *concetto* of the amphitheater so important? The answer to these questions lies, no doubt, in an awareness of the way in which forms that are archetypal are simultaneously both symbolic and real.

On an intellectual level, it is the degree to which Bernini's images appear concrete that has sometimes led scholars to juxtapose his work to the symbolic abstraction of forms characteristic of architecture from Alberti onwards.[25] For Kitao, Bernini's addition to Saint Peter's "is not merely *like* an amphitheater . . . but *is* itself one" (Kitao 1974, 30); the clarity of the idea, in other words, places the image beyond metaphor and in contrast to abstraction.[26] Yet how far away is Bernini, in fact, from those Renaissance intellectuals who felt that simple formal perfection could visually symbolize the Divine? After all, he himself tells us in his *giustificazione* that the circle is the shape most perfect and divine;[27] here the artist is already equating symbolic and real space. While

25. One of the most striking examples of the concreteness of Bernini's spatial imagery is seen in his use of what appear to be opera boxes for framing the sculpted portraits of the Cornaro family in his *Ecstasy of Saint Teresa*.

26. Kitao (1974, 29–30) in general takes issue with Wittkower's proposal that, in the design of the Piazza Obliqua, "Bernini's *concetto* is no more than a metaphor."

27. This view was also stated many times by Kircher and became a major element in his interpretation of the *crux ansata*: "per circulum, puram divinitatis formam" (1652–54, $2^2.508$).

this is not the place to address at any length the influence of Classical thought on Renaissance esthetics or the relationship between imitation and the Renaissance cult of the antique,[28] on one level at least, the rage for the antique, the esoteric, and the occult had as its goal the encyclopedic accumulation of images categorized by reference to major archetypes. Not only is Kircher's *Oedipus Aegyptiacus* filled with tables and diagrams that equate figures from various traditions, but he himself persistently employs throughout his writings the word "archetype" to refer to the characteristic nature of primordial forms (*Supremi Numinis Archetypi*). His interest in what he called a "World Spirit" (*Anima Mundi*) is just as important as his and the pope's attention to pagan prefigurations. Thus, while in the works of iconologists such as Cesare Ripa the sixteenth century saw the development of symbols to truly esoteric levels, it is also true that certain pagan and Christian legends came (as did the prefigurations of Mary) to be deliberately equated, being taken in the seventeenth century as elaborations of themes that were simpler and more nearly primordial.[29] For Bernini, the proof that certain archetypes could be simultaneously symbolic and real rests in his coherent, persistent, and ingenious use of theatrical imagery—imagery that itself had a long pedigree that was both theatrical and archetypal of Divine maternity. When Bernini portrays himself as David by having a mirror held in front of him by the "hand of God" in the form of Cardinal Maffeo Barberini (soon to be Pope Urban VIII),[30] and when he has the statue positioned in such a way that the audience must assume the role of Goliath (Fig. 42),[31] he is not only suggesting to us that life is a theater and that art is a means by which we

28. See, e.g., Lee 1967, esp. chap. 1. It is also worth mentioning in this context the extensive influence of Aristotelianism at the Roman College during Kircher's day.

29. See, e.g., Seznec [1940] 1953.

30. As Vernant (following Redfield [1975]) says of the Greek epic hero, "he but sees himself in the mirror others hold up to him" (Vernant 1986).

31. The question of point of view in Bernini's *David* is a complicated one. Hibbard, Pope-Hennessy, and Wittkower all have emphasized the fact that the *David* is governed by a dominant, frontal point of view, while Kenseth has recently challenged this interpretation by calling attention to the fact that the viewer, in the context of the work's original position, would first have seen David from behind and, thus, initially assumed his role as hero (Kenseth 1981). Though this perspective leads to a very interesting interpretation of the work, we can, in fact, only stand beside David; we cannot assume his dramatic part. The only role that the work really permits us to play completely is that of Goliath—a role that has its fullest impact once we have walked around the statue and looked at David (Bernini) face to face.

FIG. 42. Gian Lorenzo Bernini, *David* (1623: Rome, Galleria Borghese): Bernini's complex performative view of his work is here epitomized, in that his *David* is actually a self-portrait; in viewing the work, his audience, thereby, must take on the role of protagonist. (Photo: R. Wittkower)

realize this fact; he is also telling us that it is art, imitating what is archetypal, that gives life meaning.[32] We see Bernini, in other words, not only as David, but as all other mythical figures, such as Perseus, who through Divine intervention become heroes by defeating some monster. When God's representative on earth holds the mirror for Bernini, it is as primordial an experience as when Athena did the same for Perseus;[33] only this time the magic mirror shows not, as did Athena's, the hideous opponent as Gorgon or Goliath, but the hero, Bernini, backstage preparing for battle. And it is here that Bernini moves onto an intellectual plane shared by the greatest minds of his day[34]—here also where he makes good his commitment to the truism that the only object of which we have both objective and subjective knowledge is our own body.[35] And there can be no doubt about his belief that beauty

32. Here the notion of art as mirror of the universe is given a most literal meaning—one, moreover, that had its origin in the revival of mirror symbolism at the birth of the Renaissance. It is particularly interesting, from the standpoint of performance and microcosmic/macrocosmic relations, to note that mirrors played a special role in pilgrimages. According to Goldberg, "the holy nature of mirrors lay in the manner in which they were employed by the pilgrims. They would hold these mirrors up to the sacred relics to catch them in a reflection. When they returned to their villages, they exhibited their mirrors to friends and relatives, boasting that they had brought back physical evidence as well as the inspirational qualities of their pilgrimage because their mirrors had captured the reflection of the sacred scene" (1985, 139). See also Schwarz 1959, 103.

33. This is an allusion of which Bernini would, no doubt, have approved.

34. What I mean here is not simply that Bernini is engaging in a clever reversal of roles with his audience, but that he is actively participating in an empirical reversal, a theater of mirrors, in which viewers become protagonists. And it is precisely this mirroring that imaginative thinkers (ever since Giulio Camillo and his memory theater of the early sixteenth century) believed could *realize* the universal in concrete form. Indeed, as Bernheimer argues of Camillo, it is entirely possible and in keeping with his Neoplatonic beliefs "that the visible presence in his scheme of all the creative entities in the world would have a magical effect on man's mentality" (1956, 230). The magical transformation occurs, in other words, as all humanity literally sees itself, and is seen, in reflection.

35. Indeed, Cardinal Roberto Bellarmino, whose posthumous portrait Bernini executed in 1624, was widely known for his view that nothing is closer to us than ourselves. Moreover, the circumstances surrounding Bellarmino's death and burial were, themselves, a kind of redemption of Counter Reformation arguments for the Divine's being realized in material things; for, when exhumed, Bellarmino's corpse was discovered to have an incorrupted torso (Lavin 1968b, 242–43). Bodily incorruption was, and still is, thought to be a sign of divinity, and Bernini's sculpting of Bellarmino in imitation of the pose in which these incorrupted parts were found not only reminded his fellow Jesuits of Bellarmino's extreme holiness; it also represented divine recognition of the Counter Reformation's focus on materiality. Ignatius's view that an understanding of spiritual things could be arrived at through meditating on corporeal ones thus gave new meaning to the relation between the physical and the spiritual. Bernini's sculpture is very much, therefore, a kind of divinely sanctioned "incorporation."

rested primarily in the understanding and interpretation of its formal proportions, for this "was a divine thing—its origin was in the body of Adam, made by God after his own image. . . . Perfect proportion lay in the shape of a man" (Hibbard 1965, 174).[36]

Was the artist as man/hero also, then, a divinely inspired progenitor? Certainly, in the realm of symbolic interrelations he would have to be; but where, we must ask, is the evidence for stating that this belief was held by Bernini? The answer may lie in his devotion to Saint Ignatius of Loyola and in the degree to which the object of meditation, as in Tantric yoga, is on microcosmic/macrocosmic relations, and, particularly, on making the symbolic synonymous with the actual through emphasizing the continuity that underlies creative thought and creative, or procreative, acts. Bernini was aware, as much as his Jesuit friends were, that meditation for Ignatius specifically included meditation on the events of the life of Christ, of which those pertaining to the Virgin Mary were of particular significance. The *Spiritual Exercises* of Ignatius were so much connected to the cult of the Virgin that the rumor prevailed that they had been partially dictated by her, and Ignatius's devotion was so strong that he let an entire year pass between his ordination and the performance of his first Mass in order "to prepare himself and to beg our Lady that she might desire to place him with her Son" (Spence 1984, 242–43). What Ignatius means here is not simply that they be spiritually close, but that the cloistered monk see himself "as a symbol of Christ within the Virgin's womb" (ibid., 259). We know this in particular because many of the basic ideas of the *Spiritual Exercises* of Ignatius can be traced to the *Vita Christi* of Ludolph of Saxony (Bodenstedt 1944, 77), among them Ignatius's treatment of Mary and how a devotion to her could be realized.[37] According to

---

36. "Tombant ensuite sur la matière pour laquelle il est venu, il a dit que le beau de toutes les choses du monde, aussi bien que de l'architecture, consiste dans la proportion; qu'on peut dire que c'est une partie divine, puisqu'elle tient son origine du corps d'Adam, qui a été non-seulement fait des mains de Dieu, mais qui a été formé à son image et semblance; que la variété des ordres de l'architecture a procédé de la différence du corps de l'homme et de femme, et des différentes proportions que l'on y voit, et a ajouté plusieurs autres choses sur cette matière qui nous sont assez familières" (de Chantelou [1930] 1972, 19–20).

37. See also Zarncke 1931. Given Bernini's treatment of Saint Teresa in the Cornaro Chapel, it is interesting to note that the *Vita Christi* also had an important influence on her. One suspects that Bernini was well aware of this influence when he sculpted her. The sexual suggestiveness of the work was widely known and became the object of con-

scholars of the period, the goal of such meditating is to be able to see "some real relationship between spiritual reality and outward physical objects which are used to symbolize them. The process . . . becomes vital to the re-ordering of one's perception of the meaning of the world. By constructing ever deepening systems of allegory and analogy, a kind of redemption of the senses becomes possible" (Conway 1976, 10). Aside from a graphic description of a mnemotechnics that provides for "certain theological attitudes towards material objects" and permits a "kind of meditation in which devotional ideas are presented in concrete and tangible ways" (ibid., 17), what we are surely observing here is a quite explicit attempt to equate microcosmic and macrocosmic structures. Artworks—namely refined, outward, visible experiences—become vehicles for reaching some kind of fundamental truth.[38] For Ludolph, it is in the combination of the active and the contemplative "in which are signified [as in Ricci's memory palace, or Sacks's twins] those who are worthy to be presented before the *face* of God" (ibid., 35; my emphasis). The meditative experience, thus, involves the imagining of figures that become "keys to a code designed to present to the understanding *in a single flash* a whole kind of doctrine" (ibid., 36; my emphasis). Figurations become, in other words, "another language designed to communicate quickly to the reader the entirety of a certain aspect of teaching . . . devices for the quick storage and easy retrieval of theological information" (ibid.). The significance

---

siderable humorous discussion. Among the more famous responses was that of the eighteenth-century French scholar and magistrate Charles de Brosses, who, upon seeing the work, remarked, "If this be divine love, I know it well!" One might object to the role of the Incarnation for the devout Bernini, but there is nothing inherently wrong, for the followers of Ignatius, with realizing images of procreation, provided the meditation is enacted in the proper frame of mind. The tendency to conflate romance and spiritual activity was definitely a part of Teresa's view of meditation (Bodenstedt 1944, 83), and it is only when we read Teresa's description of her ecstasy that we see how thoroughly creative thought and procreation are conjoined.

38. In the Counter Reformation, this belief in the necessity for the material realization of religion through art was based on a commitment to a process of objectifying universals and to balancing "the natural tendency of the human mind toward thinning out in areas of higher generality" (Bernheimer 1956, 231); and it is to addressing this natural tendency that the mnemotechnics of the memory theater was directed from the very beginning. The image of the *theatrum* "as a place of assembly or a marketplace" (ibid., 230 n. 34) is, thus, no less unexpected than the fact that the basilican form of architecture is itself based upon the Roman marketplace. Both theater and basilica are, in other words, idealizations of the place in which objects are ordered and arranged for easy access and retrieval.

of art for the persistence of memory is, therefore, *apparent* in the merging of the symbolic and actual, for the Virgin herself becomes a memory theater, "a castle into whom Christ entered" (*Vita Christi*, pt. 1, chap. 61, 2.122; see Conway 1976, 83), so that the cloistered monk can, indeed, be "compared to Christ in the womb" (Conway 1976, 83). In resolving the paradox of spirit and matter, the artist focuses on the substantiality of art, since "man's grasp of invisible spiritual things depends upon a grasp first of all of visible bodily things" (ibid., 86). Bernini, thus, becomes thoroughly involved in the process of creation because the mnemonic palace that is the instrument of creation is synonymous with what is created as well as with the vehicle of creation.[39] Approach Christ there, Ludolph tells us, "with a devout heart, so that seeming to descend from the bosom of the Father into the womb of the Virgin, like another witness with the angel of the Holy Conception, you may continue in pure faith, and wish joy to the Virgin Mother who is thus made fertile because of you" (ibid., 126).[40]

It is by placing himself in the role of divinely inspired progenitor—as David had been for the family of Christ, or Perseus for the Greeks—that Bernini equates, through the Piazza Obliqua, the physiology of procreation with the imagery of the theater. As Lavin has pointed out, it is precisely the awareness that *someone*, that Bernini, had generated a certain response that makes his theatrical imagery so whole, so complete, so mondial (Lavin 1980, 1.154–55). It is the artist's knowledge that *he* is the creator, the progenitor, of the *theatrum mundi*, upon which

39. As Lavin says of Bernini's baldachin for Saint Peter's, "Bernini treats a volume of real space as the site of a dramatic action, in which the observer is involved physically as well as psychologically. The drama takes place in an environment that is not an extension of the real world, but is coextensive with it" (1968a, 39).

40. Conway points out, as we have seen in previous chapters, that the art of intense visualization is based on a meditation technique as much as it is on mnemonics (1976, 127–31); however, it is interesting to see that these recommendations are not restricted to Ludolph or Teresa, having to do with the syncretism of Cabalistic meditation (Yates 1966, 177) and other works on meditation (such as Thomas à Kempis's *Imitation of Christ*) that are important for understanding both Bernini and Ignatius. Nor do the consequences of these recommendations go unapplied in painting. It is worth noting, throughout the Renaissance, how many scenes of the Annunciation "read" from left to right, placing the viewer looking at the loggia, building, or transept in such a way as to suggest that the event is taking place at a crossing—indeed, at times at a basilican crossing—so that the event occurs, on the microcosmic level, precisely at the protective juncture at which the *crux ansata* is protected and impregnated. The message that is brought to the Virgin is, then, surely made fertile as the Word is made flesh.

the Divine performance occurs, that links Bernini's own perception of himself to the Piazza Obliqua and, ultimately, to the Divine—a self-awareness lying "in a series of interlocking conceits which link the theater and art on a level that can only be described as metaphysical" (ibid., 155). It is this sense of himself as creator that enables Bernini to engulf his audience by employing the imagery of both physical and metaphysical creation. For Bernini, no doubt, the mirror of God showed not only his own face, but the Divine, "uterine" stage existing through the mirror—the stage on which life is acted out just as life is lived, where artifice is obviated completely, a place where one unconsciously becomes part of an artistic performance by participating in a monumental space that is symbolic and real at one and the same time (Fig. 43). It is this mirror that Bernini has in mind when he incorporates images of the Piazza Obliqua into the scenery of his *Due Teatri*;[41] and it is that same mirror that he employs when he, in turn, envisions this *Due Teatri*—where the stage becomes a structural "portico" between a real and an imagined audience—as taking place before Saint Peter's. Here architectural symbol becomes real space: art no longer *represents* life, but is life itself.

For Bernini, to be sure, the mirror of Athena showed not simply

41. According to the description of Massimiliano Montecuculi (Kitao 1974, 22–23), "the stage was prepared with a 'flock of people partly real and partly only feigned' so arranged that, when the curtain had fallen for the opening of the play, the audience saw on stage another large audience who had come to see the comedy. Two braggarts, played by Bernini himself and his brother Luigi, then appeared on stage, one facing the real audience and the other the fictitious; and recognizing each other in no time, they went on to claim, each in turn, that what the other saw as real was actually illusory, each firmly convinced that there was no more than one theater with its audience in the half he was facing. The confusion of realities in mirror image thus heightened, the two finally decided 'that they would pull a curtain across the scene and arrange a performance each for his own audience alone.' Then the play was performed to the real audience, that is, the main act to which what preceded was only a pleasant prelude. But through the play another performance was supposed to be taking place simultaneously on the second stage introduced by Luigi; the play was, in fact, 'interrupted at times by the laughter of those on the other side, as if something very pleasant had been seen and heard.'

"At the end of the play, the two braggarts reappeared on the stage together to reaffirm the 'reality' of the illusion. Having asked each other how they fared, the impresario of the fictitious performance answered nonchalantly that he had not really shown anything but the audience getting up to leave 'with their carriages and horses and accompanied by a great number of lights and torches.' Then, drawing the curtain, he displayed the scene he had just said he had shown to *his* audience, thus rendering complete the incredible reversal of reality and illusion to the confused amazement of the real spectators, who were now finding themselves ready to leave and caught in the enchanting act of feigning the feigned spectators."

FIG. 43. Aerial view of the Piazza Obliqua during Easter benediction: the masses—both Christian and pagan—throng onto the Divine world-stage, where symbolic space is coextensive with real architectural form. (Courtesy Anton Schroll & Co.)

the monstrous adversary, but a remarkable conceit that was both sub-lime and subliminal. It is Bernini's and Alexander VII's acute awareness of the relationship between metaphysics and art that permits the Piazza Obliqua to function simultaneously as an amphitheater and as a symbol of the Divine womb. It is the Piazza Obliqua before Saint Peter's where Bernini, finally, is able to stage Aristotle's remarkable dictum that what makes the world one will be what makes a man.[42]

.   .   .

Because our bodies are the only things of which we have both objective and subjective knowledge, both the symbolism of the body and no-tions of how the integrity of body-image boundary is maintained in-variably become the loci of our most explicit statements on the for-eign. By this I mean not only how "symbols" of the body are formed but, more important, how categories descriptive of the body are ar-ticulated. For this reason it is appropriate to conclude a study of no-tions of the foreign with a speculative essay in which body-image is seen in relation to the very *idea* of culture. In the final chapter and the Epilogue I will argue that an awareness of bodily pollution, and the awareness of mental illness in particular, is contingent upon what we take "culture" to be.

42. See Clark 1975, 47.

PLATE I. Kenneth Noland, *New Day* (1967: synthetic polymer on canvas, 89½″ × 184¾″; New York, collection of the Whitney Museum of American Art; purchase, with funds from the Friends of the Whitney Museum; 68.18): while formalist critics have argued that paintings such as Noland's represent the purest form of art, others argue that, unless one views them in an appropriately artistic context, they are easily mistaken for decorative designs.

PLATE 2.   Mark Tobey, *Edge of August* (1953: casein on composition board, 48″×28″; collection of The Museum of Modern Art, New York; purchase): Tobey's highly meditative abstractions are, despite their lack of figurative content, still emotional and illusionistic.

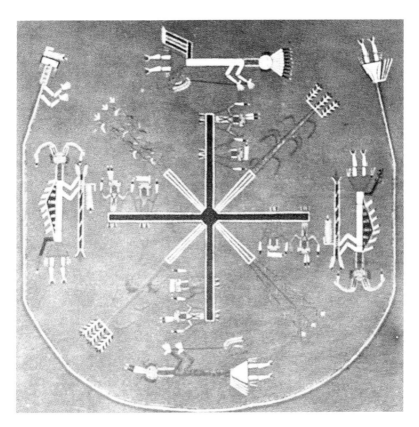

PLATE 3. Whirling Logs sandpainting (Navajo, ca. 1970): in contrast to much anti-illusionistic contemporary art, Navajo sandpainting is meant graphically and cosmically to situate a patient undergoing treatment. (Courtesy KC Publications)

PLATE 4.   Alexander Buchan, *Inhabitants of the Island of Terra del Fuego in their Hut* (1769): Buchan had been hired by Sir Joseph Banks as an illustrator on Cook's first voyage. Though meant to produce illustrations that would delight Banks's friends back in England, Buchan shortly after creating this work died of an epileptic seizure. (By permission of the British Library)

PLATE 5.   William Hodges, *A View Taken in the Bay of Otaheite Peha (Vaite-piha)* (ca. 1775–76: Lode, Cambs., Anglesey Abbey): Hodges was taken on as illustrator for Cook's second voyage in 1772. The artist was meant to record atmospheric conditions for the scientists on board. (By permission of the National Trust)

PLATE 6.   J. M. W. Turner, *Rough Sea with Wreckage* (1830: Clore Gallery, The Turner Collection, Tate Gallery, London / Art Resource, New York): Turner's highly "atmospheric" painting clearly exaggerates the monumentality of nature and the role of man as an alien element in it.

PLATE 7*a*. Nancy Holt, *Sun Tunnels* (Great Basin Desert, Utah, 1973–76): set on the solstitial axes, these concrete tubes were intended to result in a kind of cosmic reorientation. (Artist's photos)

PLATE 7*b*. *Sun Tunnels* (alternate views). (Artist's photos)

PLATE 8.   Giuseppe Arcimboldo, *Portrait of Rudolf II as Vertumnus* (ca. 1590: oil on wood; Stockholm, Skoklosters Slott): Arcimboldo created extraordinary portraits out of the unusual juxtaposition of ordinary forms. The resulting caricatures are an affront to the psychological seriousness that normally accompanies the consideration of portraits.

5

Culture as Self: The Stranger Within

Joints: whole and not whole, connected-separate, consonant-
dissonant.

Heraclitus, Fragment 10 Diels-Kranz
(trans. Kathleen Freeman)

I. ONTOLOGY AND FREEDOM

In an early and now rather neglected essay on the stranger, Georg Simmel suggests that our socially determined categories of insiders and
outsiders also pose moral questions about the fundamental nature of
what we understand, in the modern world, to be our inalienable rights
and liberties. His intention, in raising the issue of morals, was not so
much to enter the domain of constitutional law as it was to point to
the absolute connection between ontology—particularly, the social dimensions of object relations—and morality. For Simmel, objectivity
(i.e., the cultural category of what constitutes an object) may well be
the primary determinant of human freedom, since individuation—at
least as we understand it—implies the existence of an individual as object, one who is "bound by no commitments which could prejudice his
perception, understanding, and evaluation of the given" (Simmel
1950, 405). Freedom for us has, in this view, no meaning without there
being, at least hypothetically, one "objective" observer, one individual
who is detached, individuated, perfectly distinguished.

The principle of objectivity, one could argue, underlies our entire
notion of freedom, since one cannot have a purely conceived category
of what it means to be "free" without detachment, without distinguishing absolutely one individual from another, and, on the cultural
level, without separating "us" and "them." The more we deemphasize
the symbolic interconnectedness of "things" (their dependence), the

more we glamorize what it means to be "free," to be entirely independent; the more we deny that one individual is "like" another, the more
we sanctify the fact that each of us is, indeed, quite "different." This
argument leads to my first thesis—namely, that a lack of interconnectedness becomes part of commodification of the self, of our perception that the independence we take to be part of our freedom is also
part of the interchangeability of equals. Later, we shall see how commodification (the "desymbolization" of objects) has cultural implications for the self, and particularly how in American culture "freedom"
can become a millenarian excuse for disengaging—on the social, individual, and biological levels—the self from its environment.

Viewed as a marker of individuation, "freedom" is, in fact, an avul-
sive term—something that has meaning only by virtue of its capacity
to distinguish and separate; and, conversely, the very distancing that is
the natural concomitant of the process of objectification means that
objectivity, as Simmel (ibid.) points out, can actually be defined as freedom itself. Taken to its logical conclusion, absolute freedom is synonymous with a total ignorance of the "outside," and outsiders become completely unknown because we lack any point of reference by
which they may be compared—they become mystified and exoticized,
rather than assimilated or understood.

These, surely, are not new observations; many clichés remind us
that we cannot know ourselves without knowing what we are not, or
that, as Milton argued in his *Areopagitica* (though his topic was freedom of the press), we cannot employ the standards of our limited experience to judge the appropriateness of another form of life. But
what is regularly neglected (and this is Simmel's point about the supposed difference of the stranger) is the degree to which we actually
need a concept of the strange. It is because we cannot know the incom-
parable that we need a less alien "other" for self-definition; for, in alienating others, we, by extension, alienate the self. Strangers, in other
words, are enough like us, and only enough unlike us, to be heuristi-
cally useful. Or, as Goffman once polemically argued, "it is not to the
different that one should look for understanding our differentness, but
to the ordinary. The question of social norms is certainly central, but
the concern might be less for uncommon deviations from the ordinary
than for ordinary deviations from the common" (Goffman 1963, 127).

Indeed, Goffman goes so far as to argue that by degrees everyone is a deviant from the ideal;[1] Goffman's "normal deviant" tells us enough about difference to remind us of what it is to be free (distinguished, independent), but not enough to leave us, categorically speaking, high and dry. The "normal" is itself *made up* of the "deviant" in the same way, paradoxically, that the "normal" body is, according to Canguilhem ([1966] 1989), contingent upon the pathological one. Strangers are like us but different. Indeed, what American can claim to have articulated a concept of an "ordinary" body of people or an "ordinary" physical body that is less covert than his or her concept of the "strange"?

It is precisely for this reason that the concept of the stranger is central to—even, perhaps, the central metaphor for—any discussion of the body. For the human body is the sole object in the universe of which we have both objective ("different") and subjective ("same") knowledge, the only thing, moreover, about which we can both lack consciousness and be maniacally self-conscious.[2] And it is because of the singularity of this self-awareness that both the symbolism of the body and notions of how the integrity of one's body-image boundary is maintained invariably become the arena of our most explicit statements about the strange and the foreign.

By this I mean not only how "symbols" of the body are formed but, more important, how categories descriptive of the body are articulated (see, e.g., Martin 1987), and, in particular, how strange bodily states are described. An awareness of how we describe our own bodily conditions, perhaps better than anything else, indicates to us just what we

1. "Even where widely attained norms are involved, their multiplicity has the effect of disqualifying many persons. . . . In an important sense there is only one complete unblushing male in America: a young, married, white, urban, northern, heterosexual Protestant father of college education, fully employed, of good complexion, weight, and height, and a recent record in sports. Every American male tends to look out upon the world from this perspective. . . . Any male who fails to qualify in any of these ways is likely to view himself—during moments at least—as unworthy, incomplete, and inferior. . . . The general identity-values of a society may be fully entrenched nowhere, and yet they can cast some kind of shadow on the encounters encountered everywhere in daily life" (Goffman 1963, 128–29). Perhaps this is the reason that in America actors can make the most successful politicians, and why some social critics feel that Americans would prefer a monarch to a president.

2. So-called psychosomatic illnesses are, thus, taken as having a component that we should control but either will not or cannot. They are, in other words, deliberate signals about outside relations and, as such, are viewed pejoratively.

mean by the word "strange," and who or what, in fact, it is that we take to be a "stranger." Those strangenesses of the body each of us experiences are our "strangers" within, which both define and separate us as individuals, which both disengage us and make us "free." Indeed, "body" and "culture" are metaphorically identical—so much so, that an awareness of bodily pollution, and the awareness of mental illness in particular, is contingent upon what we take "culture" to be. For this reason, it is appropriate, perhaps essential, to conclude a study of "otherness" and its relation to culture with a consideration of the body *as* culture—as a locus for what we *are*, and as a stage for identifying all the strangers that we insist we are not—to show how our sense of our selves (psychologically, physically, socially) is the primary means by which we recognize culture.

II. WHAT IS CULTURE?

I have seen the way food [*kaikai*] is produced in Australia. The white men will not keep anything secret from us any longer.

Yali, Papua, New Guinea

If by culture we mean "the sum total of ways of living built up by a group of human beings and transmitted from one generation to another," then the determination of culture is, necessarily, the product of the formulation and articulation of notions of the foreign—of what it means to be a stranger and, similarly, what it means to act "strangely."[3] It is quite logical, in other words, that an awareness of what mental illness is must be contingent upon the idea of culture, since we arrive at culture through the formation of cultural canons, which do not so much preclude certain sorts of behavioral diversity as literally *internalize* diversity, bringing—through their formation as our particular cultural canons—the outside in.

I have tried to offer in this book a number of examples of the process by which outsiders are assimilated; however, it is important to emphasize at this stage just how much the notion of a culture (or a nation)

---

3. In fact, what we call "culture" so much determines how we define mental illness that those in charge of asylums in the nineteenth century, when psychiatry began making its move to be recognized as a science, were called "alienists" (Gilman 1988, 183ff.; Littlewood and Lipsedge 1989).

as a bounded domain is embedded in other, equally bounded cultural categories—not only "selves" as bounded domains, but disciplines as bounded domains of inquiry, area specialties as the exclusive turf of a particular group of researchers, or professional specializations as the legal prerogative of those who are certified. In each of these cases, a canon is established by *eliminating* the outside from the scope of the category that one seeks to define. We rely, sometimes almost exclusively it seems, upon the construction and reconstruction of an evolutionary sequence of events that simultaneously excludes outsiders and provides some basis for justifying our social rules and actions.

Thus, we minimize diversity by reflecting on who we are, by achieving, that is, a self-conscious state that is not only accepted but considered desirable. What is "transmitted from one generation to another," in other words, is a set of rules and laws about how certain kinds of diversity are precluded, how what distinguishes "us" from "them" is a function of refining what we are over time. A world in which we are simply "the people" is transformed into a world in which we are a certain *kind* of people. We achieve identity as we achieve self-knowledge, in that self-consciousness becomes a part of our awareness of otherness. We exchange an externalized diversity for a diversity in our image of an individuated body. Our "culture" becomes, thus, not only an agreed-upon way of living, but a "cultivation of microorganisms" whose complex relationships may or may not be organically proportional to the macrocosm of which they are a part. It is this notion of organic disproportion that also makes diseases "strange"; for diseases, like strangers, function as organic members of a group "in spite of being inorganically appended" (Simmel 1950, 408). Diseases, one might even argue, become not only indicators—signs—of foreignness but imitators of what we ourselves are.

III. SOCIAL DEATH BY SUGGESTION

> Efficacy, itself, is a cultural construct.
> Arthur Kleinman

There are few things in life more troubling than seeing a friend despair at being mistreated by those whose profession it is to assure our mental health. While observing a proper respect for those who make it their

FIG. 44.   James Ensor, *The Bad Doctors* (1895): Ensor's macabre etching of
the healer's art evokes, in spite of or because of its satirizing, his real anxie-
ties about the effectiveness of the medical profession. (A. Taevernier
collection)

business to safeguard our sanity, most of us, no doubt, can think of
someone close who has suffered the alienation that results when pride
and simple dignity compel one to become hostile to the prospect of
psychological salvation and the enviable sense of acculturation that is
perceived, rightly or wrongly, to exist around us. For those who have
no experience of such despair, a trip to the Musée d'Art Brut in Lausanne, a visit to the Prinzhorn Collection at the University of Heidelberg, or a glance at the work of certain critics of the medically macabre
(e.g., James Ensor's bizarre depictions of medical malpractice, as in
Fig. 44) is enough to instill a sense of how discomforting is the prospect of not feeling at ease with the condition of mental health care.

Think for a moment about a single, sobering fact—that, as Kroeber
pointed out long ago, "neurotics appear to become numerous and
characteristic in populations among whom religion has become deca-

dent and 'enlightenment' active, as in the Hellenistic, Roman Imperial, and recent eras" (Kroeber [1920] 1979, 23). How is it possible, one asks, that these neurotics, these sufferers of acute anxiety and compulsive antisocialism—these "strange" people—flourish mainly in "enlightened" social contexts? Are we largely distinguishing here between cultures in which religion is central and those in which it is not? Perhaps, but the thrust of Kroeber's insight is directed more toward the self-consciousness of "enlightenment" and the social conditions that stimulate a preoccupation with introspection. While the idea that modern society exacerbates these conditions is a truism that we need not belabor, the question of real anthropological significance is, Why do we continue to let it do so? What cultural myths are important enough that their survival takes priority over our very own? No easy question, but undoubtedly one that can be clarified considerably by examining the relationship between such myths and those strangers we find capable of polluting our persons, those things that we call diseases.

What is disease, and how do we understand it? Recognized by *the absence of a condition of well-being*, "disease" refers to any departure from a healthy state and, in particular, to those departures that deteriorate or destroy the organism involved. Diseases are recognized, that is, by the pathological conditions they give rise to—an easy situation to assess when one is confronted by diseases that are life-threatening, but very complex when considered immunologically. Too much of a good thing is detrimental to a healthy state, but just enough of even the potentially lethal can be power-engendering. Viewed as a kind of social immune response, neurosis operates as does an autoantibody, and neurotic behavior is, by analogy, an extension of a hypersensitivity that is destructive if not potentially morbid. To say that neuroses do not occur in certain non-Western cultures is to say that the mechanisms for recognizing certain pathological conditions are not present, that the "pathos" or suffering that is the sign of alienation does not, as it does in the West, form part of a recognizable social institution or a particular category of thought. This is not to say that human suffering is not experientially the same for all cultures; only that particularizing it activates it conceptually and categorically. In, for example, what is traditionally called "Western thought," everyone has sufficiently assimilated and inculcated the idioms of self-consciousness and psychoanalysis so that these are the main avenues by which we define what is appropriate and inappropriate behavior. Indeed, so crucial are these categories that they provide the dominant cultural mechanism by which the boundaries of acceptable behavior are established and regulated; one could even argue that the mechanism by which we set the boundaries of acceptable behavior is the same mechanism by which those boundaries are dissolved.[4] The implications of this awareness for images of the self are often misunderstood; our most difficult conceptual problems, that is, are frequently the result of a systematic dissolution of categorical boundaries through highly patterned, imitative processes. Metaphors of imitation, therefore, are perhaps more revealing of how mock-forms subvert categories than are metaphors of chaos or the military metaphors regularly employed in establishing the domains of self and other.[5]

Viewing things from this vantage, we are compelled to ask ourselves just why it is that our professional healers help codify the category of the mentally disenfranchised, not only accepting but promoting the culturally given cult of alienation.[6] For all our modern understanding, we must sadly accept that, after death by automobile, suicide takes the lives of more of our young adults than any other mode of dying, and the rate of curing in our institutions for the mentally insane is shockingly poor. Why, it must be asked, do so many young adults choose to take their own lives rather than participate in the therapeutic strategy that is culturally prescribed? And why, so

4. Likewise, liminal antistructures—to use Victor Turner's category—not only are defined by reference to the standards they both imitate and subvert, but also help define those very standards. Hence, we frequently see evidence of the imitation and overt mimicry of acceptable behavior by what are taken to be deviant or subversive groups. A pathogenic analogue to this kind of imitative dissolution or subversion occurs in autoimmunity, where "it appears that antigenic 'mimicry' is a persistent feature of the struggle between self and pathogen" (Cohen 1988, 55).

5. On mock-form and imitation, see Napier 1986, esp. chap. 1.

6. Later in this chapter I will argue that part of the answer to why alienation is culturally endorsed must surely have to do with the extent to which we have legitimized millennial ideas as part of culture. In other words, polluted states (states of consciousness as well as political states) have to be abandoned for higher ground. Because we are cut off from microcosmic/macrocosmic relations, we do not focus on the maintenance of balance, the reciprocity of "black" and "white"; rather, we live in constant anticipation of colonizing what we take to be unpolluted frontiers. The Balinese attach themselves to the navel of the earth, whereas we dream of the pioneer life or the weekend retreat, the house in the country wherein we may "really" be ourselves.

often, do alienated groups within a culture imitate or parody their own plight by acting out the very roles that have alienated them? Here, again, answers do not come easily; but when they do come, they point to the fact that ours is a culture that lacks a certain sophistication about notions of the person and about the visceral character of so much of what is referred to as psychosomatic illness. For us, hardships experienced while maintaining important cultural ideals—wounds, to use the military metaphor, that are received in the line of duty—reinforce the radical categories of foreignness upon which physical as well as social diseases are based, but those that stem from challenges to the effectiveness of our social institutions are, as is natural, viewed pejoratively.

Strangers within our midst are, indeed, the strangest of all—not because they are so alien, but because they are so close to us. As so many legends of "wildmen," wandering Jews, and feral children remind us, strangers must be like us but different. They cannot be completely exotic, for, were they so, we could not recognize them. They are—as I have argued throughout this book—outsiders brought into the center of culture, people within our own culture who are stigmatized, or outsiders who are enough like us or aware enough of who we are to influence us by exercising a special alien power. Strangers are, in fact, definers of culture, and those cultures that have been shown historically to be the most open to the outside are also those that are the longest-lived, since they are most likely to cultivate a sophisticated mythology by which the outside is approached and assimilated. How we manipulate outsiders conceptually thus designates them as either harmful or helpful—either as dangerous themselves, or as bolsterers of our cultural immunity, reinvigorating our capacity to sustain outside influences, foreign pollution, social disease.

That the symbolic structure of disease pathology is identical to the symbolism of the foreign is an idea readily verified by a quick look at the vocabulary employed in describing how diseases may lead to a morbid condition. For us, the concept of "psyche" assures an integrity of personality, which must not be violated; so strong is this conceptualization that our enduring sense of what we are—our mythology of the self—cannot incorporate any change so radical as to turn us into something "different"; for that would constitute schizophrenia or, at least, a kind of selflessness. Diseases, like foreigners, are things different from ourselves, and an invasion of bacteria, like so many foreign armies, leaves us petrified at the prospect of becoming polluted. Even our most highly trained scientists cannot avoid the vocabulary of the foreign when discussing how diseases take hold of a person. Moreover, the tendency is so deeply rooted that learned discussions of immunology inevitably make use of a vocabulary that can only be described as animistic. Note, for example, how we conceive of allergic reactions, of how "one cell fails to recognize another cell for what it is." Everyone knows that cells are not capable of volition, but when we need clarification of how diseases work, a cartoon in which bacteria or antigens are personified as little demons with gnashing teeth provides us with the best—indeed, the *only*—way of describing how polluting agents mask themselves and fool our loyal cells into submission (Fig. 45). There are literally thousands of works in which this visual vocabulary is employed to discuss the relationship between diseases and the organisms they threaten. In fact, one could argue that this kind of model is the *only* one to which we have access.[7] Our model of what makes a person, therefore, is based on the radical categories of the strange, the foreign; little wonder that we do so poorly with diseases that do not easily fit this conceptualization, or that do not reveal themselves (as foreign) until sometime later.[8]

In "Voodoo Death," Walter Cannon's now-famous article of 1942, Cannon describes how, among Australian aborigines, death by suggestion occurs through the onset of shock in victims at whom a fatal bone has been pointed. The signs and symptoms are classic: after an initial surge, blood pressure drops, the heartbeat becomes weak and irregular, the skin cold and clammy. Within a few days, the victim dies. What happens physiologically is understandable; however, sociologically, the situation is much less certain. Why is it that death by suggestion occurs in some cultures and not in others? Or why, at least, does it occur—or why is it recognized as occurring—more frequently in certain cultures?

7. For a good example of the popular use of the vocabulary of warfare for discussing diseases, see Jaret 1986.

8. Here, particularly, the idea of a "slow virus" is worth considering because of the conceptual ambiguity—the transformation, the masking, the categorical mutation—implicit in the word "slow." See, e.g., Sontag 1988, 94.

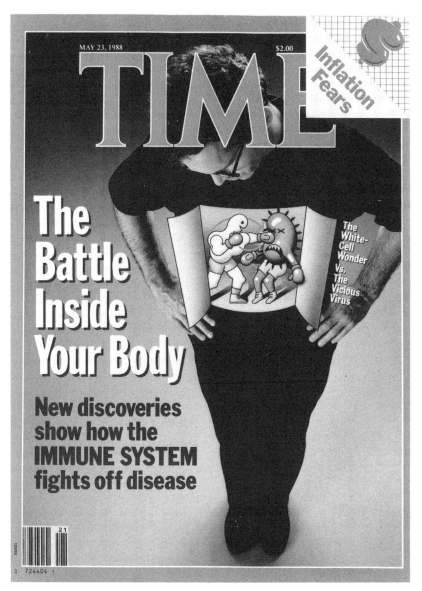

FIG. 45. "The Battle Inside Your Body" (*Time*, May 23, 1988): though we are all familiar with the sort of military metaphor commonly employed in explaining the most mystifying illnesses, we have yet to ask why we resort in these instances to conceptual categories and modes of description that can only be characterized as "animistic." (© Time, Inc., 1988; reproduced by permission)

For members of "enlightened" cultures—that is, cultures that actively promote a cult of self-consciousness—the answers to these questions usually consist of simple statements about ignorance or the power of superstition; but a closer look at the Australian case suggests a set of circumstances that are, perhaps, sociologically and intellectually more complex. Typically, after the bone has been pointed at the victim, the family begins preparations for mourning. Death is a foregone conclusion, and the beleaguered soul, if not already in shock, soon arrives at that state upon seeing his friends and family bidding him farewell. Cruel, it may seem to us, but not much different in principle than the send-off one gets as a mental outlaw, a social castoff relegated to an asocial asylum for the mentally disabled; for, indeed, we openly promote the very thing we wish to abolish by dividing the mentally ill into a separate category, the category of the socially disenfranchised.[9] Furthermore, we assume that this constitutes a responsible, ethical, and humane response to the tendency on the part of the mentally ill to cross the threshold out of the social. We cannot get better until we admit to being ill; but the ill are members of an excluded category, the radical opposite of the healthy norm.[10] One is asked to rejoin society by admitting that one is not part of it—a paradox of the first order. But, given this alienation, what is yet more paradoxical is the fact that the mentally insane also become for us the focus of what "enlightenment" is; for it is also insanity, as Sontag (1978, 40) points out, "that is thought to bring consciousness to a state of paroxysmic enlightenment." The enlightened, that is, seek out analysis on many levels. More important, it is insanity—the "strange"—that defines what "normal" means, as when mental patients call one another crazy, or when people who live in the streets of our cities proudly refer to themselves as bums. The enlightened, that is, are not only those who are able to achieve reasonable levels of socialization, and those who are socialized rarely realize the degree to which they are indebted to "strangers" for understanding what acceptable behavior is, or what "acceptable behavior" means.

9. While the literature on this problem is extensive, a brief look at the writings of Goffman or Foucault, for example, will give one a sense of its depth.

10. An example of the social consequences of even approaching this "cult of alienation" occurred in the 1988 presidential campaign when Republican propagandists implied that Michael Dukakis was unfit for the presidency because he might have consulted a psychologist.

The knowledge that disease exists is a form of enlightenment, and enlightenment of the critical faculties is, in a social sense, diseaselike, because it is divisive; it excludes and distinguishes when what is frequently required by the disabled is inclusion, superficiality, and a deemphasis of self-consciousness. Enlightenment is fine for those who are self-confident, but the category of the mentally ill is distinctively asocial and does not, therefore, provide in itself the basis for confidence and resocialization. This absence suggests to us why "analysis"—that is, the self-conscious breaking down into parts—frequently fails; it also indicates the extent to which self-consciousness is based upon a notion of the person that, as we shall see, makes all of us strange. But the fundamental problem—and it is an ethical one, and perhaps even an esthetic one[11]—has to do with the conceptualization of disease itself and how diseases are categorized, with pollution by strangers, with the stranger within, and with the myths by which strangers are conceptualized and culturally dispatched.

What, one may ask, does the categorizing of diseases have to do with ethics? To answer this question, we must consider not ethics, as we commonly understand the term, but ethos—that is, the characteristic way of performing an action, the manner, the custom. For it is precisely in cultures for which religion and custom are one—for so-called unenlightened cultures—that neurosis, as such, becomes uncommon, or, at least, unrecognized.[12] In this sense, neurosis may be viewed as an aberration of self-criticism, in which "enlightenment" leads not only to an awareness of cultural pluralism but to an exhibition of the self-contained and self-justifying neurotic impulse. Our notions of what a culture means socially are identical to our notions of what a culture is clinically; our model of how patients "fight" cancer through the hypnotic visualization of memory landscapes in which a battle takes place is reflected in our conceptualizations of cancer as a hermetic culture in which cells change identity (whatever this could possibly mean), creating microcosms, "selfish" (and "selflike") entities that reproduce uncontrollably. That our immune system takes part of the body as its own enemy is as much a statement of culture (in both a

---

11. Because these categories have performative consequences, the fundamental problems posed by self-consciousness also have—as I hope this entire study shows—a significant esthetic dimension.

12. See above, Chap. 2, n. 23.

social and a biological sense) as it is a description of something that is actually observable. We assume that there is a "system," in other words, because the body regularly responds in a characteristic way, because certain series of responses regularly repeat themselves; however, one might as easily characterize the problem—particularly considering the extent to which problems of immunity manifest themselves *on the skin*—as the body's inability to come to terms (in a sense that is *simultaneously* symbolic and biological) with the value of systems as such: that is, with its environment. Immunity is what establishes body-image boundary as much as what threatens it, and, since body-image priorities are cultural phenomena, so are the mental constructs that we call "immune systems," and so too are the memory landscapes in which body-image is rendered meaningful. For us, mental disease necessitates a recognition of and a devotion to the idea of a psyche that forms one hermetic, atomic element out of the plurality of categories that constitutes a person—a belief in the existence of one psychological element that can, as can a tumor, grow disproportionately with respect to the organism to which it is connected but by which its relative size is not governed. Looked at in this way, it is startling to consider just how the pathology of cancer, for example, parallels certain patterns of aberrant behavior that detrimentally exaggerate a particular element of character; more startling still to confront the respective dominance of these conceptualizations of disproportion today on the "stage" of the physical, on the one hand, and of the mental, on the other.[13]

But the issue of relative size—the integration and proportioning of categories—is not only ethical; it is also symbolic and esthetic. Einstein's popularization, in physics, of the view that a theory had to be simple and beautiful—even elegant—to be probable has its corollary in the demands for symbolic relativism commonly evidenced in cultures that have not achieved "enlightenment."[14] In the Hindu view, as we have seen, the fact that the macrocosmic must reflect the microcosmic demands that symbols themselves be primordial, and that

---

13. That the idea of "staging" cures offers the right metaphor here is evident not only from the use of drama in contemporary therapy, but in the traditional use of symbols of transition in the very structure of certain curing centers (e.g., the Greek Asclepieion at Pergamum).

14. Enlightenment might be compared here with what Clifford Geertz (1964) has called "internal conversion."

beauty be recognized in the reflection of proper proportion rather than through unique aberration—even when that disproportion results in what we call artistic genius. As the epitome of uncontrollable individualism, both the image of the artist and that of the mentally insane are mirrored in the volition—the egotism and independence—we attribute to our own cells in diseases of proportion.

In Bali, everything outside oneself, and even things within oneself, are potential strangers (*jaba*), since every kind of Balinese character radiates from an idealized center; body-image boundary is, in other words, very carefully monitored because its existence and location are not taken for granted. One is quite careful about establishing what is outside, and both psychological and physical ailments are, thus, recognized as having their bases in types of pollution. In consequence, there exists a tremendous awareness of orientation, to the degree that one is constantly aware of one's environment. This kind of careful orientation in the physical as well as the ideological world is largely responsible for the common view that the Balinese are, one and all, "artistic"; but it is also responsible for their acute awareness of things "outside," of the subtle boundary maintenance that is required to keep themselves affectively "oriented." My point is that the Balinese have rationalized, and are therefore consciously aware of, how close the strange is and, indeed, how essential it is for self-definition. We, conversely, promote myths that encourage us to flee from the strange, myths that isolate us in the name of protecting our freedom, our individuality.

Diseases of proportion, whether they be pathological or symbolic, are paradoxically the hardest to comprehend in "enlightened" cultures, because they conform in structure to the notion of the person, the human body-image, that a radical monotheism necessitates, and, in conforming to that notion, exploit it. They exploit, that is, the view of personhood whereby uniqueness becomes a goal in itself;[15] individuality in this respect is unique only insofar as it is unequal. It is because diseases of proportion so much parallel the structure of the person in

15. In the Hindu view, this is the precise paradigm for designating the ultimate form of evil. The most evil are not those who are outsiders, but those who follow all the prescriptions for achieving enlightenment, but in turn use that knowledge to the disadvantage of others, even of the gods themselves.

"enlightened" cultures that we are, formally, least capable of curing them. Our romantic notions of mad genius—of the neurotic artist or unacculturated scientist, of the meteoric rise of a film star or political figure—parallel the structural relation of a tumor to its host. This argument is proferred to suggest not that conformity be idealized, but only that our insensitivity to context and to conformity of proportion is formally at the basis of those diseases—mental or physical—that we find most troubling intellectually, most "strange." Uniqueness is, therefore, not only an individual's distinguishing feature but also what isolates one; it makes famous but it can also—as so many clichés remind us—destroy. More to the point, our radical isolation of the "strange," and the fleeing from it that our favorite cultural myths promote, encourages in us an ignorance of just how much we rely upon the "strange" for self-definition.[16]

IV. AGAINST OTHERNESS

against: in opposition to, contrary to; toward, so as to press on.
Webster's

For Neoplatonists or Augustinians—or, for that matter, all monotheists—what is most "strange" invariably is defined as the total disengagement of personality from the object-person. In today's world, Goffman's well-dressed, highly educated, polite, white Anglo-Saxon male (see n. 1) is as readily a description of the average homosexual as it is of Goffman's unstigmatized male of the 1950s. Not surprisingly, in a truly "free" environment, what is most "traditional" becomes itself a veil for those who transform traditional mores and basic beliefs. In fact, there is no better way of calling attention to one's freedom than to place oneself deliberately in a social category where appearance is not what it seems—where the conflation of traditionally separate categories becomes embodied in a particular person.[17] Impersonation be-

16. To repeat Turner's categories, one could also describe this reliance as the categorical need for antistructures and liminality.

17. Social relations in a stratified context, conversely, may function as much to remind one of who one is not (to remind one that other modes of thought do, indeed, exist) as to codify group identity by reference to a paradigmatic role model embodied only in a single person (Goffman's perfect WASP male). While I once heard a radio news-

comes part of power to the degree that authority and "acting" go hand in hand. For the Balinese, the most treacherous kind of impersonator is one who wears no mask at all in a context in which everyone else is masked; for such a person either is uninitiated (and, therefore, "outside") or is intentionally engaged in manipulating the most clever of masks—for in certain forms of drama both the gentle and noble characters as well as the evil ones (who disguise themselves in noble forms) may appear unmasked. Both the demonic narcissist (the one who is "free" to conflate social categories) and the generic idealization of pureness (Goffman's example of the one and only perfect individual) utilize the same visual category to make completely different statements. A social minority that wears the appropriate emblem in order to be readily identified as "outside" is much more easily accounted for than one that wears the cloth of purity but speaks the word of danger.

As with T. E. Lawrence among the Arabs, otherness becomes a codifying feature of what we understand "free" to mean; the word suggests an acceptance of standards, but also a certain disengagement from those particular behavioral standards that provide no obvious commentary on the self. More mysterious still, it indicates a willingness on the part of the "free" individual to indulge self-consciously in his or her own freedom—to make self-conscious, romantic, and even eccentric statements about the singularity of one's life. This process ultimately depends upon an actualization of the exotic within one's own world view; in order, that is, for one to know oneself, daily life must be understood as a continual exchange between what—as the Balinese say—one can see and what one can't, between our reaction to the kinds of events that trouble us in a minor way from day to day, and the sense that "outsiders" actually have the ability to see the same events in a distinctively "different" way.[18] Such voyeuristic (literally "reflective") or, to be less critical, such self-referential modes of living are rigorously devoted to the sustenance of personal meaning without "oth-

caster refer to America as being "*in* President Reagan," the rest of society finds itself sensitized to those differences that set each individual apart from the "perfect" example, making every minor psychological lesion into a defining feature of personhood.

18. It is worth noting here the power that is to be had, particularly within millennial contexts, by one who is widely traveled, or who, at least, can lay claim to a certain worldliness.

erness," without actively needing others in order to experience the importance of the unknown for self-definition. Or, conversely, because one's own self is thought to be least known, that "otherness" most like the self—one's mirror image—represents, indeed, the essence of exoticism. The totally "free" individual cannot "know" the world through contrast, because all contrasts are meant to be embodied in the unique self and in replications of it.[19] "Freedom," here, means not needing the unknown for self-management, because the unknown has been embodied in one's own self-doubt—hence democracy's romance with confidence-men and its fascination with crime, its obsession with uniqueness and its underlying conviction that "equal" can only mean "selfsame."[20] In democracies, of course, the assimilation of the exotic is nearly impossible, since true diversity is so often antithetical to the selfsameness that constitutes the dead-level condition of daily living. Unlike highly stratified societies, where systems of inequality institutionalize "difference" and therefore demand more complex forms of social interaction, democracy cannot promulgate both social diversity and selfsameness without a millennial scenario (a socially determined performative text) that is both evolutionary and monotheistic—a scenario wherein the "other" is ritually overcome by "self" through the living out of important cultural myths.

In America, for example, the triumph of millennialism in the realm of social thinking no doubt poses the greatest of all threats to human liberty, since millennial thinking, by definition, can neither envision a sophisticated concept of the foreign nor sustain any rational construction of a future. Certainly, the concept of "society" by any definition

19. The correct image for describing this condition is, perhaps, not the single mirror, but a set of barbershop mirrors, in which one reflection leads to an infinity of other copies of itself.

20. By contrast, social orders that depend upon an explicit—rather than our implicit—form of hierarchy lack all such guarantees for individuals. What they are, however, very good at is socialization, since the separation of skills and duties that they necessitate creates an interdependence in any given group of individuals and, hence, a notion of self that is more socially oriented. The growth of democracy in India, for example, has not resulted in equal rights for women, because the system of dual inequality (the absolute separation of domains of power among men and women) is still perceived as more central to social identity than the freewheeling disconnectedness that democracy inculcates. Where Indians seek to protect the traditional family unit and (despite the sometimes ghastly consequences for women entrapped by dowry requirements) traditional forms of marriage, Americans live with an ever-increasing number of broken families and an appalling level of social alienation.

is founded on evolutionary—or, at least, developmental—thinking; but where millennialism differs from other sorts of evolutionary thought is in its lack of any kind of continuous future. Its apocalyptic vision permeates decisions at all levels as its story unfolds. The absence of any sophisticated American foreign policy during periods when millennial myths are prevalent, or of any real interest in, or complex awareness of, the foreign by either its citizens or the press that panders to them, regularly illustrates just how dependent millennial beliefs are upon distancing the "outside" and making it unknown. Because the foreign is what must be escaped, it is both central and peripheral: peripheral in that it must be kept unknown and seemingly irrelevant; central in that this deliberate ignorance creates a hysteria among millennialists about the prospect of being unknowingly polluted by that unknown. In millennial contexts, in other words, the "foreign" is central as a general idea, but meaningless as an articulated category of thought. Homophobia is, thus, not just a fear of social minorities (of "other" people), but a central condition of the millennial democracy.

V. HYSTERIA RULES

> I didn't have cancer. I had something inside of me that had cancer in it, and it was removed.
>
> Ronald Reagan

Does somatic hysteria, itself, give rise to millennialism?[21] And can the significance we attach to millennialism as a form of "social disease" be correlated to an obsessive concern with the "strange" forms of somatic corruption we perceive as existing within another social category or among members of another culture? Is social hysteria, in other words, itself responsible for the post-Enlightenment asymmetry in which we become obsessed with the unknown other in a way that those we study are not obsessed (Fabian 1983)? Is even the discipline of anthropology, in the end, a form of post-Enlightenment hysteria?

   To get some sense of how these issues might be related, it is useful to consider an example of how the integration of mind and body in another culture provides a clear indication of the way in which social

---

21. For a discussion of the epigraph to this section, see Sontag 1988, 1989.

metaphors have "medical" implications. Though I have elsewhere in this study discussed the relationship between ontology and body image and, in particular, the relevance of Tylor's view of "animism" for psychoanalysis (see Chap. 2, "The Animated Memory"), it is worth reconsidering the problem of animism as it relates to pathology. For it is not so much the case that other cultures refrain from subdividing the categories that constitute a person; far more interesting are the ways in which such categorical subdivisions are connected and integrated into patterns of social behavior. Unless we are fully capable of imagining the real implications of such ideas for patterns of behavior, we are unlikely to succeed in increasing our understanding of the logic of "animism." Tylor's description of the undisturbed sleeper whose "soul" wanders beyond the body (1913, 1.428–31) may strike one as merely a charming way of describing the mysterious world of dreams. But expanding the horizons of such a belief into the world of day-to-day social interactions yields a picture of the body image that is considerably more complex. For the "soul" may be led to wander not only in sleep; it may also be startled from the body—through fright, through ingesting some cathartic substance, or even, in some cultures, by a simple sneeze.

But this is not to say that such a disengagement of "soul" is always taken to be a bad thing. Though the Balinese (to expand upon my earlier examples) avoid frightening situations and deemphasize them socially so as to avoid such "soul" loss, I would argue that the entire pattern of events in a ritually charged atmosphere is designed to give special meaning to just such a physiological experience. Death, naturally, is the clearest event in which disengagement is ritually articulated; however, possession states also utilize established patterns for experiencing an absence of self, and especially the loss of soul that is caused by startling another or oneself. During possession, that is, one may be startled in a *meaningful* way; one may be encouraged to experience a kind of transformation that has social meaning. The sort of hysteria that comes when one's gods and ancestors take possession of one's own body results not in the draining of one's life force, but in what Marcel Mauss called a "total prestation," an experience that has meaning on all levels, including not only the social and religious, but the physical, metaphysical, moral, esthetic, and economic as well.

FIG. 46. Balinese masks (Batubulan, Gianyar, Bali): in the foreground we see depicted on the face of the monstrous Barong the ambivalence that is alternatively horrific or humorous, depending on the context in which it is invoked. Around the Barong are a number of other mask types that also display this ambivalence. (Photo: author)

For the Balinese, the face that epitomizes this physical condition is that of an ambivalent monster (Fig. 46),[22] the face itself displaying an expression of arrest that has a variety of meanings (from horror to humor) depending on the social context in which it appears. It is also a face that represents the natural sensory capacities of the somatosensory and the motor cortexes and, as such, is a "superficial" (i.e., "on-the-skin") manifestation of one's total sensory capabilities, conflated into a complex bundle of sensations that constitute the expression of startle or arrest, and that achieve their meaning (horrific *or* humorous) through the performative context in which they are elicited. Without a proper context, the overstimulation of the senses results in "soul"

22. For discussion, see Napier 1986, 217–23.

loss—a kind of continuous emotional percussion that weakens the person through excess, eventually driving the "soul" out from the organism, the body, that is its host.[23]

How does this Balinese attitude toward loss of self relate to other forms of pollution that manifest themselves on the skin, that is, to other forms of somatization? Used as a model for immunological disorders, the decontextualized barrage of overstimulation results in the progressive weakening of the individual. Most humans, similarly, possess the capacity to mount a defense against invading viruses, but in certain instances they cannot produce the quantity of cells required to purge the organism, such failures of the body being often disproportional, the result of a progressive weakening. The immunological corollary to the Balinese expression of arrest (or, for that matter, to the facial image of the Greek Gorgon) is the riot of immunological stimuli that is at the basis of anaphylactic shock (of either psychogenic or other "physical" origin), the progressive destabilization by which "self" and "not-self" coalesce in a destructive, rather than a constructive, set of interactions. Indeed, the parallel between this Balinese exegesis of such weakening and patients' descriptions of immunological disorders is, as it were, "striking"; lupus sufferers, for example, will often focus on the very active or even hyperactive life they once lived as a way of not only contrasting their present inactivity, but suggesting that they may have simply surpassed, through constant stimulation, some somatic threshold. Three important observations can be made here.

The first is that there is a similarity between Balinese descriptive language and immunological discourse. For the Balinese, enlightenment is frequently rendered in pugilistic language. Palm-leaf manuscripts tell, quite literally, how the lights get turned on, especially when one is struck like a lightning bolt by Śiva's staff. The Balinese are stunned much as Western intellectuals are "struck" by creative thoughts and Western drug addicts take "hits" of their favored drugs.

The second is that an attention to the depleting effects of stress is cross-cultural but the meaning of stress is not. Freud's well-known idea that the mind is "first and foremost a device designed for mastering

---

23. As with overexposure to television violence, one becomes stupefied by this loss of self.

excitations which would otherwise be felt as distressing or would have pathological effects" (Freud [1914] 1957, 85) can, as McDougall demonstrates ([1982] 1985, 81–106), have new meaning for immunology. But this is as far as the similarities go, since stress, as the stagnation of "psychoneuroimmunology" has shown, is as unquantifiable as it is socially negotiated. Two people exposed to the same stressful stimulus will, even under extreme conditions, have very different reactions, much as the same appalling living conditions can give rise to both sociopaths and so-called normal people, even if the former type predominates. Studies of psychiatric recidivism, in fact, have demonstrated that successful coping strategies (e.g., "acting normal") may indeed be consciously developed by those who feel they have no hope of normalcy, while those who return again and again to psychiatric institutions vent stress through a persistent belief in the efficacy of the system (Corin 1990, 170–85). Stress, indeed, can actually be creative and invigorating under the right circumstances, so much so that its effects cannot be extracted from the more complex domain of social interaction in which it has meaning: one may become deathly ill by the depletion of energy that results from overstimulation of the organism (as in allergic reactions); one may become (as in autism, or certain forms of shock, or even through an overexposure to TV violence) simply dulled, stupefied, deadened; but one may equally become very productive and creative (like "troubled artists," traditional shamans, or those who "make it" by overcoming a life-threatening illness through "self-help"). Stress may be either sensitizing or desensitizing; it may, furthermore, sensitize us in destructive or creative ways.

Though it is perhaps premature to suggest that the opposition between immune deficiency and immune hyperactivity is only immunology's Cartesian straw man, in psychotherapy such an argument can be pursued through the third and final observation about the cultural dimensions of Balinese somatization and the somatic dimensions of immunology that we label "psychic." It may be assumed without stirring much debate that one of the basic tenets that psychoanalysis inherits from Descartes is that conscious thought is both the distinguishing feature and the goal of human activity. While we will consider this assumption more directly in the Epilogue, it is important to note that this tendency is, as much of the non-Western world illustrates, neither a necessary nor a contingent condition of being human. A predilection for reflexive, self-conscious introspection can vary significantly across cultures and even, indeed, within any given group of individuals. Furthermore, there is nothing universal to indicate that human development should necessarily evolve from subjective to objective thought to the degree that we are justified in inveighing against the appearance of the former among mature adults as retrograde. The popular concept of the "Freudian slip" is frequently held out to us as evidence of psychic connections that we have failed to bring to consciousness, and our analysts take it as a major conceptual victory to put together such associations for us. But subliminal agendas can be viewed as having been "discovered" (or uncovered) only when they occur in cultures that suppress their elaboration; and our fascination for dissecting them with the aid of a psychoanalytic lens that is culture-specific, no doubt, owes more to Descartes and Darwin than it does to Freud. Indeed, from the standpoint of subjective, associative—what some call "regressive"—thought, these associations may be self-evident and even banal.

Though the Cartesian dimensions of cellular theory need their own separate study, or several such studies, the degree to which understanding these dimensions is sociosomatic (rather than psychosomatic) should now be clear: what for the neuropathologist is an immunological or autoimmunological mystery is, for the Balinese, a condition of decontextualized emotional stimulation. We discuss to little effect the psychogenic basis of shock and susceptibility to disease, while the Balinese endeavor to articulate social paths upon which such stimulation produces an experience—be it constructive or destructive—that is socially contextualized and controlled. They, in other words, attempt to accommodate pathological conditions that are ontologically ambivalent, to provide a social framework for assessing them, rather than to isolate them as weapons of psychological destruction.

Considered from this perspective, we can easily identify the Western—and, particularly, the contemporary American—tendency to capitalize upon ambivalent situations in self-destructive ways. No doubt one of the best examples of this turning upon the self may be evidenced in what the anthropologist Gregory Bateson called a "double bind." A double bind occurs when an individual is placed in a situation of having to decide between alternatives that are only negative, the classic cases occurring in parent–child relationships in which the latter may be provided a choice between two options that both reflect negatively on his or her own socialization. Situations that are socially ambivalent or not easily categorized are used by a parent to instill fear and dependence, or, in terms of the present discussion, to remind the child that it does not know its way in the world because it lacks the sort of judgment that is necessary for self-knowledge. While Bateson ascribed considerable anxiety to individuals who regularly have to undergo such oppression, what is important for this discussion is the fact that, as Bateson (1972) also points out, such situations tend to create a tremendous dependence of child upon parent, since the device is often employed to intimidate children as they attempt to express their independence, and, in particular, their capacity to make decisions about their place in the world. The double bind, while making a child more dependent upon the judgment of the parent, also instills a lack of confidence about establishing ontological categories. Ambivalence here becomes threatening and fear-inducing, so much so that, if it is employed without restraint, the child develops an almost paroxysmal self-consciousness. Every instance that is socially ambivalent, where one is not certain of one's place, becomes an instance in which one's response to the experience of being startled is to turn against the self rather than toward the world outside, or in which the response is directed outward only after the individual can no longer absorb additional stimulation.[24] Instead of legitimating the outwardly directed "fight" response by finding a constructive avenue (such as possession) through which it may be socially legitimized, we overstimulate the "flight" (fright) response, by which that particular "hysteria" is turned against the self. The double bind is a device for inducing self-doubt— even a Gorgon-like petrifaction—when the individual confronts ambivalence or uncertainty; socially, we employ it to intimidate one another. The double bind, thus, becomes a way of imposing "hysteria" upon the self, since, as a culture, we refuse to institutionalize those avenues of personality development that suggest any ambivalence about

---

24. Thus, we have the well-known examples of individuals who seem suddenly, and without apparent provocation, to lose control—or, in Malay terms, to run *amok*.

self-knowledge while simultaneously maintaining that there can be no such thing as a *positive* "loss of self."

The double bind provides the paradigmatic case of how we use ambivalence to destroy others rather than to suggest ways by which ontological conditions that are not easily categorized may be understood *socially*; as continual stimulation of the immune system causes its deterioration—a not-knowing of the self—so too the double bind creates a repeated startling into fright that weakens the individual's social immunity. No wonder, then, that we feel we can isolate certain "types" of individuals who are more prone to immunological disorders, since the psychogenic factor in disease is mirrored by social mechanisms that have the same "reflexive" consequence. If, that is, immunological dysfunction can be exacerbated by "psychogenic" factors, then those social conditions that overstimulate an unfulfilled concern for self-knowledge give rise to a kind of social autoimmune response, an incapacity to distinguish effectively self and other. And if threat is constantly invoked each time the individual expresses his or her "freedom" to redefine social space, then the choice of fight or flight in situations of startle and arrest will always result in flight into self-doubt. It is no wonder, then, that those who are unhappy about seeing themselves defined through systems of opposition (e.g., dual inequality) are often members of a social group (e.g., homosexuals) that seems to have a higher rate of immunological disorders.[25] Indeed, from a Balinese perspective, a solution to AIDS or other immunological or autoimmunological malfunctioning should—from the standpoint of how one becomes socially immune—necessarily be discovered in the effects (what we would call the neurobiology and biochemistry) of the flight/fight–startle complex; for it is in the ambivalence made possible by that moment that an intellectual transformation becomes at all possible.[26] Here, refiguring the self in physical terms is coextensive with a belief about efficacy that is culturally structured.

25. The so-called psychogenic factor in immunological disorders is, of course, widely debated. What is significant, however, for the present discussion is not *how great* a role such factors play, but the fact that a susceptibility to immunological disorders may at all be influenced psychologically and, in turn, statistically influence certain socially determined categories of people who are considered "outside."

26. For the Balinese, this emotional complex is visualized, as noted earlier, in the horrific "Face of Glory," which is seen above temple gates and in masks. This image of

This "social" analogue for immunity (our inability to understand immunology *socially*) indicates how we have failed as a culture to bridge profitably the gaps between biology, psychology, and everyday human relations; but it also suggests to us directions for future understanding. For to say that certain kinds of "social" autoimmunity depend upon a wrongly conditioned response of self to other is also to say that individuals caught within that web of interactions condition themselves neuroimmunologically for such misapprehensions to take place on the biochemical and pathological levels.

In contradistinction to the traditional notion of psychosomatic illness—where we proclaim the existence of psychogenic factors without providing any avenue by which an understanding of them might advance our treatment of disease—we now see just *how* social is our construction of disease pathology and, moreover, how central are our *social* metaphors for our understanding of what disease is. Thus, it follows that, in order to refigure the way we look at our most intellectually complicated physical afflictions, we must refigure the social metaphors that define the body and the ways in which "bodies" (both human and microbiological) interact.

VI. FEAR OF THE FOREIGN;
OR, THE BORAX FACTOR

Infirmity is as much a catalyst of culture as it is a construct thereof.

John Palmer

Of the cultural myths that define American life, certainly the most dominant have to do with a love of individual freedoms (from one another and from government)[27] and the pioneering spirit that is continually associated with American history, with moral fiber, with capitalistic enterprise. While glorifying the pioneer, Americans rarely admit to the millennial characteristics of pioneering, to the role of such millennial dreams in the foundation of American culture, and to the

---

transition and transformation is, according to their *lontar* (palm-leaf) manuscripts, epitomized in the physiological effects of *kacubung* (*Datura*, *Brugmansia*). No doubt this ideological and biological nexus would also color their understanding of what we call "immune deficiency."

27. Ronald Reagan once described democracy as "not a system of government, but a way of keeping people free of government."

FIG. 47.   Ronald and Nancy Reagan: making full use of his television experience as host and mythologizer for the serial program "Death Valley Days,"
the millennial wagon master is shown here "trail-blazin' for tax reform" in
Missouri. (*Newsweek*, September 16, 1985; photo: Larry Downing)

ramifications of millennial thinking for how Americans, in turn, deal
with things "outside." When Ronald Reagan symbolically held out a
wagon train as the microcosmic symbol of his America (Fig. 47), he
epitomized a fundamentally American millennial notion, which recon-
firmed a basic cultural tendency to assuage social hysteria by patron-
izing it. The effects of that tendency are mainly seen in the inclination
on the part of Americans to abandon—in the name of psychoanalytical
sensitivity—a necessary commitment to their places of origin or to any
sort of microcosmic/macrocosmic awareness. "If you don't like it
(reality, the way things 'are'), leave it," one so frequently hears. The
statement reflects not only the reactionary invitation to "put up or shut
up"; it also reflects what is largely considered a positive response to
environmental difficulties—namely, the freedom to go elsewhere,
preferably accompanied by a twenty-mule team hauling purificatory
soap. We set ourselves up, that is, as a melting pot, and then spend all

our time developing myths of escape from diversity, from the stranger. This is not the assimilation of the foreign, but the flight from it.

One might even argue that the entire nation is immersed in millennialism, and that millennialism not only is the cause of a constant wandering in search of yet another achieved status, but is also at the basis of the rapid resettling both of individuals and of the vast financial empires that rule modern life. Though these conditions may appear—as, for example, a Marxist might argue—to have different sources, from the millennialist perspective (that is, from the standpoint of a radical transformation) the two go hand in hand, since a rite of passage demands the desymbolization of all things in order that they may be reconstituted.[28] It cannot be coincidental, in other words, that a country based upon the commoditization of objects and the dissolution of "total prestations" (to recall again Marcel Mauss's description of social exchanges that are symbolically rich) is also a country in which the liminal state of seeking out frontiers has been institutionalized into a permanent condition. The real question is whether or not that institutionalization of liminality is, in fact, another state altogether.[29] Is modern life, in other words, an example of extended liminality, or has the rite of passage, to extend the metaphor, actually been completed?

Are we already in a new "settled" condition? To my mind, we are not. And my answer stems from the fact that our acquired "freedoms" have yet to result in anything like a considered reevaluation of our new status, a redefinition of a new social notion, a resettlement among strangers, both cultural and personal—in other words, a *recontextualization*. We have not, as it were, emerged from our liminal condition into a new status that incorporates or assimilates the freedoms we experienced during "resettling"—during, that is, the period of colonization—into a condition that is both physically and metaphorically *oriented*. American culture is, indeed, cognitively entrapped in a rite of

28. Such actions as shaving the heads of initiates, or giving up civilian clothing (e.g., in the military), illustrate the significance of desymbolizing (reducing to sameness) at transitional moments both people and the objects that define them.

29. Van Gennep's classic description of a rite of passage ([1908] 1960)—including a separation from the profane world, a transformational experience, and a readmission into society—has been widely employed by anthropologists as an analytic tool. Victor Turner built upon the concept of liminality to show how in certain social situations (e.g., in the America of the 1960s) a liminal period of transformation can be prolonged enough to have the appearance of being a permanent condition (e.g., 1969, 106–13, 145–65).

passage, and it has, moreover, yet to emerge from its romance with liminality. Like Marlow's shipmates in Conrad's *Heart of Darkness*, we are still shooting from the coast into the darkness of Africa, firing randomly into the emptiness in which colonizers behave in ways that they never would were they at home.[30] And in the absence of the dignity that a sense of environmental connectedness assures, we wander aimlessly and sometimes violently, the sons and daughters of "settlers" finally cut loose from their parents' memories of a place of origin. One cannot, of course, turn back from such a psychosocial transformation, because a rite of passage is also a rite of birth into self-consciousness. Once one enters into it—whether to reemerge or not—one is forever changed. No matter what one does, one cannot regain the same sense of a fixed origin, the same sense of place. For this reason, *reorientation* cannot simply involve a nostalgic attempt to recover—as Americans attempted to in the 1960s—a lost past in which people were meant to be connected to the land. What, then, might it be?

In positive terms, our continued efforts to eradicate in America the kind of inalienable status that is the basis of the caste system or the traditional British aristocracy help insure the perpetuation of the constitutional rights we value. However, unless we are able to be entirely confident about those values, the result is yet one more millennial dream in which pioneers break camp, taking the "few good men," as so many of our cultural myths tell us, to a new horizon. Regrettably, in these situations many are left behind, including those less fortunate individuals that for traditional Hindus reveal that the world will always be a mixed place, requiring an informed sense of balance.

One need only look to the predominance of "horizons" in American genre painting, the absence of human beings in "nature" photography, or the obsession in modern society with holidays and vacation homes (where one can express one's "true" emotions about the "outside") to see that our emotional commitments so often lie elsewhere.

---

30. Reading Conrad's *Heart of Darkness* alongside van Gennep's *The Rites of Passage* is most illuminating, in that the novel so accurately reflects those formal features of rites of transition that had been isolated by French sociologists of Conrad's day. Indeed, when looked at in this way, the novel reads very much like a literary rendition of French anthropological thought, from its symbol of the Fates (who initiate Marlow's period of transition), to the harlequin Russian (who guides the initiate through the liminal, transitory state), to the inversion of factual evidence on Marlow's part once he has reentered normal (European) society.

Clearly, these proclivities are older than American culture and have their bases in a larger Romantic tradition. But, increasingly, we lament the internalization of otherness by hoping against hope that there yet exists another kind of otherness to fill the existential emptiness that is the consequence of our cult of self-indulgence.

Why, we need to ask, are contextualization and orientation important at all? The answer is simply that they enable us to make distinctions, to establish beginnings and endings, to *organize* categories, and, thus, to complete transitions. Above all, they enable us to create new cultural myths and, in so doing, to establish a foundation upon which new daily actions may be interpreted. Without other myths to replace the millennial ones, there is very little chance of changing categories; for if millennialism is dependent upon a radicalization, if not an ignorance, of the foreign, then it stands to reason that the desymbolization of object relations will continue to reinforce the conviction that the millennium is upon us—that, like the "cargo" cultists of Melanesia, we can lay waste our environment because it is superfluous to the Second Coming.

Without such myths the conditions of living alter significantly, and a belief in a future reemerges. For, certainly, the devaluing of millennial thinking has concrete implications. Believing that the world will persist, for example, demands that "defense" involve less a protection against foreigners for those now living than an assurance that current decisions derive from a wish to provide better conditions for future lives. What is more, the two agendas are clearly not the same; for imagine environmental protection being funded by those concerned with "defense": one readily senses the kind of categorical transformation that the changing of myth enables. Today, we think of "defense" as protection against "foreign" governments; but, clearly, a nation so fearful of the foreign that it pollutes itself from within with chemicals and hardware is more concerned with the preservation of a certain form of nationhood than with the physical preservation of its citizens. What really needs to be questioned is the idea of a nation-state that regards its own identity and mythology as more important than the survival of the very individuals who inhabit its lands, create its myths, and maintain them. "Live Free or Die" goes the hotly debated motto of the State of New Hampshire.

Why isn't "the environment" a matter of "defense"? The only reason for its not being so is that we are unable, as yet, to refigure any sense of connectedness—since "commodification" implies the infinite exchange and replaceability of all things, there is no relative contextualization of one thing over another, no sense that relative position helps promote situational responsibility. Here, the best evidence comes from the behavior of the great capitalists—arguably the world's best commodifiers and millennial dreamers;[31] for capitalism demands above all else a freedom of individual ambition that is without environmental constraint. Indeed, the fundamental capitalist pursuit is exactly that of the millennialist—namely, to exercise the freedom to move elsewhere once a particular environment has been sapped of its resources.

This moving elsewhere, moreover, is such an essential feature of the pioneer myth that pioneers need not respect cultural boundaries or existing social responsibilities, except when doing so proves convenient.[32] And as long as such an ideology prevails, there is little need to think about the deteriorating consequences of defense hysteria, since new categories by which such concerns might be refigured have not emerged.[33] In the world of commodification, a "land of opportunity" can only be a land of cheap exploitation, one where "defense"—as so many "cargo" cults show us—by definition includes the capacity for self-destruction.[34]

In short, there can be no allegiance to a collectivity for whom object

31. I say this because one need only see how predictably traditional objective prestations ("gifts," in Marcel Mauss's terminology) are commodified—symbolically devalued —in millennial movements to understand why our greatest capitalists are often our most outspoken millennial dreamers.

32. The examples are nearly innumerable, but think of the conceptual oddity whereby our richest corporations set up in the cheapest (i.e., most symbolically "free") environments while promoting propaganda that suggests their working in the best interest of a collectivity. Like those oil companies that register tankers in low-tax countries and then lean on taxpayers to protect them from those very powers when the political climate takes a turn for the worse, the millennialist's "cargo" is thoroughly devoid of environmental specificity.

33. One consequence of America's being "inside [former] President Reagan" is that when he goes, so does the country. (Who, then, should care about such things as the half-lives of radioactive isotopes, or "national debts"?) Indeed, a problem common to many American children is the sense of doom that characterizes the self-unmaking of their self-made parents—the parental conviction, that is, that the millennial transformation is unrepeatable and that it, therefore, must unfold within their generation.

34. In Melanesia, for example, it is common for "cargo" cultists to abandon their fields, destroy their livestock, and, in general, ignore all responsibilities relating to the continuation of life on earth.

relations are entirely commodified. In the absence of an actively nourished symbolic interdependence among things or among individuals
as social beings there exist no relative bases for responding to others in
a considerate and morally responsible manner. Mauss's understanding
of how symbolic connectedness engendered sympathetic behavior has
its natural corollary: one could equally argue that capitalism—the totally free marketplace—is little more than a means of undermining democracy's moral agenda. Indeed, a government's allegiance to a free
marketplace may even be construed as signifying a total absence of
"patriotism," since a "patriot," one must remember, is less a political
animal than "one who loves his or her *land*."[35]

Odd though it may seem, most national problems reveal themselves
as more generated by and dependent upon those myths and stereotypes
that offer the culturally sanctioned category of personhood—upon culturally rendered categories of thought that specify individuality—than
by any fact of experience. In other words, the maintenance of certain
forms of self-centered myth is often more important than learning
either about life itself or about the great varieties of human experience
that can be known—unless one is willing to argue that there is no life
other than that proffered in myth. Finally, then, we need to ask
whether or not we are, indeed, even *willing* to refigure our dominant
social metaphors; and there is much evidence to indicate that we are
not. Cannon's bone-pointing Australians—who mourn to death a very
much alive relative in the throes of entering shock—provide the exotic
parallel to Goffman's or Foucault's rendition of the "alienating" myths
of personhood that dominate modern life; we too, in other words,
continue to induce psychogenic double binds that spare our myths but
not our lives.

Were such "refiguring" possible, it could only come by way of rad-

---

35. Here, the notion of landed gentry becomes especially relevant; for, like India,
America provided an opportunity for those without extraordinary status in Britain to
assume status values in the Colonies. One need only look at the signers of America's
famous colonial documents to see how much the Constitution of the United States was,
to some extent, an experiment of privilege whose success depended on the wisdom and
cosmopolitanism of its signers. The kind of measured, humanitarian restraint demonstrated in Franklin's wish that U.S. forces should not fire upon Captain Cook (because
he was engaged in an endeavor deemed beneficial to mankind) would, as Henry Steele
Commager has argued (1975, xviii–xix), have been most unlikely had Franklin not had
the complex awareness of the foreign that he cultivated by spending considerable time
abroad.

ically transforming basic categories: on the physical level, this means reassessing the entire range of military metaphors that not only dominate immunology, but define what, in fact, it is; on the social level, it means reassessing our conceptualization of the foreign enough to realize that, like the autoimmune aggressor, we often subscribe to myths that encourage the self to be its own worst enemy. For it is only through such social and biological reassessments of the dominant myths that provide us with our conceptualization of the "foreign" that a transformation in social understanding becomes at all possible.

The problems posed by millennialism for the assimilation of the foreign can be discussed only briefly here, but they are, nonetheless, important for an understanding of how notions of "otherness" are uniquely influenced by culture. Like the millennialist who abandons what cannot be understood, the "foreign" foils for self-definition that specify otherness are mirrored by that bacterial model of disease in which we attribute volition and independence to biological aliens and, in so doing, deem them "exotic." We know that disease is "alien"— that is, unknown—but we have no framework for reconnecting what is "different," because we depend upon that opposition for self-knowledge.[36]

How will we actually permit the diseased person to venture into uniqueness if, fundamentally, we define by making analytical distinctions that are pluralistic, not to say divisive? States of ill health are always defined in terms of a pluralism of parts, and the entire field of immunology is based on the idea that recognition and defense govern the internal war that is waged by the cells of an organism. Our skin, being the part of us *par excellence* that responds to *superficial* ("socio-somatic") difficulties of the immune system, is treated by our dermatologists and allergists, while the surgeons who excise cancer are the medical profession's version of the fighter pilot—out for "visceral" gratification in the name of curing, the healer warriors of the modern world.[37] Volition and intention become the concepts epitomizing this

---

36. One could, similarly, attribute the absence of a Reagan foreign policy until the end of his administration to a demand for maintaining similar radical categories. Under the terms of the millennial pioneering myths of which he was so fond, he, indeed, *could* have no detailed foreign policy. Note, also, how abysmal in general is the coverage of "foreign" affairs by American news media, and how exceedingly poor is the average American's so-called geographic literacy (itself an oxymoron).

37. See Napier 1986, 80–82, on *hērōes iatroi*.

aggressive pluralism that defines the self. While in theory intellectual "monotheists," we have internalized our polytheism—forced ourselves to deny it while openly utilizing it in every effort we make at an internal self-description that is morally complex. Such infighting within the self seems to be a permanent part of an organism's sense of proportion; and it should, therefore, not strike us as odd that among the first Greek physicians were its mythological warriors. Nor should it surprise us that symbols that formally dissolve oppositions—joints, the pineal body, the skin, autoimmunity—become the focus of a culture's social and mental balance, a battleground on which its toughest intellectual, moral, medical, and ethical issues are either compounded or solved.

Why, we need to know, if our notions of self-balance are based on pluralistic models, do we so much deny the idea of a pluralism of the self? Do we affirm the *self* through denying the theories by which we understand the actions of its cells? Are we so far away from a social system that reinforces the unification of the plural through collective activity that we cannot risk admitting any plurality of self to a theater that goes beyond the skin and risks, therefore, being "superficial"? Certainly the violent reactions of autistics to changes in habit or behavioral patterns suggest for us how few models those in distress may actually allow to codify symbolic unity. In the absence of social or religious symbols that dissolve reciprocities and unite opposites, our single symbol that does so becomes the self—distinguished by definition, disenfranchised by the notion of ritual (organized collective activity) as an entirely mechanical, repetitive thing, in which innovation and group dynamics become unlikely if not impossible. We label autistic behavior "ritualistic" as a damnation of an autistic individual's inability to cope with innovation, without realizing that autistic people are ritualistic because their sense of disenfranchisement has led them to grasp at the fundamental patterns that unite individuals into coherent social wholes. The presence of ritual—of patterns that in real terms unite through reciprocity—is not the problem of autistics, but their one primordial link to others. Ritual behavior among them is, I would argue, as much a statement about how tenaciously we as a culture cling to the cult of the individual as it is a demonstration of their aberrance. Here it is important to realize that while the pattern of a ritual may appear eternally fixed—even repetitive—frequently it is not. In cul-

tures in which ritual becomes the stage for the unification of the plural—as in a Sri Lankan healing rite or a Balinese temple festival—each
new ritual event becomes the occasion for a group's reassessing itself
interpersonally through the personification of good and evil forces, of
the radical oppositions that people must resolve both for the culture as
a whole and within themselves.

What such innovative ritual patterns suggest about foreignness—
about revising our own curing methodologies, as well as our conceptualizations about diseases of proportion—is that diseases of proportion can only be cured through creating something that is their reciprocal, some mock-form of what causes them. Like Bernini's double
theater,[38] in which each person is "remembered" in a contextualizing
mirror image, otherness is understood only through connectedness. In
physical diseases of proportion, we are, it seems, often delayed in con-
ceptualizing appropriate avenues of research as much by our faith in
the disproportion characteristic of things exotic (like intellectual genius) as by anything else. We now take as a discovery the realization
that such diseases (certain forms of cancer, for instance) cannot be
cured unless the exotic compounds devised to treat them in some way
mimic—as do all personae—the forms they wish to transform. Indeed,
we have great difficulty understanding how mimicry—the "actualization" of superficiality—can be a life-engendering thing, even though
"any natural opposition to the growth of tumours," as Medawar has
pointed out, "is almost certain to be immunological in character and
to be the outcome of an immunological reaction of much the same
kind as that which leads to the rejection of foreign transplants" (1982,
163). Odd though it may seem now, one should not be at all surprised
were the cures for many diseases of proportion to be discovered within
the organism itself—having perhaps been forced, for whatever "physical" or "psychological" reasons, into conditions of homeopathic disproportion and opposition not unlike those that define individuals both
physically and mentally, and that, therefore, form the basis for our
conceptualization of the foreign, of what is "outside," of what disease,
in fact, is. If, as Genette says, the mirror image is the perfect symbol
of alienation (1966, 22), then surely the most alien of things is, in a

38. See above, Chap. 4, n. 41.

sense, something very like us—like AIDS, a distinctly human thing, not a form of life, but a reflective image, a caricature that we recognize by its genetic code.

In mental diseases of proportion, "enlightened" cultures may, therefore, require a type of ceremonialism that is innovative. In the West, innovative therapeutic ceremonies have occurred experimentally, and for the mentally unsocialized as part of hypnotic therapy; but their situational and experimental character is perceived to be part of a unique—even desperate—strategy for inducing change; whereas they need, rather, to become statements of what all groups are by definition. In other words, such innovative group activity needs to be perceived as normative rather than as abnormal or experimental—as assimilative and conditioning, rather than exceptional and indoctrinating. For as long as we perceive group therapy as indoctrinating, so long will autistics rely on their own rituals rather than on the social rituals to which they cannot permit themselves blindly to subscribe. So long as we have no regular group ceremonies wherein the personae at work within each of us can proudly take the stage in our own memory theaters, so long will we isolate yet further those who suffer from autism and encourage our young adults to take themselves to their own perdition.

Epilogue:
A Social Theory of the Person

Every theory of the world that is at all powerful and covers a large
domain of phenomena carries . . . within itself its own caricature.

Levins and Lewontin,
The Dialectical Biologist

I. WITHOUT STRANGERS WITHIN

Though Descartes's *cogito ergo sum* was certainly less solipsistic than the
theories of many post-Enlightenment thinkers who have laid claim to
him as their forebear, Descartes may, nonetheless, be credited for having given rise to the popular notion that valuable experiences are particularly those that can be brought to the level of self-conscious reflection. This idea of thought as the proof of existence is, of course, itself
an indisputable solipsism; all, in this view, that is to be gained by *ego
cogito ergo sum* can be had by the word *ego*; for its converse is an absurdity: one cannot "not think and, therefore, not be" any more than
one can say of others who have not had one's thoughts that they do not
exist either outside of or as a part of one's experience. If one considers
the existence of other cultures, that is, one merely accepts that there
are things that one does not know, not that others do not exist because
one does not know them. Indeed, one might even argue that living
with uncertainty is what makes the practice of anthropology a potentially creative endeavor.

This is not an auspicious juncture at which to take up even a rudi-
mentary discussion of self-consciousness as a cultural construct; I raise
the giant problem only to show how wonderful solipsisms are for creating obstacles for any morally responsible cross-cultural theory of
personhood: the more, that is, we argue that we can know only our-

selves, the more we imply that knowledge is only self-centered. As an ontological category, self-centeredness is as much at the mercy of language and cultural canons as is any other experiential category; the more we imply that knowledge is self-centered, or that the only knowledge we value is self-conscious cognition, the more we relieve ourselves of the burden of the unknown by cutting it out, from the start, as unknowable. The more we devalue any sort of experience that is not reflexive or narcissistic, the less capable we are of appreciating any sort of value in the alien.

Like anthropology itself, secure notions of culture demand equally strong invitations to the unknown, to the degree that "others" are not only trivialized caricatures—simple foils for accumulating allies—and, by extension, it is those societies least capable of dealing with potential "otherness" that depend most regularly on the kind of evolutionary hierarchy that places alien modes of thinking on some inferior cognitive plane. Though one could argue, along these lines, that the Enlightenment brought with it a complete incapacity for engaging otherness—indeed, that it brought mainly a kind of expropriation or cultural cannibalism—probably the single major obstacle to a meaningful engagement of alien theories of personhood, at least in this century, has been Freud's evolutionary view of the person, by which the final objective of analysis was, and yet remains, to bring to consciousness (that is, to make valuable) all the mental errors and simian urges hidden in each person's beginnings. In psychoanalysis, more than anywhere else, we combine the view that "value" equals "the bringing to consciousness" with the equally culture-specific notion that one evolves out of experiences focused on a loss or uncertainty of self into those that are purely self-conscious. One need only think, for example, of the troubled anthropological literature on altered states of consciousness, or of how few forms of self-loss we, as a culture, tolerate, to see how much we have come to accept a vision of the self that is most associated with depth psychology in general and a Freudian critique of primary processes in particular. Indeed, an attempt to find a single notion of dissociation that we treat positively will reveal just how much we have accepted the idea that not being self-conscious is a function of regressive, infantile activity. Even the most innocuous forms of dissociation (such as, say, ecstatic dancing) are regularly part of the categorical baggage of base racism and banal elitism. And, despite the awareness among psychoanalysts of the need for and value of regressive activity, the evolutionary concept, along with its devaluation of dissociative states, has survived intact; these are still, that is, regressive, rather than progressive, forms of mentation.

But aside from being quite blatantly a cultural construct, Freud's idea of what makes a person a better individual also makes for some troubling dilemmas that call into question the ability of psychiatric categories to function cross-culturally. When, within our own tradition, it can be said that "there is no convincing evidence that psychoanalytic treatment as such is efficacious" (Medawar 1982, 70), the prospect of employing psychoanalysis as a universal analytic system seems grim indeed. From Malinowski onwards, anthropologists have had to admit that they have yet to locate, for example, a single case of primal patricide that had anything like the kind of cultural significance Freud suspected would be universal, and the field of cross-cultural psychiatry continues to demonstrate that the application of psychoanalytic categories to other cultures often produces embarrassing results. One need only think of how a randomly selected group of psychoanalysts would respond to Balinese trance "dancing" to see the folly of adopting a system of analysis that is not acutely aware of the need for what Kleinman has called "indigenization" (1980, 55–56), the process by which a specialization can become interwoven with a popular reality. But while part of Freud's own fear of conflating self and other is evidenced in his treatment of the "animistic" primary processes that each of us should overcome in the natural course of personal growth, what is troubling about many other cultures, and about what is most unknown within our own culture, is that things simply do not work that way. What might otherwise be called a confused self-image is often central to the most advanced forms of cognitive reflection; furthermore, some forms of subject-object conflation can be shown to play not a contingent but a necessary role in such thinking.

Throughout this book I have endeavored to address this problem, not through a critique of psychoanalysis but by examining the topic of modes of thought through the vehicle of attitudes toward otherness. As a final commentary on this problem, I would like to add a psychosocial consideration of immunology to the more strictly social considerations undertaken in the last chapter; for, now that we have introduced the problem of how culturally articulated concepts of the self are played out in a critique of "others," it is worthwhile asking if immunology has any particular features that make it more useful than other cultural categories for such a discussion.

Just why, we may ask, should immunology have any special significance for a discussion of self-consciousness and dissociation? If the answer does not appear obvious, it may be helpful to recall the social nature of the Latin word *immunis* as describing the freedom from certain forms of social interaction, and, in particular, an exemption from public service. Being "immune," or having immunity, in other words, has as much to do with forms of social reciprocity (or, as it were, their absence) as it does with bodily states; rather, bodily states are themselves extensions of forms of reciprocity that are social. In the Roman case, the evidence for this fact comes, as Mauss has shown, in the *nexum*—that is, the formal, binding transaction between debtor and creditor by which the former pledges his or her own liberty as security for a debt incurred (Mauss 1967, 46–53). Now bodily reciprocity, the "primary process" by which an individual is embedded in his or her environment, is at the very heart of what we have come to know as the science of immunology. In immunology, in other words, we have an excellent example of a domain of inquiry that—though ostensibly an outgrowth of "our" way of thinking—has, willy-nilly, resisted Freud's developmental scenario; indeed, if anything, immunology demonstrates just how important it is for us to be able to employ so-called regressive, primary notions quite openly when we enter domains that we least know. It is my intention not to give an inventory or a scholarly analysis of the theoretical literature on the topic or to reiterate, except by way of summary, the points made in the last chapter, but to show how important it is to consider the significance of entertaining a nonsolipsistic—that is, a social—theory of the person. It is important to state clearly that an argument for a social theory of the person is not simply another argument for anthropological relativism; it is not to say that all cross-cultural studies guided by an overarching theory are doomed from the outset. Rather, as we shall see, a social perspective is significant because of its ability to accommodate the multiplicity of complex voices that make up the unique and sometimes antithetical responses of individuals to the categories that govern the particular culture of which they are a part. Moreover, a social theory—because of its focus on how metaphor facilitates socialization—recognizes the possibility that the way in which self-consciousness is valued is itself a cultural construct. The relativist decries the application of Western concepts to other cultures while justifying that culture's own ethnocentrism; the social theorist simply admits that all such constructs—even the universalist ones—are culturally defined and constrained, and that culture as such becomes meaningful insofar as: (1) it offers categorical patterns of meaning; (2) these patterns, in turn, facilitate individual change through forms of dissociative activity largely governed by metaphor; and (3) the utilization of such metaphors gives rise to an enormous range of potential responses among individuals. Given the significance in the modern world of what we have labeled "scientific" activity, it stands to reason, therefore, that our most significant cultural metaphors can be found not outside "science" but within it.

Though the subject of science and metaphor, and metaphor and immunology in particular, deserves a lengthy and detailed study, it may be profitable here to raise two simple questions that highlight just what relevance immunology has for refiguring depth psychology and, especially, for reevaluating the significance of the *social* dimensions of person formation. These two questions are specific. Why are metaphors so prevalent in describing certain illnesses? And why does there appear to be a correlation between the complexity of an illness (e.g., AIDS, cancer, rheumatoid arthritis) and the degree to which metaphor is called upon to explain it?

Part of the answer to these questions certainly lies in a better understanding of the correlation between levels of metaphorical activity and degrees of dissociative mental activity: in the context of an individual dealing with the uncertainties of personal change and psychological transformation, there is clearly a relationship between change and (on the one hand) those metaphors that distance (and therefore suppress) self-conscious reflection at those uncertain periods between changing mental states, and (on the other hand) the social categories that include or exclude individuals as participants in such changes. Conversely, Freud's conviction that memories were fixed moments in the past that required analytic excision becomes crucial to a radically static kind of Cartesianism by which what makes one oneself is the conscious fixation of such memories, the elimination of metaphor by admitting to a certain series of events that we take to be "facts." What we would like to believe, and what our cultural canons tell us to believe, is that loss of self is a weaker form of humanness, and that individual strength comes of being enough self-aware to see through the masks that metaphor holds up to us—to see the real person whose fixed memories make us "really" what we are. However, there are a number of important flaws to such a view. I wish, here, merely to restrict myself to those having a social anthropological dimension.

First of all, metaphor, having a broad cultural basis, invades all experience wherever and whenever uncertainty permits it to do so; it takes up the empty spaces, to use a visual image, created by the absence of self-conscious thought. Though some physicians, for example, would like to think that they employ the metaphor of "the body at war with itself" because their patients are too poorly educated to appreciate a more accurate "scientific" language, it is clear that this argument is, itself, part of the cognitive tyranny exercised by a particular cultural canon that separates fact and fiction (or, say, science and art) in a way that cannot be corroborated through actual experience. Ask researchers, for instance, if they "really believe" that a particular cell thinks such-and-such—that is, that cells have volition—and you will usually be rewarded with a laugh, if not a resounding no; but take the anthropological tack: watch the researcher in his or her daily routine and you will soon find, as Latour has cleverly shown of science in general (1987), that something very different takes place. Setting aside the role of metaphor and fantasy in creative discovery—where researchers ride cells through the bloodstream, imagine themselves as inside their microscopes, or participate in cell warfare—in the absence of the self-conscious reflection brought forward by the interview, metaphor, as it were, invades freely the otherwise "factual" environment of everyday research activity. It is the social collectivity of culture that silently or overtly inveighs against the use of words like "savage" or "man"; and, in immunology, it is culture that leads a scientist from a self-conscious denial of the idea that cells have volition to an unself-conscious research strategy dominated by the notion that those same cells have "strategies"—that they "invade," "protect," or "recognize" one another. No amount of direct questioning by an anthropologist will deplete the cultural meaning that is sustained by entitling an introductory immunology course at the Harvard Medical School "Identity: Microbes and Defense." What we have here is less the "work of culture" (where an animated culture goes about its business) than the "working of culture" (the collective utilization of "communicative norms that legitimate specialized and context-dependent vocabularies" [Kleinman and Good 1985, 30]).

The "social" question, then, is why do we seem, almost naturally, to move *in the direction* of metaphorical language whenever we (and I mean by this even the most self-aware of us) are not engaged in self-conscious reflection? My argument is that we do so not out of weakness, but because a major function of collective ideation is to provide ready avenues for what I will call *selective dissociation*—avenues that make it possible to engage patterns of socialization and self-presence that are not overtly narcissistic. I have already outlined in each chapter of this study a number of examples of what I have in mind here, examples in which a collective, cultural mirror replaces an individual one. From the "social" perspective, it becomes abundantly clear that the sort of homage to self-consciousness that we take as synonymous with intellection is in the end not only unadventurous; worse yet, the idea of self-consciousness can itself become the cultural apologist's bastion.

In this line of thinking, Freud can be seen as much as a spokesperson for Western culture as an interpreter of it, since his view of the person so thoroughly depends upon an awareness of the radical distinction between self and environment. This is, I think, what Pocock has in mind (though his target is rather different) when he criticizes the "pusillanimity" of those who take anthropological "reflexivity" as a daring theoretical step; for "they write," he states, "as though they are inarticulately angry at the world for having betrayed their too long cherished confidence in its objective stability" (Pocock 1988, 214). The point that needs to be emphasized here is not only the incredible neoconservatism, the radical distancing and objectification that characterize this form of solipsistic anthropology, but the alienation of any domain of experience not already known by calling it unknowable. It is this kind of polarizing that has become the common property of the naive Cartesianism practiced by many postmodern anthropologists, in which the objectivity of things is enough simplified and caricatured that one can presume to know at all times what separates self and other. More important, however, is the degree to which such objectifying misses the entire logic by which, in certain forms of symbolic exchange, one is drawn to "know" another person or a thing by offering some initial prestation—that is, a symbolic (in psychoanalytic terms, a "regressive") liberating of a part of oneself through actively endowing some exchangeable "fetish" with personal meaning. In other words, we need not fall into metaphorical or poetic language to see that one can maintain a fairly distinct set of categories that separate subjects and objects while still seeing that these can become meaningfully conflated through some dynamic symbolic engagement. Indeed, the capacity of metaphor symbolically to "invade" experience in the absence of self-conscious reflection suggests, if anything, that Descartes's credo tells us only that there are significant domains of intersubjective experience that a naive "objectivity" disallows us from knowing, domains that, for want of another word, might be called "artful." One might even argue that the better socialized one is, the more sensitive one becomes to an "artful" engagement of what Werner and Kaplan refer to as the dynamic "autonomization" of symbolic forms (1963, 40).

We need not, therefore, turn to poetry or another form of art proper to see the merits of conflating subject-object relations in ways that many psychoanalysts would find unhealthy. Unless, as I said, we take as our task being apologists for our own culture, so-called regressive thinking is less the sign of an unstable person (though surely it is a concomitant of instability) than it is a natural state to which we return at every moment not controlled by culturally prescribed self-conscious reflection. These are states (as, for example, Duerr [(1978) 1985] has argued) that are experientially much closer than the canons imposed by our cultural categories would have us believe; and the proof of their proximity is the extent to which we go out of our way to denigrate all forms of experience not characterized by self-consciousness. Rejecting the conflation of subject and object as "regressive" is part of the oath that every aspiring intellectual takes upon the Bible of post-Enlightenment experience; it is our promise not to engage in uncondoned forms of original thought. This is precisely why philosophers find metaphor so problematic. Mary Hesse, as I remarked at the outset of this book, speaks of metaphor as if its challenge were quite profound; and while the difficulties posed by metaphor for contemporary philosophical thought may, indeed, be as profoundly baffling as she would have us think, its profundity comes as much from what it exposes about the recalcitrance of philosophy as from the capacity of metaphor to move us onto another fantastic plane of mental activity.

As I have tried to show, the use of metaphor as an avenue of selective dissociation is not always as exotic an activity as our experiential canons make it out to be; metaphor ("bodily warfare" in immunology) is—despite what warnings to the contrary we find culturally meaningful—at our very door, always ready to provide us with a way of apprehending what is "other" and unknown. The proof is, as we shall see in a moment, to be found not only in the way that metaphor intervenes through selective dissociation whenever self-conscious reflection is not at its most active, but also in the degree to which this perspective enables us to set aside the embarrassments of applying a psychoanalytic view of regressive behavior to much of what other cultures profess to be symbolically meaningful.

II. IMMUNOLOGY AND COGNITION

Part of my argument in this book has been that anthropology is the premier discipline for refiguring theories of the person because of its focus on "other" cognitive states. Compared to philosophy or depth psychology, it is far better positioned to be critical of the canonical mannerisms that invade those disciplines traditionally charged with the explication of the intellectual bases for cognition. Psychology (like some forms of psychological anthropology) distances us from bizarre forms of thought by exoticizing them or making their thought processes "taboo." And philosophy (which, in a cross-cultural sense, is anything but empirical) necessarily inveighs against those modes of thinking that purport to transcend normal experience "and to be incommunicable by any kind of analogy with it" (Berlin 1968, 34). Anthropology, at least, has at its foundation an invitation to attempt to experience difference. We can, of course, give up "reflexively" in advance; but far more demanding intellectually is the act of opening the door before us—entering the quite real temple space, which is a redaction of symbolic activity as much as it is an ethnographic reality. Nothing except psychological condemnation prohibits us from, for example, entertaining the idea that the world revolves around an *axis mundi* that provides a set of values capable of affecting "symbolic" actions in the "real" world. The idea is before us as clear as can be: anthropology offers a different way of looking at microcosmic/macrocosmic relations that need not be at all exotic or so tied to an "other" cultural way that we must give up in advance or retreat into the tidy haven of intellectual thought that culture provides for us. Being abroad makes the unexpected more plausible, but the strong at heart can figure out such a system in Manhattan as well as in Bali or pre-Classical Greece or seventeenth-century Rome, with children at play, or in the asylum. Such experiences may be entertained in the context of modern science: indeed, the topic of modes of thought ought, perhaps, to be our central concern if, truly, we desire to refigure the notions of selfhood that are embedded in our theories of what binds us to one another or makes us "immune" to such interrelations.

Whether we are dealing with an immunological hyperactivity, as in autoimmune diseases (such as rheumatoid arthritis or systemic lupus erythematosus), or the opposite breakdown and failure of that system (as in AIDS), the problem of how the interactions of microentities are described is largely the same—a problem of distinguishing "self" and "not self." The problem of self-recognition is, and has been since the inception of immunology as a legitimate domain of scientific inquiry, "crucial to the whole understanding of antibody formation" (Nossal 1969, 99). The clinical significance of this observation is clear, if nowhere else, in the frequency with which people with immunological disorders are told by health-care professionals and in the popular literature that the body is waging a war with the self.

The undeniable prevalence of this metaphor begs to be analyzed, and some recent literature has centered on the use of metaphors of conflict in immunology. Most critics have focused on the capacity of metaphor to hide other agendas: Sontag, to name the best-known writer on the topic, argues "that illness is *not* a metaphor, and that the most truthful way of regarding illness—and the healthiest way of being ill—is one most purified of, most resistant to, metaphoric thinking" (1979, 3); Martin's work (1990) on this topic isolates, among other things, how military metaphors used in describing states of ill health perpetuate cultural stereotypes and gender bias; Scheper-Hughes wonders about "the irreconcilability of an anthropological knowledge that is largely 'esoteric' (concerned with 'otherness'), subjective, symbolic, and relativist with a biomedical knowledge that is largely mundane [and] universalist in its claims, concrete, objective and radically materialist" (1990, 191); and Haraway goes so far as to describe immunology as "a map drawn to guide recognition and misrecognition of self and other in the dialectics of western biopolitics" (1989, 4).

Though each of these arguments is supported by the weight of both moral indignation and ethnographic fact, the present study focuses less on what metaphor disguises than on the question of why such metaphors have the affective currency that, clearly, they do. In an era of astonishing scientific change, even more astonishing is this fact of experience: that the truly animated and ideologically primitive pathogenic metaphor of cell "warfare" should survive these changes and that cells should continue to be described as if they had volition and intentions. As Allan Brandt has recently argued in response to Sontag, knowing the actual biological causes of a particular disease does little to demystify it: knowing the cause of AIDS, for example, leaves it no less richly metaphorized (1988, 417). Indeed, "disease cannot be freed of metaphor" (ibid., 416), and the connection is abiding not only when the threat of disease is used to incite conformity, justify religious dogma, or facilitate particular political agendas. "Rather than decrying the metaphorization of disease, it seems more appropriate to analyze the process by which disease is given meaning" (ibid., 418). My task, then, is not to explain away this phenomenon, but to accept the reality of its sociological prevalence. Though one cannot help but subscribe to that same moral concern expressed by those who have considered the question of the relationship between metaphor and immunology, we have yet to address the problem on a simple cognitive level: why, we must again ask, do we use metaphor at all in describing certain illnesses? And why, strangely, do we use the most highly metaphorical language when speaking of those illnesses about which we are most troubled—factually, intellectually, conceptually? Is it not entirely counterintuitive to tell someone deeply oppressed by the pain of cancer or AIDS that they are not what they thought they were, that some alien thing has taken them over, that they are losing, and may already have entirely lost, the capacity to affect their own identity?

Not strange at all, perhaps, if what we are witnessing is the categorical separation of some harmful agent from the self. But consider the actual anomaly of telling someone who is already suffering that their body is at war with their "self"; this is not exactly what one would call positive reinforcement. Insofar as experience is usually the best judge, those of us who have suffered from immune disorders or severe allergies have at least a basic "ethnographic" awareness of the degree to which such experiences can produce a sense of profound disorientation.

If telling someone who is ill that his or her body is at war with itself seems counterintuitive, then why do we do it? The answer is that it is sometimes a very helpful thing to do; and there is much to be gained by accepting this fact and building upon it. People often do feel better when they can salvage a "self" from a ravaged body; we learn to deal with illness by setting it up as something against which we can define (even through dissociation) a better condition of selfhood. But what is important is less the fear of "indoctrination" that we often perceive as synonymous with any activity not governed by self-conscious reflection; more significant is the simple acceptance that this splitting-off of the self from its experience is so frequently how personal meaning is established and an experiential strategy set in place. It is through the dissociated manipulation of culturally relevant metaphor—rather than, solely, through self-conscious introspection—that one positions oneself to engage in the cognitive battle or game that misfortune necessitates. Canguilhem describes this juxtaposition of the pathological as an essential dynamic in identifying what is normal ([1966] 1989, 239–40):

The normal is not a static or peaceful, but a dynamic and polemical concept. Gaston Bachelard . . . has rightly perceived that every value must be earned against an anti-value. It is he who writes: "The will to cleanse requires an adversary its size." When we know that *norma* is the Latin word for T-square and that *normalis* means perpendicular, we know almost all that must be known about the area in which the meaning of the terms "norm" and "normal" originated, which have been taken into a great variety of other areas. A norm, or rule, is what can be used to right, to square, to straighten. To set a norm (*normer*), to normalize, is to impose a requirement on an existence, a given whose variety, disparity, with regard to the requirement, present themselves as a hostile, even more than an unknown, indeterminant. It is, in effect, a polemical concept which negatively qualifies the sector of the given which does not enter into its extension while it depends on its comprehension. The concept of right, depending on whether it is a matter of geometry, morality or technology, qualifies what offers resistance to its application of twisted, crooked or awkward.

The reason for the polemical final purpose and usage of the concept of norm must be sought, as far as we are concerned, in the essence of the normal-abnormal relationship. It is not a question of a relationship of contradiction and externality but one of inversion and polarity. The norm, by devaluing everything that the reference to it prohibits from being considered normal, creates on its own the possibility of an inversion of terms. A norm offers itself as a possible mode of unifying diversity, resolving a difference, settling a disagreement. But to offer oneself is not to impose oneself. Unlike a law of nature, a norm does not necessitate its effect.

What is important in Canguilhem's elusive polemic is that the presence of a norm necessitates its opposite—not its actual antithesis, but a devalued "other." Pathology, like any other *logos* or form of cognition, is a mechanism for creating a mirror image, for knowing through constructing a devalued opposite that can, hopefully, be manipulated. Controlling of "otherness" is, therefore, facilitated by codifying the alien through metaphor and by dynamically engaging those metaphors through myth. Indeed, if a myth is to be at all powerful, capable of providing a satisfactory basis for responding to new and unknown events, it must successfully engage its powerful "other" by this dynamic process. It is this engagement of powerful, even overpowering, cultural metaphor that accounts for the sense of deficiency that is commonly elicited by the contemplation of the normal, versus the florid richness that describing the pathological can give rise to. In the latter case, the pathological is engaged through metaphor and controlled through thematically enrolling it in a culturally meaningful scenario—in immunology, that is, through mystifying or otherwise elevating the mischievous power of the pathogen, and then conquering it by any heroic metaphorical device that may devalue it.

Devaluation most frequently takes place through caricature, which is not, at least primarily, a manipulation of the grotesque. Rather, it is the end result of a dynamic process, a method, first, for empowering the "other" by giving it an identity, and, second, for embodying it through the assimilation of its devalued form. The dynamics of this process account for the obvious structural similarity that exists between myth and scientific theory, on the one hand, and the less obvious and widely overlooked similarity between the process of promulgating a particular scientific theory and the mechanics of hero epic on the other. As with anthropologists denouncing their Victorian ancestry, in both cases the implanting of a new order is accompanied by a recognition and a caricaturing of one's intellectual forebears. This is why "men of science," as the old gender-biased diction goes, deal with their theoretical ancestors in the same way as cultural myths deal with otherness; in both cases a sketch in shorthand, a caricature, or a "black box," becomes the static captured image—the portrait, the war trophy, the corpse, the hunted head—of an immobilized other.

One answer, then, to the question of why metaphorical language appears to prevail in conditions of the greatest conceptual uncertainty is that the cultural categories embedded in myth provide—as they do for science and hero epic—a way of dynamically engaging uncertainty. This dynamic process enables us to name the "other" (and, therefore, to separate it from self), to tame or devalue it through caricature (to let particular signs stand for the whole), and to assimilate and embody its static form (as portrait, trophy, black box, etc.). As we shall see, this process need not be intentional or calculated; indeed, it is in the nature of myth to provide open avenues by which such processes may be engaged unconsciously or even covertly. The cultural categories embedded in myth provide us with culture-specific ways to employ metaphor in separating self from other.

III. SELECTIVE DISSOCIATION:
A NONSOLIPSISTIC THEORY
OF PERSONHOOD

Because norms are articulated through either overt or covert cultural categories, a major part of refiguring immunology will demand a re-visioning of the cognitive sciences in general and psychopathology in particular. From the standpoint of efficacy, there need be no formal distinction made within a culture between a conscious creative engagement of the ambiguities of "otherness" and an unconscious or "primary" process in which apparently we do not control that engagement. Indeed, the entire anthropological literature on rites of passage demonstrates that lasting personal change is more frequently made possible through processes that remove attention from individuals and focus on placing them within culturally valued performative paradigms. Since difference—as anthropology regularly demonstrates—is itself a cultural construct, "otherness" may be therapeutically engaged by cultural systems that call attention to the uniqueness of individual experience as well as by those that openly devalue the unique as aberrant (even if covertly encouraging the realization of the self through an obsessive attention to myth or another culturally recognized form of cognitive engagement). Dominant myths may indeed become a primary way of engaging in selective, perhaps even routinized, forms of dissociation; far from being that suppressed, less than desirable, form of psychosocial development that must be overcome through self-conscious activity, myth (with metaphor as its vehicle) steps forward at every juncture to enable individuals to deal with the constant change that marks nearly every moment in one's life. And it is anthropology, not psychoanalysis, that shows the way to discussing the positive channels, the culture-specific avenues, by which "self" may be disengaged ("lost") to good effect.

Even to broach this topic is, of course, to violate a major taboo of psychoanalysis, but again and again we evidence—through myth, through rites of passage, through trance and the significance placed on altered states of consciousness—the fact that it is not just what can be brought to consciousness that has value; or, to put it another way, the deliberate suppression of certain nagging concerns by an individual can bring on a sense of liberation that is positively invigorating. This deliberate suppression may occur in any culture, but it is more likely to take shape where the "heroic" behavior characteristic of self-conscious activity is devalued. Status distinctions in Bali, for instance, provide a conscious mechanism for avoiding the troubling consequences of fame; I have been told more than once about the removal of supposedly powerful objects because of an individual's wish not to become the servant of a spiritual force that could, as well, provide real personal gain. Every culture has its Faustian dilemmas, though each, also, has its own system of values by which the demonstration of individual power is admired, scorned, or limited.

But how, we must ask, can an argument that, after all, concerns itself with the social dimension of myth be perceived as an affront to the kind of personhood given over to us through psychoanalysis and depth psychology in general? It is an affront because it forces us to ask whether culture as such has canonically limited the purview of what we are willing to see as meaningful and valuable. Thus, instead of condemning all unself-conscious individual change as the by-product of the brainwashing of the weak, we force ourselves to look more directly at the ethnographic reality of psychological experience and realize that, while as a culture we value self-conscious reflection, this activity is far from the only way that individuals experience meaningful personal change. Interestingly, the best evidence for this argument comes not from the application of psychoanalytic theory to other cultures, but from new research on the brain, on the one hand, and from non-Western psychotherapy on the other.

Among the more interesting results of recent scientific research on the brain has been the realization that memories seem to be not "a permanent record of past events" (Rosenfield 1988, 161), but, as anthropologists struggling with alien modes of thought have known for some time, a categorizing process; understanding the way that particular circumstances and the objects that are part of those events are related means sorting information by testing new data against existing categories (ibid., 193): "Recognition of an object requires its categorization. And categories are created by *coupling*, or correlating different samplings of . . . stimuli. This is best achieved through mappings that create a variety of possible groupings of the stimuli, and relating different mappings to each other." Memories are not, in this view, fixed events but fluid paths of neural activity superimposed upon one another—not static moments that need to be psychically excavated, but processes of recategorization in which neural paths ("images") are formally recombined. In fact, recent work with highly creative individuals has demonstrated the extent to which the unlikely superimposition of images functions in the making of significant discoveries; scientists, it seems, quite regularly articulate new identities by employing what Rothenberg has labeled a "homospatial process," in which one actively conceives "two or more discrete entities occupying the same space" (1988, 444). Indeed, the role of metaphor in creative superimposition suggests that we must not immediately conclude that controlling something necessarily means bringing it to consciousness, that we take seriously the essential role of metaphor for Rothenberg's subject (a Nobel laureate microbiologist), who "visualized himself superimposed upon an atom in an enzyme molecule in constructing a scientific theory" (ibid.).

Metaphors and the cultural values that bring them to life provide, in other words, not only avenues for unself-conscious dissociation, but avenues through which one can dissociate selectively and creatively. Deindividuation is not, therefore, only to be connected with a loss of self that is unhealthy, for the active and selective control of such activity enables one to articulate ideas that are entirely new. Likewise, memory is a "recombinant" process; for in order to combine, we must (to continue the genetic metaphor) be engaged in the dynamic generation of new creative images (i.e., neural patterns) that are experimentally categorized. What is more, the fact that memories are dynamic "events" rather than static "things" is easily proved. An individual will, for example, often return to a particular place when trying to "remember" some "thing"—that is, piece together an experience—because in returning to a place, one is more able to reengage the neurally generated sequence of images onto which an idea is attached by duplicating the dynamic situation that initially gave rise to it.

Now what, one might ask, does anthropology have to do with neurology and its effects on psychoanalytic theory? The answer is quite simply that, despite what neurology tells us about memory, we are still left with establishing value through categories that are culturally governed, even if the process of categorization may be studied in the laboratory. What is discovered in creative thought, in other words, is meaningless unless it has a sociocultural referent; and whatever theories may be applied in attempting to evaluate the neurological evidence, they remain themselves subject to the demands of culture. The entire discipline of psychoneuroimmunology, thus, will certainly founder without a heavy dose of cultural anthropology, for no greater reason than the fact that stress is only crudely quantifiable, if it can be quantified at all, since the values that mark categorical boundaries as "stressful" vary among cultures, among individual members of a given society, and among individuals experiencing the same event.

The relationship between neurology and psychotherapy similarly depends upon values that are culture-specific. While Rothenberg is very careful in his studies of creativity not to confuse the *superimposed* images employed by his brilliantly creative subjects with the more *conflated* images employed by children, "primitives," and the mentally impaired, what anthropology tells us is something quite different— namely, that conscious superimposition and regressive conflation differ only in the way that a particular culture values or devalues certain sorts of object relations. Here, we are dealing with phenomenology, in the strictest sense in which it was originally construed by Husserl—that is, as a kind of radical empiricism. Indeed, as I have tried to argue, the major difference between the two ontologies outlined—between images that are superimposed and those that are conflated—is that the former is, necessarily, more controlled by conscious activity, while the latter is motivated more by cultural categories, by "myth," and, most significantly, by those metaphors that step in, in the absence of self-consciousness, as mediators between persons and things. How these processes are valued varies significantly across cultures, but the processes themselves appear to have a universal purview.

The degree, therefore, to which any group of individuals values the separation of objects in the construction of specific "memories" is a matter of cultural persuasion. Whether, that is, we envision two separate things superimposed upon one another, or merge two superimposed things into an objective conflation, is largely a function of whether or not our culture tells us that the latter is a regressive form of animism that devolves from some lower form of cognitive life, or, more simply, from not having matured properly as a human being. It is the conflation of images or their separation that is a cultural peculiarity; what is universal is the process of bringing these images ("neural paths") together in some dynamic formal relation, the dynamic *event* that constitutes the creation of a memory through the testing of something unknown against what is already known—that is, through categorization. And it is here, precisely, that cross-cultural clinical psychiatry comes into play.

Except in a few rare circumstances where a kind of methodological pluralism has been applied to the cross-cultural study of psychic states (Bateson's *Naven*, for example), the field of cross-cultural psychiatry has become, rather, a battlefield of two major camps with lots of negotiators variously positioned in their midst. On the one hand are those who would have other cultures seen as so sociocentric that they compulsively deindividualize to the degree that they offer a theory of the person completely incommensurable with the sort of ego that dominates post-Enlightenment thinking. On the other are those who would have us think that individuals are valued the same in every cultural context, the "self" being a universal construct. This latter camp is, of course, enormous, and carries with it the full weight of morality, since its concern for the rights of individuals is an overriding one. In the vanguard today, however, is neither camp, since the battlefield itself is being shaken by those non-Western clinicians and theoreticians who find themselves caught between the rock of psychoanalysis and the hard place of cultural fact; for it is here that the realities of constructive, cosmopolitan therapy actually reside. In the words of Eguchi (1991) 444–45:

> Within the field of psychiatry, the "universalistic" approach attempts to classify and systematize all illnesses around a nucleus of universal syndromes. On the other hand, the "particularistic" approach tries to minutely classify psychiatric maladies as illnesses particular to certain regions. If there is such a thing as clinical "reality," it lies balanced somewhere on the thin line between these two conflicting methods. If it leans too much to either side, I believe that it loses its power to assist in treatment within a complicated context. . . . In order to achieve the necessary balance between the two approaches, we must rethink the

function of diagnosis. We must abandon the attempt to force a multi-faceted reality into the fractionalized sort of framework provided by instruments such as the DSM-III or the ICD-10. Instead, we must see diagnosis as a tool enabling us to recognize that the multi-natured reality we call illness is an "event," not a "thing." This we can do by holding up various concise criteria (codes) and observing the ways in which the phenomenon (the illness we are dealing with) deviates from each of them. It is only through use of the latter approach that we can see the phenomenon in its three-dimensional fullness, resting on a grid composed of the points where the various criteria (codes) intersect. This contrasts with the purely two-dimensional view we get when we try to fit the whole thing into a single model, to narrow it down to a single "reality."

The act of diagnosis should not be an attempt to fit a particular phenomenon into one set of criteria or another. Rather, its function is to force the person making the diagnosis to recognize where and how the actual phenomenon *deviates* from the criteria. Paradoxically, a diagnosis is only useful when it fails to encompass a phenomenon, when the discrepancy between the diagnosis and the actual occurrence leads to a more multi-faceted understanding.

As a matter of fact, when we observe the exchanges between a patient and psychiatrist, we find that diagnosis is *not* used to try to arrive at a single correct understanding (although it may be that the psychiatrist is not aware of this fact). To put it another way, the patient's symptoms may be seen as a form of popular "art de faire" (de Certeau 1984) in response to certain social and cultural codes (including the diagnosis). In turn, the psychiatrist brings into play an even more convoluted "art de faire," and it is only when that is effective that we can say that psychiatric treatment has borne fruit.

Even when Western diagnostic standards dominate the treatment setting (as is almost always the case in anything termed "psychiatric treatment"), what actually happens is that the healer makes use of popular, indigenous, so-called "particularistic" methods. However, because the process is too delicate to be described and recorded, as Eisenberg (1981: 245) has pointed out, psychiatric treatment is always left with an element of what seems to be coincidental, non-linguistic, or even magical.

I have quoted this passage at length, not because it summarizes points already made by other writers (e.g., Eisenberg 1977, 1981; Kleinman 1977, 1980; de Certeau 1984), but because its focus on illness as a negotiated *event* in a non-Western context (in this case, fox possession in rural Japan) illustrates, first, how the reality of "becoming better" is a reality that derives from the conflation of the universal and the particularistic. Like what neurology suggests to us about the creative process in general, and what we now know about memories, in particular, "getting better" is itself a creative, even artistic, process, in which new categories are created by superimposing the peculiar onto the more static, universalist model. Like memories, illnesses too are not "things" but dynamic events out of which new "things" (categories, labels, codes, canons) are created. Second, the passage is significant because what is richly pathological occurs on what would be for psychoanalysis the exotic testing ground of rural Japanese fox possession. Here we have, in other words, an excellent example of the need to rethink so-called primary processes cross-culturally, and it is no accident that it is precisely in the anthropological domain of "animistic" activity, in which subject and object are conflated, that *selective dissociation* steps forward as the primary challenge to psychoanalytic theory and self-conscious "value" theory in general. Here, the argument against the exclusivity of self-referential introspection as the locus of "meaning" and "value" is quite simple; for, setting aside the abysmal record of psychoanalysis actually to cure through intense self-conscious thought (that is, the logical contradiction of deliberately attempting a release from self-consciousness), it is equally possible that such phenomena as depression, conversion hysteria, and what is commonly called hypochondriasis may be adaptive, creative mechanisms that "help rechannel anxiety released by the uncertain, potentially disabling, life-threatening aspects of [certain] diseases" (Liang et al. 1984, 18). If what we know of metaphor as a creative vehicle is any sign (e.g., Kittay 1987, 117–25), not "knowing" oneself may, as anthropologists have repeatedly demonstrated, be as much a part of a willingness to recreate, a desire to generate new forms of meaning, or a need to find something "artistic" in suffering, as it is a sign of a dysfunctioning person; and the cross-cultural evidence, in particular, points to the many ways in which *culture* can provide avenues for a creative, constructive *loss* of self.

   This so-called loss of self leads us, as we have seen, directly into the domain of selective dissociation; but it is important at the outset of a summarizing of this idea to realize that to engage the idea of dissociation as a potentially positive part of personhood is not to engage in a complete damnation of the "self" as it is understood in the West. For in the first case, my argument may be viewed as a direct extension of a certain kind of self-awareness; as Eguchi points out in the above-quoted passage, the prevalence of psychoanalytic categories in *any* discussion means that one cannot develop a new understanding without using them, even if only in caricature. Morcover, psychoanalysis has, for better or worse, accumulated enough allies, to use Latour's paradigm, that it cannot but be the dominant explanatory model in all cosmopolitan discussions of "personhood." One need not, that is, be an apologist to recognize the cultural significance of the categories culture provides, and one should no more argue for the legitimacy of alien ways of doing things than one should abandon one's own culturally established proclivities as corrupt, morally bankrupt, and hopelessly unsalvageable. Moreover (and even more certainly), one cannot embody an unself-conscious state, and one can no more decide to lose oneself in anonymity than one can escape one's past by self-consciously dwelling on it. Though we may assume that lasting and meaningful adjustment of one's psychological condition can come only through introspection, it is equally clear that one cannot put such introspection behind oneself once finished with it. Like the person dying of cancer who is informed that part of himself is devouring "him" (whoever "he" may be in such a context), the individual under analysis will not recover from every wound by reopening it. One cannot, therefore, return from self-consciousness to some kind of naive, participatory bliss, any more than one can reverse a rite of passage in which a permanent change of social estate—a lasting transformation—has taken place.

The third reason for recognizing a value in those particularistic elements that loom large in many non-Western psychoanalytic contexts is, in addition to the above arguments, that in openly engaging them we are able to formulate a better understanding of how selective dissociation influences personal development whenever self-conscious reflection subsides as the dominant locus of "meaning." Like the regular unself-conscious use of "animistic" categories among immunologists, what the prevalence of conflating metaphors in conditions of uncertainty tells us is something quite at odds with the objectives of depth psychology, if not something quite opposite, about the real nature of individual change: this is, namely, that we "overcome" uncertainty—we "become"—through selective dissociation, through a deliberate letting-go in which the force of culturally generated symbolic thought takes hold of that part of us that we have released *and engages it in a complex and highly dynamic world of symbolic activity*. Since illness can be defined only as an absence of a condition of well-being, the goal of such dissociative states is not the self-conscious reflection of one's disability—it is not, in other words, always to be found in the "support group," in which aberration itself has a certain normality—but the goal is to find the strength to place one's illnesses in the context of that condition of well-being, whatever it may be in a particular social context. As one lupus sufferer put it: "I tried the support groups but found them very unrewarding; I'd prefer to spend my time feeling a part of my friends who are healthy." As with an aged Balinese woman who denies illness its legitimacy by transporting her drinking water despite her arthritis, or as with the Biblical Job, or the Christian saint, who bears up under suffering that is anything but justified, not legitimizing an illness by not *realizing* it in the social world becomes more than an act of suppression. Being with healthy people, in other words, can *in the right circumstances* (and, perhaps, *only* there) provide one with a mirror of what one desires, to the degree that "illness" is not simply being displaced, delegitimized, or alienated. In this regard, lupus finds its social "cure" in the same domain of collective activity as does the demonic possession of a Balinese trance, in which the many hands of fellows directing, as it were, activities at the borders of culture become the most powerful mechanism for coming to terms with those strangers within each of us.

•   •   •

In this Epilogue, I have tried to summarize the general arguments made in this book by indicating the degree to which I believe the development of personhood to be a "sociosomatic" phenomenon. Though what I have called "selective dissociation" may be most readily studied in non-Western or exotic Western contexts (i.e., in the fine arts or in creative thinking generally), it is only the prohibitions of a cultural canon that keep us from becoming better acquainted with the effects of dissociative mental activity in our daily lives. Indeed, though our most "exotic" local examples come from the literature on multiple personalities, each of us has had the experience of traveling from one point to the next without an accurate recollection of the journey. To have such an experience is both an actual example of a dissociative activity as well as a metaphor for thinking about what dissociation itself might mean. We need not, that is, be capable of playing a musical theme while discussing metaphysics, or even playing in one key while singing in another, to understand how dissociation is something readily accessible, and something, furthermore, that can be developed to good effect. The point, though, that must be emphasized is that there are observable dissociative processes that function as significantly as does self-conscious reflection in the development of the person. These processes are not the negation of self-consciousness, but the deliberate re-creation of the self through the engaging of metaphors that enable us selectively and creatively to imagine.

Bibliography

Aleandro, Girolamo. 1616. *Antiquae Tabulae Marmoreae Solis Effigie, Symbolisque Exculptae Accurata Explicatio*. Rome.

Alexiou, Margaret. 1974. *The Ritual Lament in Greek Tradition*. Cambridge.

Altheim, Franz. 1929. "Persona." *Archiv für Religionswissenschaft* 27: 35–52.

Andrewes, A. 1982. "The Tyranny of Peisistratus." In *The Cambridge Ancient History*, 2d ed., vol. 3, pt. 3, ed. John Boardman and N. G. L. Hammond, 392–416. Cambridge.

Appadurai, Arjun, ed. 1986. *The Social Life of Things: Commodities in Cultural Perspective*. Cambridge.

"Atilt over *Tilting Arc*." 1981. *Art News* 80(10): 12, 14, 19.

Auping, Michael. 1983. "Earth Art: A Study in Ecological Politics." In *Art in the Land: A Critical Anthology of Environmental Art*, ed. Alan Sonfist, 92–104. New York.

Avalon, Arthur [Sir John Woodroffe]. 1959. *Śakti and Śākta: Essays and Addresses*. 5th ed. Madras.

Bailey, B. L. 1940. "The Export of Attic Black-Figure Ware." *Journal of Hellenic Studies*. 60: 60–70.

Baker, Elizabeth C. 1983. "Artworks on the Land." In *Art in the Land: A Critical Anthology of Environmental Art*, ed. Alan Sonfist, 73–84. New York.

Baldinucci, Filippo. [1682] 1966. *The Life of Bernini*. Trans. Catherine Enggass. University Park, Pa.

Banks, Sir Joseph. 1896. *Journal of the Right Hon. Sir Joseph Banks during Captain Cook's First Voyage*. Ed. Sir Joseph D. Hooker. London.

Barb, A. A. 1953. "Diva Matrix: A Faked Gnostic Intaglio in the Possession of P. P. Rubens and the Iconology of a Symbol." *Journal of the Warburg and Courtauld Institutes* 16: 193–238.

Barnett, R. D. 1956. "Ancient Oriental Influences on Archaic Greece." In *The Aegean and the Near East: Studies Presented to Hetty Goldman*, ed. Saul S. Weinberg, 212–38. New York.

———. 1960. "Some Contacts between Greek and Oriental Religions." In *Éléments orientaux dans la religion grecque ancienne, Colloque de Strasbourg, 22–24 mai 1958*, 143–53. Paris.

Barthes, Roland. 1957. *Mythologies*. Paris.

Bateson, Gregory. 1958. *Naven*. 2d ed. Stanford, Calif.

———. 1972. *Steps to an Ecology of Mind*. San Francisco.

Battcock, Gregory. 1969. "Marcuse and Anti-Art." *Arts Magazine* 43(8): 17–19.

———, ed. 1973. *Idea Art: A Critical Anthology.* New York.

Becker, Howard S. 1982. *Art Worlds.* Berkeley and Los Angeles.

Beidelman, T. O. 1986. *Moral Imagination in Kaguru Modes of Thought.* Bloomington, Ind.

Benthall, Jonathan. 1969. "Technology and Art, 9: The Relevance of Ecology—Part II." *Studio International* 178 (917): 207–8.

———. 1971. "Newton Harrison: Big Fish in a Small Pool." *Studio International* 182(939): 230.

———, ed. 1972a. *Ecology in Theory and Practice.* New York.

———. 1972b. *Science and Technology in Art Today.* New York.

———, ed. 1974. *The Limits of Human Nature: Essays Based on a Course of Lectures Given at the Institute of Contemporary Arts, London.* New York.

Berlin, Isaiah. 1968. "Verification." In *The Theory of Meaning,* ed. G. H. R. Parkinson, 15–34. London.

Bernheimer, Richard. 1956. "Theatrum Mundi." *Art Bulletin* 38: 225–47.

Besig, H. 1937. "Gorgo und Gorgoneion in der archaischen griechischen Kunst." Dissertation, Friedrich-Wilhelms-Universität zu Berlin.

Bianchi, Ugo, ed. 1970. *The Origins of Gnosticism: Colloquium of Messina 13–18 April 1966.* Studies in the History of Religions: Supplements to *Numen,* vol. 12. Leiden.

Boardman, John. 1972. "Herakles, Peisistratos and Sons." *Revue Archéologique* 1: 57–72.

———. 1976. "A Curious Eye Cup." *Archäologischer Anzeiger* 3: 281–90.

Bodenstedt, Sr. Mary Immaculate. 1944. *The "Vita Christi" of Ludolphus the Carthusian.* The Catholic University of America Studies in Medieval and Renaissance Latin Language and Literature, 16. Washington, D.C.

Boehmer, Heinrich. 1921. *Loyola und die deutsche Mystik.* Berichte über die Verhandlungen der Sächsischen Akademie der Wissenschaften zu Leipzig, Phil.-hist. Klasse, 73.1. Leipzig.

Bois, Yve-Alain. 1985. "La pensée sauvage." *Art in America* 73(4): 178–89.

Bonner, Campbell. 1950. *Studies in Magical Amulets, Chiefly Graeco-Egyptian.* Ann Arbor, Mich.

Borsi, Franco. 1980. *Bernini.* Trans. Robert E. Wolf. New York.

Brandt, Allan M. 1987. *No Magic Bullet: A Social History of Venereal Disease in the United States since 1880.* Expanded ed. New York.

———. 1988. "AIDS and Metaphor: Toward the Social Meaning of Epidemic Disease." *Social Research* 55: 413–32.

Bron, C., and F. Lissarrague. 1984. "Le vase à voir." In *La cité des images: Religion et société en Grèce antique,* 7–18. Lausanne.

Burkert, Walter. 1970. "Jason, Hypsipyle, and New Fire at Lemnos: A Study in Myth and Ritual." *Classical Quarterly,* n.s., 20: 1–16.

———. [1962] 1972. *Lore and Science in Ancient Pythagoreanism.* Trans. Edwin L. Minar. Cambridge, Mass.

———. 1979. *Structure and History in Greek Mythology and Ritual.* Berkeley and Los Angeles.

———. [1972] 1983. *Homo Necans: The Anthropology of Ancient Greek Sacrificial Ritual and Myth.* Trans. Peter Bing. Berkeley and Los Angeles.

———. [1977] 1985. *Greek Religion.* Trans. John Raffan. Cambridge, Mass.

Burnham, Jack. 1971. "Hans Haacke's Cancelled Show at the Guggenheim." *Artforum* 9(10): 67–71.

Cacciari, Massimo. 1987. "Animarum Venator (Hunter of Souls)." *Artforum* 25(6): 70–77.

Canetti, Elias. 1978. *Crowds and Power.* Trans. Carol Stewart. New York.

Canguilhem, Georges. [1966] 1989. *The Normal and the Pathological.* Trans. Carolyn R. Fawcett and Robert S. Cohen. New York.

Cannon, Walter B. 1932. *The Wisdom of the Body.* New York.

———. 1942. "'Voodoo' Death." *American Anthropologist* 44: 169–81.

Capasso, Nicholas J. 1985. "Environmental Art: Strategies for Reorientation in Nature." *Arts Magazine* 59(5): 73–77.

Carrithers, M., et al., eds. 1985. *The Category of the Person.* Cambridge.

Carroll, Lewis [Charles L. Dodgson]. 1939. *The Complete Works of Lewis Carroll.* London.

Cartari, Vincenzo. 1626. *Le imagini de gli dei delli antichi.* 2nd ed. Ed. Lorenzo Pignoria. Padua.

Casson, Lionel. 1959. *The Ancient Mariners: Seafarers and Sea Fighters of the Mediterranean in Ancient Times.* New York.

———. 1971. *Ships and Seamanship in the Ancient World.* Princeton.

———. 1984. *Ancient Trade and Society.* Detroit.

de Certeau, Michel. 1984. *The Practice of Everyday Life.* Trans. Steven Rendall. Berkeley and Los Angeles.

de Chantelou, Paul Fréart. [1930] 1972. *Journal du voyage en France du cavalier Bernin.* New York.

———. [1877–84] 1985. *Diary of the Cavaliere Bernini's Visit to France.* Ed. Anthony Blunt. Annot. George C. Bauer. Trans. Margery Corbett. Princeton.

Clark, Kenneth. 1939. "Introduction," in Roger Fry, *Last Lectures,* ix–xxix. New York.

Clark, Stephen R. L. 1975. *Aristotle's Man: Speculations upon Aristotelian Anthropology.* Oxford.

Clay, Diskin. 1982. "Unspeakable Words in Greek Tragedy." *American Journal of Philology* 103: 277–98.

Clifford, James. 1981. "On Ethnographic Surrealism." *Comparative Studies in Society and History* 23: 539–64.

———. 1985. "Histories of the Tribal and the Modern." *Art in America* 73(4): 164–77, 215.

———. 1988. *The Predicament of Culture: Twentieth-Century Ethnography, Literature, and Art.* Cambridge, Mass.

Cohen, Irun R. 1988. "The Self, the World and Autoimmunity." *Scientific American* 258(4): 52–60.

Cole, Herbert M., and Chike C. Aniakor. 1984. *Igbo Arts: Community and Cosmos.* Los Angeles.

Collingwood, R. G. 1958. *The Principles of Art.* New York.

———. 1964. *Essays in the Philosophy of Art.* Bloomington, Ind.

Collins, James. 1973. "Things and Theories." *Artforum* 11(9): 32–36.

Commager, Henry Steele. 1975. *Jefferson, Nationalism, and the Enlightenment.* New York.

Conason, Joe. 1986. "Homeless on the Range: Greed, Religion, and the Hopi-Navaho Land Dispute." *Village Voice,* July 29: 19–26, 73.

Conway, Charles Abbott, Jr. 1976. *The "Vita Christi" of Ludolph of Saxony and Late Medieval Devotion Centered on the Incarnation: A Descriptive Analysis.* Salzburg.

Corin, Ellen E. 1990. "Facts and Meaning in Psychiatry: An Anthropological Approach to the Lifeworld of Schizophrenics." *Culture, Medicine and Psychiatry* 14: 153–88.

Crane, Diana. 1987. *The Transformation of the Avant-Garde: The New York Art World, 1940–1985.* Chicago.

Croon, J. H. 1955. "The Mask of the Underworld Daemon—Some Remarks on the Perseus-Gorgon Story." *Journal of Hellenic Studies* 75: 9–16.

Danforth, Loring M., and Alexander Tsiaras. 1982. *The Death Rituals of Rural Greece.* Princeton.

Danto, Arthur C. 1964. "The Artistic Enfranchisement of Real Objects: The Art World." *Journal of Philosophy:* 571–84.

———. 1973. "The Last Work of Art: Artworks and Real Things." *Theoria* 39: 1–17.

———. 1981. *The Transfiguration of the Commonplace: A Philosophy of Art.* Cambridge, Mass.

———. 1986. *The Philosophical Disenfranchisement of Art.* New York.

———. 1987. *The State of the Art.* New York.

Davis, Natalie Zemon. 1975. *Society and Culture in Early Modern France.* Stanford, Calif.

Deitch, Jeffrey. 1976. "Daniel Buren: Painting Degree Zero." *Arts Magazine* 51(2): 88–91.

Dempsey, Charles. 1966. "The Classical Perception of Nature in Poussin's Earlier Works." *Journal of the Warburg and Courtauld Institutes* 29: 219–49.

Detienne, Marcel. [1972] 1977. *The Gardens of Adonis: Spices in Greek Mythology.* Trans. Janet Lloyd. Sussex.

D'Onofrio, Cesare. 1967. *Gli obelischi di Roma.* 2d ed. Rome.

Doty, William G. 1981. "Mythophiles' Dyscrasia: A Comprehensive Definition of Myth." *Journal of the American Academy of Religion* 48: 531–62.

———. 1986. *Mythography: The Study of Myths and Rituals.* University, Ala.

Duerr, Hans Peter. [1978] 1985. *Dreamtime: Concerning the Boundary between Wilderness and Civilization.* Trans. Felicitas Goodman. Oxford.

Eco, Umberto. 1976. *A Theory of Semiotics.* Bloomington, Ind.

Eguchi, Shigeyuki. 1991. "Between Folk Concepts of Illness and Psychiatric

Diagnosis: *Kitsune-tsuki* (Fox Possession) in a Mountain Village of Western Japan." *Culture, Medicine and Psychiatry* 15: 421–51.

Eisenberg, Leon. 1977. "Disease and Illness: Distinctions between Professional and Popular Ideas of Sickness." *Culture, Medicine and Psychiatry* 1: 9–23.

———. 1981. "The Physician as Interpreter: Ascribing Meaning to the Illness Experience." *Comprehensive Psychiatry* 22: 239–48.

Emlyn-Jones. C. J. 1980. *The Ionians and Hellenism: A Study of the Cultural Achievement of the Early Greek Inhabitants of Asia Minor.* London.

Entwistle, A. W. 1981–82. *Vaiṣṇava Tilakas: Sectarian Marks Worn by Worshippers of Viṣṇu.* London.

Evans-Pritchard, E. E. 1937. *Witchcraft, Oracles and Magic among the Azande.* Oxford.

Fabian, Johannes. 1983. *Time and the Other: How Anthropology Makes Its Object.* New York.

Fernandez, James W. 1986. *Persuasions and Performances: The Play of Tropes in Culture.* Bloomington, Ind.

Foerster, Werner. 1972–74. *Gnosis: A Selection of Gnostic Texts.* Ed. R. M. Wilson. 2 vols. Oxford.

Foster, Hal, ed. 1983. *The Anti-Aesthetic: Essays on Postmodern Culture.* Port Townsend, Wash.

———. 1985. "The 'Primitive' Unconscious of Modern Art." *October* 34: 45–70.

Foucault, Michel. 1965. *Madness and Civilization: A History of Insanity in the Age of Reason.* Trans. Richard Howard. New York.

Frankfort, H. 1944. "A Note on the Lady of Birth." *Journal of Near Eastern Studies* 3: 198–200.

Frascari, Marco. 1985. "A 'Measure' in Architecture: A Medical-Architectural Theory by Simone Stratico, *Architetto veneto.*" *Res* 9: 80–90.

Freud, Sigmund. [(1922) 1940] 1955. "Medusa's Head." In *The Standard Edition of the Complete Psychological Works of Sigmund Freud,* ed. and trans. James Strachey et al., 18.273–74. London.

———. [1914] 1957. "On Narcissism: An Introduction." In *The Standard Edition of the Complete Psychological Works of Sigmund Freud,* ed. and trans. James Strachey et al., 14.67–107. London.

Fried, Michael. 1967. "Art and Objecthood." *Artforum* 5(10): 12–23.

Frontisi-Ducroux, F. 1984. "Au miroir du masque." In *La cité des images: Religion et société en Grèce antique,* 147–60. Lausanne.

Gallo, Robert C. 1987. "The AIDS Virus." *Scientific American* 256(1): 46–56.

Gardner, Paul. 1985. "The Electronic Palette." *Art News* 85(2): 66–73.

Geertz, Clifford. 1964. "'Internal Conversion' in Contemporary Bali." In *Malayan and Indonesian Studies Presented to Sir Richard Winstedt,* ed. J. Bastin and R. Roolvink, 282–302. Oxford. [Reprinted in William A. Lessa and Evon Z. Vogt, eds., *Reader in Comparative Religion: An Anthropological Approach,* 4th ed. (New York, 1979), 444–54]

———. 1973. *The Interpretation of Cultures: Selected Essays*. New York.

———. 1983. *Local Knowledge: Further Essays in Interpretive Anthropology*. New York.

Gell, A. 1985. "How to Read a Map: Remarks on the Practical Logic of Navigation." *Man*, n.s., 20: 271–87.

Genette, Gérard. 1966. *Figures: Essais*. Paris.

van Gennep, Arnold. [1908] 1960. *The Rites of Passage*. Trans. Monika B. Vizedom and Gabrielle L. Caffee. Paris.

Georgiev, Vladimir I. 1973. "The Arrival of the Greeks in Greece: The Linguistic Evidence." In *Bronze Age Migrations in the Aegean: Archaeological and Linguistic Problems in Greek Prehistory*, ed. R. A. Crossland and Ann Birchall, 243–56. London.

———. 1981. *Introduction to the History of the Indo-European Languages*. 3d ed. Trans. Jana Molhova and Bistra Karadjova. Sofia.

Gernet, Louis. [1968] 1981. *The Anthropology of Ancient Greece*. Trans. John Hamilton, S.J., and Blaise Nagy. Baltimore, Md.

Gilman, Sander L. 1988. *Disease and Representation: Images of Illness from Madness to AIDS*. Ithaca, N.Y.

Goffman, Erving. 1961. *Asylums: Essays on the Social Situation of Mental Patients and Other Inmates*. New York.

———. 1963. *Stigma: Notes on the Management of Spoiled Identity*. New York.

Goldberg, Benjamin. 1985. *The Mirror and Man*. Charlottesville, Va.

Gottlieb, Carla. 1976. *Beyond Modern Art*. New York.

Gould, Cecil. 1982. *Bernini in France: An Episode in Seventeenth-Century History*. Princeton.

Grant, R. M. 1966. *Gnosticism and Early Christianity*. 2d ed. New York.

Greenberg, Clement. 1961. *Art and Culture: Critical Essays*. Boston.

Gregory, Christopher. 1982. *Gifts and Commodities*. London.

Griaule, Marcel. [1948] 1965. *Conversations with Ogotemmêli: An Introduction to Dogon Religious Ideas*. London.

Hahn, R., and Arthur Kleinman. 1983. "Belief as Pathogen, Belief as Medicine: 'Voodoo Death' and the 'Placebo Phenomenon' in Anthropological Perspective." *Medical Anthropology Quarterly* 14(4): 3, 16–19.

Hall, Edith. 1989. *Inventing the Barbarian: Greek Self-Definition through Tragedy*. Oxford.

Hall, James. 1983. *A History of Ideas and Images in Italian Art*. New York.

Hall, Kenneth R. 1985. *Maritime Trade and State Development in Early Southeast Asia*. Honolulu.

Hampe, R. 1936. *Frühe griechische Sagenbilder aus Böotien*. Athens.

Haraway, Donna. 1989. "The Biopolitics of Postmodern Bodies: Determinations of Self in Immune System Discourse." *Differences* 1: 3–43.

Harnack, Adolph. 1958. *History of Dogma*. Trans. Neil Buchanan et al. 7 vols. New York.

Hartog, François. 1980. *Le miroir d'Hérodote: Essai sur la représentation de l'autre*. Paris.

Hastings, James, ed. 1914. *Encyclopaedia of Religion and Ethics*. Vol. 6. New York.

Heckscher, William S. 1947. "Bernini's Elephant and Obelisk." *Art Bulletin* 29: 155–82.

Hesse, Mary. 1984. "The Cognitive Claims of Metaphor." In *Metaphor and Religion*, ed. J. P. Van Noppen, 27–45. Brussels.

Hibbard, Howard. 1965. *Bernini*. Harmondsworth, Middx.

Hocart, A. M. [1948] 1970. "Turning into Stone." In *The Life-Giving Myth and Other Essays*, ed. Rodney Needham, 33–38. London.

Hornell, James. 1920. "The Origins and Ethnological Significance of Indian Boat Designs." *Memoirs of the Asiatic Society of Bengal* 7(3): 139–256.

———. 1938. "Boat Oculi Survivals: Additional Records." *Journal of the Royal Anthropological Institute* 68: 339–48, pls. XVIII–XX.

———. 1943. "The Prow of Ships, Sanctuary of the Tutelary Deity." *Man* 43: 121.

Howe, Thalia Phillies. 1952. "An Interpretation of the Perseus-Gorgon Myth in Greek Literature and Monuments through the Classical Period." Ph.D. dissertation, Columbia University.

———. 1954. "The Origin and Function of the Gorgon Head." *American Journal of Archaeology* 58: 209–21.

Husserl, Edmund. [1900–1901] 1975. *Logische Untersuchungen*. Halle. [Trans. J. N. Findlay, *Logical Investigations* (London, 1970)]

Jackson, D. A. 1976. *East Greek Influence on Attic Vases*. London.

Jaret, Peter. 1986. "Our Immune System: The Wars Within." *National Geographic* 169: 702–36.

Javacheff, Christo. 1973. *Christo: Valley Curtain*. New York.

Jerne, Niels Kaj. 1973. "The Immune System." *Scientific American* 229(1): 52–60.

Johnson, Mark. 1987. *The Body in the Mind: The Bodily Basis of Meaning, Imagination, and Reason*. Chicago.

Jonas, Hans. 1963. *The Gnostic Religion: The Message of the Alien God and the Beginnings of Christianity*. 2d ed., rev. Boston.

Karagiorgas, T. G. 1970. *Γοργείη Κεφάλη*. Athens.

Kenseth, Joy. 1981. "Bernini's Borghese Sculptures: Another View." *Art Bulletin* 63: 191–210.

Kepes, Gyorgy. 1970. *Arts of the Environment*. New York.

Kircher, A., S. J. 1652–54. *Oedipus Aegyptiacus*. 3 vols. Rome.

———. 1665. *Mundus Subterraneus*. Amsterdam.

———. 1666. *Ad Alexandrum VII Pont. Max. Obelisci Aegyptiaci Nuper inter Israel Romani Rudera Effossi Interpretatio Hieroglyphica*. Rome.

———. 1676. *Sphinx Mystagoga*. Amsterdam.

Kitao, Timothy K. 1974. *Circle and Oval in the Square of Saint Peter's: Bernini's Art of Planning*. New York.

Kittay, Eva Feder. 1987. *Metaphor: Its Cognitive Force and Linguistic Structure*. Oxford.

Kleinman, Arthur. 1973. "Medicine's Symbolic Reality: On a Central Problem in the Philosophy of Medicine." *Inquiry* 16: 206–13.

———. 1977. "Depression, Somatization and the 'New Cross-Cultural Psychiatry'." *Social Science and Medicine* 11: 3–10.

———. 1980. *Patients and Healers in the Context of Culture.* Berkeley and Los Angeles.

Kleinman, Arthur, and Byron Good, eds. 1985. *Culture and Depression: Studies in the Anthropology and Cross-Cultural Psychiatry of Affect and Disorder.* Berkeley and Los Angeles.

Kolb, Frank. 1984. "Die Bau-, Religions- und Kulturpolitik der Peisistratiden." In *Die orientalisierende Epoche in der griechischen Religion und Literatur,* ed. Walter Burkert, 99–138. Heidelberg.

Korshak, Yvonne. 1987. *Frontal Faces in Attic Vase Painting of the Archaic Period.* Chicago.

Kosuth, Joseph. 1969a. "Art after Philosophy." *Studio International* 178(915): 134–37.

———. 1969b. "Art after Philosophy, Part 2: 'Conceptual Art' and Recent Art." *Studio International* 178(916): 160–61.

———. 1969c. "Art after Philosophy, Part 3." *Studio International* 178(917): 212–13.

Kraay, C. M. 1976. *Archaic and Classical Greek Coins.* Berkeley and Los Angeles.

Kramer, Hilton. 1984. "The 'Primitivism' Conundrum." *New Criterion* 3(4): 1–7.

Krauss, Rosalind E. 1985a. "Corpus Delicti." *October* 33: 31–72.

———. 1985b. *The Originality of the Avant-Garde and Other Modernist Myths.* Cambridge, Mass.

Krautheimer, Richard. 1985. *The Rome of Alexander VII, 1665–1667.* Princeton.

Kris, Ernst, and Otto Kurz. 1979. *Legend, Myth, and Magic in the Image of the Artist: A Historical Experiment.* New Haven.

Krishna, Nanditha. 1980. *The Art and Iconography of Vishnu-Narayana.* Bombay.

Kroeber, Alfred. [1920] 1979. "Totem and Taboo: An Ethnologic Psychoanalysis." *American Anthropologist* 22: 48–55. [Reprinted in William A. Lessa and Evon Z. Vogt, eds., *Reader in Comparative Religion: An Anthropological Approach,* 4th ed. (New York, 1979), 19–27]

Kroll, John H. 1981. "From Wappenmünzen to Gorgoneia to Owls." *American Numismatic Society Museum Notes* 26: 1–32.

Küchler, Susanne. 1987. "Malangan: Art and Memory in a Melanesian Society." *Man,* n.s., 22: 238–55.

Kuhn, Rudolf. 1970. "Gian Lorenzo Bernini und Ignatius von Loyola." *Argo: Festschrift für Kurt Badt,* ed. Martin Gosebruch and Lorenz Dittmann, 297–323. Cologne.

Kurtz, Donna C., and John Boardman. 1971. *Greek Burial Customs.* Ithaca, N.Y.

Kuspit, Donald B. 1979. "To Interpret or Not to Interpret Jackson Pollock." *Arts Magazine* 53(7): 125–27.

———. 1984. *The Critic Is Artist: The Intentionality of Art.* Ann Arbor, Mich.

de La Chausse, Michel Ange. 1706. *Le grand cabinet romain, ou recueil d'antiquitez romaines.* Amsterdam.

Laing, R. D. 1960. *The Divided Self: An Existential Study in Sanity and Madness.* London.

Lakoff, George. 1987. *Women, Fire, and Dangerous Things: What Categories Reveal about the Mind.* Chicago.

Lakoff, George, and Mark Johnson. 1980. *Metaphors We Live By.* Chicago.

Lang, Berel, ed. 1984. *The Death of Art.* New York.

Lansing, J. Stephen. 1983. *The Three Worlds of Bali.* New York.

Latour, Bruno. 1986. "Visualization and Cognition: Thinking with Eyes and Hands." *Knowledge and Society* 6: 1–40.

———. 1987. *Science in Action: How to Follow Scientists and Engineers through Society.* Cambridge, Mass.

———. [1984] 1988. *The Pasteurization of France.* Trans. Alan Sheridan and John Law. Cambridge, Mass.

Laurence, Jeffrey. 1985. "The Immune System in AIDS." *Scientific American* 253(6): 84–93.

Lavin, Irving. 1968a. *Bernini and the Crossing of Saint Peter's.* New York.

———. 1968b. "Five New Youthful Sculptures by Gianlorenzo Bernini and a Revised Chronology of His Earlier Works." *Art Bulletin* 50: 223–48.

———. 1980. *Bernini and the Unity of the Visual Arts.* 2 vols. New York.

Lawrence, Peter. 1964. *Road Belong Cargo: A Study of the Cargo Movement in the Southern Medang District, New Guinea.* Manchester.

Lawson, J. C. 1910. *Modern Greek Folklore and Ancient Greek Religion: A Study in Survivals.* Cambridge.

Lee, Rensselaer W. 1967. *Ut Pictura Poesis: The Humanistic Theory of Painting.* New York.

Leenhardt, Maurice. 1970. *La structure de la personne en Mélanésie.* Milan.

Levins, Richard, and Richard Lewontin. 1985. *The Dialectical Biologist.* Cambridge, Mass.

Lévi-Strauss, Claude. [1975] 1982. *The Way of the Masks.* Trans. Sylvia Modelski. Seattle, Wash.

Lévy-Bruhl, Lucien. [1949] 1975. *The Notebooks on Primitive Mentality.* Trans. Peter Rivière. Oxford.

Liang, Matthew H., et al. 1984. "The Psychosocial Impact of Systemic Lupus Erythematosus and Rheumatoid Arthritis." *Arthritis and Rheumatism* 27(1): 13–19.

Littlewood, Roland, and Maurice Lipsedge. 1989. *Aliens and Alienists: Ethnic Minorities and Psychiatry.* 2d ed. London.

Long, Timothy. 1986. *Barbarians in Greek Comedy.* Carbondale, Ill.

Luria, A. R. 1963. *The Mentally Retarded Child.* Trans. W. P. Robinson. New York.

———. 1976. *Basic Problems of Neurolinguistics.* Trans. Basil Haigh. The Hague.

MacClancy, Jeremy. 1986. "Mana: An Anthropological Metaphor for Island Melanesia." *Oceania* 57: 142–53.

———. 1988. "A Natural Curiosity: The British Market in Primitive Art." *Res* 15: 163–76.

Magnuson, Torgil. 1986. *Rome in the Age of Bernini.* Vol. 2. Stockholm.

Markoe, Glenn. 1989. "The 'Lion Attack' in Archaic Greek Art: Heroic Triumph." *Classical Antiquity* 8(1): 86–115 & plates.

Marshall, Sir John, ed. 1931. *Mohenjo-Daro and the Indus Civilization.* 3 vols. London.

Martin, Emily. 1987. *The Woman in the Body: A Cultural Analysis of Reproduction.* Boston.

———. 1990. "Toward an Anthropology of Immunology: The Body as Nation State." *Medical Anthropology Quarterly* 4: 410–26.

Masheck, Joseph. 1976. "The Carpet Paradigm: Critical Prolegomena to a Theory of Flatness." *Arts Magazine* 51(1): 82–109.

Mauss, Marcel. 1967. *The Gift.* Trans. Ian Cunnison. New York.

McDougall, Joyce. [1982] 1985. *Theaters of the Mind: Illusion and Truth on the Psychoanalytic Stage.* New York.

———. 1989. *Theaters of the Body: A Psychoanalytic Approach to Psychosomatic Illness.* New York.

McEvilley, Thomas. 1981. "An Archaeology of Yoga." *Res* 1: 44–77.

———. 1984. "Doctor Lawyer Indian Chief: ' "Primitivism" in 20th Century Art' at the Museum of Modern Art in 1984." *Artforum* 23(3): 54–61.

McFarland, Thomas. 1981. *Romanticism and the Forms of Ruin: Wordsworth, Coleridge, and Modalities of Fragmentation.* Princeton.

———. 1985. *Originality and Imagination.* Baltimore, Md.

———. 1987. *Shapes of Culture.* Iowa City, Iowa.

McGill, Douglas C. 1984. "What Does Modern Art Owe to the Primitives?" *New York Times,* 23 September, sec. 2, pp. 1, 16.

Medawar, Peter. 1982. *Pluto's Republic.* Oxford.

———. 1984. *The Limits of Science.* Oxford.

Mercati, Michele. [1589] 1981. *Gli obelischi di Roma.* Ed. Gianfranco Cantelli. Bologna.

Meuli, Karl. 1975. *Gesammelte Schriften.* Ed. Thomas Gelzer. 2 vols. Basel.

Meyer, Ursula. 1972. *Conceptual Art.* New York.

———. 1973. "The Eruption of Anti-Art." In *Idea Art: A Critical Anthology,* ed. Gregory Battcock, 116–34. New York.

Miller, J. Innes. 1969. *The Spice Trade of the Roman Empire, 29 B.C. to A.D. 641.* Oxford.

Mitter, Partha. 1977. *Much-Maligned Monsters: History of European Reactions to Indian Art.* Oxford.

Momigliano, Arnaldo. [1958] 1966. "The Place of Herodotus in the History of Historiography." In *Studies in Historiography,* 127–42. London.

Moor, Edward. 1810. *The Hindu Pantheon.* London.

Mylonas, George E. 1957. *Ancient Mycenae: The Capital City of Agamemnon.* Princeton.

Nadeau, J. Y. 1970. "Ethiopians." *Classical Quarterly*, n.s., 20: 339–49.

Nadelman, Cynthia. 1985. "Broken Premises: 'Primitivism' at MoMA." *Art News* 84(2): 88–95.

Napier, A. David. 1986. *Masks, Transformation, and Paradox*. Berkeley and Los Angeles.

Needham, Rodney. 1967. "Percussion and Transition." *Man*, n.s., 2: 606–14.

———. 1972. *Belief, Language, and Experience*. Oxford.

———, ed. 1973. *Right and Left: Essays in Dual Symbolic Classification*. Chicago.

———. 1975. "Polythetic Classification: Convergence and Consequences." *Man*, n.s., 10: 349–69.

———. 1980. *Reconnaissances*. Toronto.

———. 1983. *Against the Tranquility of Axioms*. Berkeley and Los Angeles.

———. 1987. *Counterpoints*. Berkeley and Los Angeles.

Neisser, Ulric. 1976. *Cognition and Reality: Principles and Implications of Cognitive Psychology*. San Francisco.

Nilsson, Martin P. [1932] 1972. *The Mycenaean Origin of Greek Mythology*. Introd. Emily Vermeule. Berkeley and Los Angeles.

Noguchi, Isamu. 1957. "The 'Arts' Called 'Primitive.'" *Art News* 56(1): 24–27, 64–65.

Nossal, G. J. V. 1969. *Antibodies and Immunity*. New York.

Obeyesekere, G. 1981. *Medusa's Hair: An Essay on Personal Symbols and Religious Experience*. Chicago.

———. 1990. *The Work of Culture: Symbolic Transformation in Psychoanalysis and Anthropology*. Chicago.

Pagels, Elaine. 1979. *The Gnostic Gospels*. New York.

Palmer, L. R. 1958. "New Religious Texts from Pylos (1955)." *Transactions of the Philological Society*, 1–35.

Panofsky, Erwin. 1955. "*Et in Arcadia Ego*: Poussin and the Elegiac Tradition." In *Meaning in the Visual Arts: Papers in and on Art History*, 295–320. Garden City, N.Y.

Parke, H. W. 1977. *Festivals of the Athenians*. Ithaca, N.Y.

Parry, Jonathan. 1989. "On the Moral Perils of Exchange." In *Money and the Morality of Exchange*, ed. J. Parry and M. Bloch, 64–93. Cambridge.

von Pastor, Ludwig Freiherr. [1940] 1957. *The History of the Popes, from the Close of the Middle Ages*. Vol. 31. Ed. and trans. Ernest Graf. London.

Peacock, James L. 1978. *Muslim Puritans: Reformist Psychology in Southeast Asian Islam*. Berkeley and Los Angeles.

———. 1986. *The Anthropological Lens: Harsh Light, Soft Focus*. Cambridge.

Pepper, David. 1984. *The Roots of Modern Environmentalism*. London.

Pettazzoni, Raffaele. 1956. *The All-Knowing God: Researches into Early Religion and Culture*. Trans. H. J. Rose. London.

Pickard-Cambridge, Sir Arthur. 1927. *Dithyramb, Tragedy and Comedy*. Oxford.

Pocock, D. F. 1988. "Persons, Texts and Morality: Marett Memorial Lecture, Oxford 1988." *International Journal of Moral and Social Studies* 3: 203–16.

Popper, Frank. 1975. *Art—Action and Participation*. New York.

Price, Sally. 1986. Review of *"Primitivism" in 20th Century Art*, ed. William Rubin. *American Ethnologist* 13: 578–80.

Rawlinson, H. G. 1975. "Early Contacts between India and Europe." In *A Cultural History of India*, ed. A. L. Basham, 425–41. Oxford.

Redfield, James M. 1975. *Nature and Culture in the Iliad: The Tragedy of Hector.* Chicago.

Reilly, P. Conor, S.J. 1974. *Athanasius Kircher, S.J.: Master of a Hundred Arts, 1602–1680.* Wiesbaden.

Robins, Corinne. 1976. "Alan Sonfist: Time as Aesthetic Dimension." *Arts Magazine* 51(2): 85–87.

Rorty, Richard, and Mary Hesse. 1987. "Unfamiliar Noises." In *The Symposia Read at the Joint Session of the Aristotelian Society and the Mind Association at the University of Cambridge, July 1987*, The Aristotelian Society, Supplementary Volume 61, 283–311. London.

Rosenberg, Harold. 1969. "Art and Words." *New Yorker* 29 (March 29): 110–21. [Reprinted in *Idea Art: A Critical Anthology*, ed. Gregory Battcock (New York, 1973), 150–64]

Rosenfield, Israel. 1988. *The Invention of Memory: A New View of the Brain.* New York.

Rothenberg, Albert. 1976. "Homospatial Thinking in Creativity." *Archives of General Psychiatry* 33: 17–26.

———. 1988. "Creativity and the Homospatial Process: Experimental Studies." *Psychiatric Clinics of North America* 11: 443–59.

Rubin, William, ed. 1984. *"Primitivism" in 20th Century Art: Affinity of the Tribal and the Modern.* 2 vols. New York.

Rubin, William, Kirk Varnedoe, and Thomas McEvilley. 1985. "On 'Doctor Lawyer Indian Chief: "Primitivism" in 20th Century Art' at the Museum of Modern Art in 1984." *Artforum* 23(6): 42–51. [Letters to the editor by Rubin and Varnedoe, with response by McEvilley]

Sacks, Oliver. 1985. *The Man Who Mistook His Wife for a Hat, and Other Clinical Tales.* New York.

Sacks, Sheldon, ed. 1979. *On Metaphor.* Chicago.

Schechner, Richard. 1985. *Between Theater and Anthropology.* Philadelphia.

Scheper-Hughes, Nancy. 1990. "Three Propositions for a Critically Applied Medical Anthropology." *Social Science and Medicine* 30: 189–97.

Schliemann, Henry. 1878. *Mycenae: A Narrative of Researches and Discoveries at Mycenae and Tiryns.* London.

Schwarz, Heinrich. 1959. "The Mirror of the Artist and the Mirror of the Devout." In *Studies in the History of Art*, 90–105. New York.

Seaford, Richard. 1976. "On the Origins of Satyric Drama." *Maia* 28: 209–21.

———. 1984. "Introduction," in Euripides, *Cyclops*, 1–60. Oxford.

———. 1987. "The Tragic Wedding." *Journal of Hellenic Studies* 107: 106–30.

Seznec, Jean. [1940] 1953. *The Survival of the Pagan Gods: The Mythological Tradition and Its Place in Renaissance Humanism and Art.* Trans. Barbara F. Sessions. Princeton.

Simmel, Georg. 1950. *The Sociology of Georg Simmel*. Ed. and trans. Kurt H. Wolff. Glencoe, Ill.

———. 1971. *On Individuality and Social Forms: Selected Writings*. Ed. Donald N. Levine. Chicago.

Smith, Bernard. 1984. "Captain Cook's Artists and the Portrayal of Pacific Peoples." *Art History* 7: 295–312.

———. 1985. *European Vision and the South Pacific*. 2d ed. New Haven.

Smithson, Robert. 1979. *The Writings of Robert Smithson: Essays with Illustrations*. New York.

Sonfist, Alan, ed. 1983. *Art in the Land: A Critical Anthology of Environmental Art*. New York.

Sontag, Susan. 1979. *Illness as Metaphor*. New York.

———. 1988. "AIDS and Its Metaphors." *New York Review of Books* 35(16 [Oct. 27]): 89–99.

———. 1989. *AIDS and Its Metaphors*. New York.

Spence, Jonathan D. 1984. *The Memory Palace of Matteo Ricci*. New York.

Stocking, George W., ed. 1985. *Objects and Others: Essays on Museums and Material Culture*. Madison, Wisc.

Stoller, Paul. 1989. *The Taste of Ethnographic Things: The Senses in Anthropology*. Philadelphia.

Stoller, Paul, and Cheryl Olkes. 1987. *In Sorcery's Shadow: A Memoir of Apprenticeship among the Songhay of Niger*. Chicago.

Strauss, Barry S. 1986. *Athens after the Peloponnesian War: Class, Faction and Policy, 403–386 B.C.* London.

Szasz, Thomas S. 1974. *The Myth of Mental Illness: Foundations of a Theory of Personal Conduct*. Rev. ed. New York.

Tambiah, S. J. 1968. "The Magical Power of Words." *Man*, n.s., 3: 175–208.

Thompson, Robert Farris. 1968. "Esthetics in Traditional Africa." *Art News* 66(9): 44–45, 63–66. [Reprinted in *Art and Aesthetics in Primitive Societies: A Critical Anthology*, ed. Carol F. Jopling (New York, 1971), 374–81]

———. 1973. "Yoruba Artistic Criticism." In *The Traditional Artist in African Societies*, ed. Warren L. d'Azevedo, 19–61. Bloomington, Ind.

Todorov, Tzvetan. [1982] 1984. *The Conquest of America: The Question of the Other*. Trans. Richard Howard. New York.

Turner, Sir Ralph L. 1969. *A Comparative Dictionary of the Indo-Aryan Languages*. London.

Turner, Victor W. 1964. "Betwixt and Between: The Liminal Period in *rites de passage*." In *Symposium on New Approaches to the Study of Religion, Proceedings of the 1964 Annual Spring Meeting of the American Ethnological Society*, ed. June Helm, 4–20. Seattle, Wash. [Reprinted in William A. Lessa and Evon Z. Vogt, eds., *Reader in Comparative Religion: An Anthropological Approach*, 4th ed. (New York, 1979), 234–43]

———. 1969. *The Ritual Process: Structure and Anti-structure*. Ithaca, N.Y.

———. 1974. *Dramas, Fields, and Metaphors: Symbolic Action in Human Society*. Ithaca, N.Y.

Tylor, Edward B. 1913. *Primitive Culture: Researches into the Development of Mythology, Philosophy, Religion, Language, Art, and Custom.* 5th ed. 2 vols. London.

Upadhyaya, U. P., and S. P. Upadhyaya. 1983. *Dravidian and Negro-African: Ethno-linguistic Study on Their Origin, Diffusion, Prehistoric Contacts and Common Cultural and Linguistic Heritage.* Udupi, Karnataka.

Vermaseren, Maarten J. 1956–60. *Corpus Inscriptionum et Monumentorum Religionis Mithriacae.* 2 vols. The Hague.

———. 1977. *Cybele and Attis: The Myth and the Cult.* Trans. A. M. H. Lemmers. London.

Vernant, Jean-Pierre. 1980. "Étude comparée des religions antiques." *Annuaire du Collège de France, 1979–1980: Résumé des cours et travaux,* 453–66.

———. 1981a. "L'autre de l'homme, la face de Gorgô." In *Pour Léon Poliakov: Le racisme, mythes et sciences,* ed. Maurice Olender, 141–55. Brussels.

———. 1981b. "Étude comparée des religions antiques." *Annuaire du Collège de France, 1980–1981: Résumé des cours et travaux,* 391–406.

———. 1985. *La mort dans les yeux: Figures de l'Autre en Grèce ancienne—Artémis, Gorgô.* Paris.

———. 1986. "The Private Man inside the City-State." [Unpublished manuscript]

Vygotsky, Lev Semenovich. [1934] 1964. *Thought and Language.* Ed. and trans. Eugenia Hanfmann and Gertrude Vakar. Cambridge, Mass.

Waley, Arthur, ed. and trans. 1938. *The Analects of Confucius.* London.

Webster, T. B. L. 1954. "Personification as a Mode of Greek Thought." *Journal of the Warburg and Courtauld Institutes* 17: 10–21.

Weiner, Annette B. 1983. "From Words to Objects to Magic: Hard Words and the Boundaries of Social Interaction." *Man,* n.s., 18: 690–709.

———. 1985. "Inalienable Wealth." *American Ethnologist* 12(2): 210–27.

Werner, Heinz, and Bernard Kaplan. 1963. *Symbol Formation: An Organismic-Developmental Approach to Language and the Expression of Thought.* New York.

Werner, Karel. 1977. *Yoga and Indian Philosophy.* Delhi.

Whorf, Benjamin Lee. 1956. *Language, Thought, and Reality.* Ed. John B. Carroll. Cambridge, Mass.

Wikan, Unni. 1989. "Managing the Heart to Brighten Face and Soul: Emotions in Balinese Morality and Health Care." *American Ethnologist* 16: 294–312.

Wilson, Bryan R., ed. 1974. *Rationality.* Oxford.

Witherspoon, Gary. 1977. *Language and Art in the Navajo Universe.* Ann Arbor, Mich.

Wittgenstein, Ludwig. 1966. *Lectures and Conversations on Aesthetics, Psychology, and Religious Belief.* Ed. Cyril Barrett. Oxford.

Wolfe, Tom. 1975. *The Painted Word.* New York.

Yates, Frances A. 1966. *The Art of Memory.* London.

Zarncke, Lilly. 1931. *Die "Exercitia spiritualia" des Ignatius von Loyola in ihren geistesgeschichtlichen Zusammenhängen.* Schriften des Vereins für Reformationsgeschichte 49.1, 151. Leipzig.

Zimmer, Heinrich. [1926] 1984. *Artistic Form and Yoga in the Sacred Images of India.* Ed. and trans. Gerald Chapple and James B. Lawson, in collaboration with Michael McKnight. Princeton.

Index

Abstraction: in art, 3–6; and concretion, 45, 49, 129; and symbolic thought, xxi, 152–53

Acconci, Vito: *Following Piece*, 66; *Way Station*, 37

Acharnians (Aristophanes), 86

AIDS (immunological disorder), 164, 175, 180, 185–86

Alexander VII (pope), 112; and humanism, 117; interest in Gnosticism, 114–20, 125, 127–28; Kircher's influence on, 115, 125

Alienation, xxiv–xxvi, 50, 171; nature of, 146–47

Ambivalence, 90–91, 95, 98, 103, 163–64

American culture: and contextualization, 167, 169–70; and environmental connectedness, 166–70; and foreignness, 166–67, 169; millennialism and, 146n, 166–70; rejection of hierarchy in, 168

Andre, Carl: *Copper-Aluminum Plain*, 27

Androgyny, 95, 100–101, 121

Animism, 7, 51–52, 65, 158; disease and, 148, 196–97; dreams and, 52, 158

Ankh: Gnostic interpretation of, 116, 125–26

Anonymity: in art, 16, 22–24

Anthropology, modern: conservatism of, 182–83

Arcimboldo, Giuseppe, 58–59

Argos (Greece), 83, 106

Aristophanes: *Acharnians*, 86

Aristotle, xxi, xxiii, 79

Arrest: expression of, 159–60

Art: anonymity in, 16, 22–24; avant-garde, xxiv, 16–17, 19–22, 45; body in, 21; and canons, 24; and contextualization, 18–22; and cultural adaptation, 74; and identity, xxiv; and illusion, 17, 26; and imagination, xxiv; innovation in, xxiv; objects in, 4n, 18–19, 32, 45, 48–49; post-modern, 48, 50. *See also*

Environmental art; Minimal art; Performance art; "Primitive" art

Art and artists, 3, 4–6, 16, 18–21, 29–33, 44–45, 66–68, 128, 133–34, 153–54

Australian aborigines: death by suggestion among, 148–50, 171

Autism: and ritual behavior, 173, 175

Autoimmunology and autoimmunological disorders, 146n, 165, 185

Autumn Rhythm (Pollock), 3

Avalon, Arthur, 101

Avulsion, 16–19, 32, 140

Axis mundi, 49, 185

Bachelard, Gaston, 188

Balinese: and concept of soul-loss, 158–60, 162; and disease, 58n, 162, 198; and foreignness, 72–75, 153; masks, 72, 155, 159, 164; ritual possession in trances, 69–70, 158–59, 178, 198; and symbolic language, 70–71, 160; worldview, 49–50, 68–69, 74, 146n, 153, 155, 174, 191

Banks, Joseph: *Journal*, 9

Barberini, Francesco, 115n, 117n, 126

Barberini, Maffeo, 130

Bateson, Gregory, 162–63; *Naven*, 194

Beating the bounds, xv–xvi

Beidelman, T. O., xxii

Benthall, Jonathan, 34–35

Berlin, Isaiah, 3

Bernini, Gian Lorenzo: *David* as self-portrait, 130–32; and design of Piazza San Pietro, 112–14, 120–26, 128, 135–38; *Due Teatri*, 136, 174; and Gnosticism, 114–15

Bodily pollution: and foreignness, 148, 152; nature of, 138, 142

Body: in art, 21; as microcosm of universe, 128; objective and subjective knowledge of, 132, 138, 141; representation of in disease states, 141, 147–48, 151–52, 172, 180–81, 197; self-awareness and the, 141–42, 153, 158

Body-image, 11, 138, 141, 152–53, 187, 197

Boundaries: in art, xxvi, 36–38, 41; of body-image, 138, 141, 152–53; in canon formation, 110–11; in ritual, xv–xviii, xxvi, 36–37, 69, 198

Brandt, Allan, 186

Buchan, Alexander, 9

Buren, Daniel, 23n, 55

Cacciari, Massimo, 58–59

Canguilhem, Georges, 141, 187–88

Cannon, Walter: "Voodoo Death," 148, 171

Canons: boundaries in, 110–11, 142–43; cultural, 107–9; formation of, xxiii, 110–11, 142–43; in visual arts, 24

Capasso, Nicholas, 38–40

Capitalism: and millennialism, 170

Cargo cults, 169–70

Carroll, Lewis: *Sylvie and Bruno Concluded*, 45

Children: and symbolic language, xix–xxi

Christo. *See* Javacheff, Christo

Clark, Kenneth, 6

Cognitive maps, 45, 48, 53–55

Commoditization, xxii–xxiii, 32, 65–66, 140, 167, 170–71. *See also* "Gift"

Conceptualization, xxvii; and imagination, xviii, xxi

Connectedness, 24, 32–33, 48–52, 54–55, 57, 65; and environmental art, 39–41; and individualism, 139–40, 171; and neurosis, 50; self and absence of, 11–13, 32, 66, 140

Conrad, Joseph: *Heart of Darkness*, 168

Contextualization: and American culture, 167, 169–70; and art, 18–22; and disease, 174; and symbolic thought, xvi–xviii

Cook, James, 8–9

Copper-Aluminum Plain (Andre), 27

Cosmology. *See* Microcosmos/macrocosmos

Croon, J. H., 85

Cultural adaptation, 74

Cultural diversity, 142

Culture: alienation within, 147; and foreignness, 142–43, 147, 153–54, 170; and memory, 193; and mental illness, 138, 141, 144–47, 151; nature of, 142–43, 147

Cybele, 114–15, 121, 124–25

Dali, Salvador: *Face of Mae West Which Can Be Used as an Apartment*, 59; *Paranoic Face*, 59

David (Bernini): as self-portrait, 130–32

Death by suggestion, 148–50, 171

Democracies: and foreignness, 157; freedom lacking in, 156–57; millennialism in, 156–57

Descartes, René, xxv, 161–62, 176, 183

Dionysus, 104, 107–9

Disease: Balinese and, 58n, 162, 198; contextualization and, 174; descriptions of, 141, 147–48, 151–52, 172, 180–81, 197; "foreign" nature of, 143, 145, 147–48, 150–51, 172; immune system and, 160, 162, 164–65; and metaphor, 146, 148, 151, 165, 172, 180–81, 185–89, 196

Dissociation, 177–78; in immunology, 179, 197; and metaphor, 180, 187, 192, 199

Dissociation, selective, 182, 184, 196; and personhood, 190, 198–99

Dogon: worldview, 11, 16, 26, 28, 31

Double bind, 162–64, 171

Double Negative (Heizer), 42

Due Teatri (Bernini), 136, 174

Durkheim, Emile, xxii

Eco, Umberto, 64

Ecology, 34, 38–39

Edge of August (Tobey), 6

Eguchi, Shigeyuki, 194–95, 197

Egyptology: and Pope Alexander VII, 115–18, 125

Einstein, Albert, xxi, 152

"Enlightened" cultures, 144–45, 150, 153–54, 175

Enlightenment, 150–51, 177

Environmental art, 38–46, 54; and connectedness, 39–41; and environmentalists, 39–44, 51n; and self, 45

Environmental connectedness: in American culture, 166–70

Environmentalists, 51n; and environmental art, 39–44

Eskimo masks, xv, xix

Evans-Pritchard, E. E., 51–52

Exchange. *See* Commoditization; "Gift"

Exoticism: in art, 1–2, 9, 11, 14, 24; in culture, 156, 172, 174, 184, 198–99

Experience: and knowledge, xxiv–xxv

Expressionism: in art, 3

Eye: in Greek mythology, 86–89, 102–3

Eye cups, 91–94, 101, 103

Face of Mae West Which Can Be Used as an Apartment (Dali), 59

Fight/fright response, 103n, 163–64

Flatness: in art, 3n, 17, 26, 27–28

Following Piece (Acconci), 66

Forehead: and Indian sectarian marks, 93, 95, 98–99; in Gorgon myth, 87–93, 96; in Indian iconography, 90, 93–101

Foreignness: and American culture, 166–67, 169; among Balinese, 72, 75, 153; and bodily pollution, 148, 152; in Classical Greece, 81, 85, 88–90, 101–6, 110–11; in definition of culture, 142–43, 147, 153–54, 170; and democracies, 157; Goffman and, 140–41, 171; millennialism and, 167, 172; nature of, xxiii–xxiv, 79, 143; Simmel on, 139–40; and strangers, 86, 142, 147; symbols and, xxiii–xxiv *See also* Otherness

Formal relations: assimilation, 117, 189; conflation, 19, 69, 193; conjunction, xxvi; disjunction, 38–39; juxtaposition, xxvi, 31; opposition, 19, 52, 56, 61n, 83, 172, 174; separation, 32, 143, 151; superimposition, xxvi, 193

Foucault, Michel, 150n, 171

Freedom: and individualism, 139–40; lacking in democracies, 156–57; nature of, 140; and objectivity, 139–40; and otherness, 153–55; in pioneer culture, 167–68, 170; Simmel on, 140

Freud, Sigmund, 160–62, 182; on memory, 180–81; on personhood, 177–79

Fry, Roger, 6

Genette, Gérard, 174

"Gift," xxii–xxiii, 7–8, 170n. *See also* Commoditization

Gnosticism, xxvii; Alexander VII's interest in, 114–20, 125, 127–28; Bernini and, 114–15; and design of Piazza Minerva, 118; and design of Piazza San Pietro, 114, 118–24, 129–30; and interpretation of St. Peter, 121; and interpretation of the *ankh*, 116, 125–26; and interpretation of Virgin Mary, 118–19, 121, 128–30; Kircher's interest in, 115–18, 126, 128–30; and the obelisk, 115, 118; popular interest in, 118–19; and uterus image, 114, 118–21, 124, 129, 136–38

Goffman, Erving, xxv, 23, 150n, 154–55; and foreignness, 140–41, 171

Gorgon: as archetype, 77–79, 88–89, 101–2, 104, 111, 132; compared to Kali, 96–97; iconography of forehead, 87–93, 96; as mask, 80, 84, 106; myth of, xxvii–xviii, 77–87, 97–98, 160, 163; origins of, 89–91, 101–6

Greece: historical connections with India, 90–91, 101, 105–6, 108–9

Greece, Classical: foreignness in, 81, 85, 88–90, 101–6, 110–11

Greece, Mycenaean: cultural change in, 79–81, 84–85, 87, 106–8, 185; death and rebirth in, 84–85; rites of passage in, 85

Greek culture, 7; rise of, 75

Greek identity: and Perseus myth, 78–81, 89, 106–11

Greek mythology: eye in, 86–89, 91–92, 102–3

Greenberg, Clement, 17

Haraway, Donna, 186

Harrison, Newton: *Portable Fish Farm: Survival Piece 3*, 34–36

Heart of Darkness (Conrad), 168

Heizer, Michael, 44–45; *Double Negative*, 42

Herodotus, 90

Hesiod, 79, 86–87

Hesse, Mary, xxv, 184

Hinduism, 96–99, 168; and *axis mundi*, 49; ritual in, xvi–xviii; symbols in, xvi–xviii, 152–53

Hippolytus, Saint, 124

Hodges, William, 9, 11

Holt, Nancy: *Sun Tunnels*, 39, 41

Homer, 79, 86, 104, 106n, 109–10

Homunculus, 103

Humanism: Alexander VII and, 117

Husserl, Edmund, 17, 62–64, 193

Hysteria: and millennialism, 157, 170; and stress, 161, 163–64

Ibeji (Yoruba figures), 29–31

Identity: and art, xxiv

Ideographs, xviii–xxi

Igbo dancing, 60–61, 72

Ignatius of Loyola, Saint: *Spiritual Exercises*, 133

Illness. *See* Disease

Illusion: in art, 17, 26

Image-making, xxiii–xxiv; and worldview, xxi

Imagination, xxi, xxiv, xxvi; and art, xxiv; and conceptualization, xviii, xxi;

Imagination (*continued*)
and juxtaposition, xxvi–xxvii; and superimposition, 192–93
Immunology and immunological disorders, 145, 148, 151–52, 160–61, 164–65, 172, 174, 187; and dissociation, 179, 197; and self-conscious cognition, 179. *See also* Autoimmunology and autoimmunological disorders; Psychoneuroimmunology
India: historical connections with Greece, 90–91, 101, 105–6, 108–9; ritual in, xviii; sectarian forehead marks in, 93, 95, 98–99
Indian iconography: forehead in, 90, 93–101
Individualism: concepts of, 14–16, 20–22, 31–32, 153; and connectedness, 139–40, 171; and freedom, 139–40; and ritual behavior, 173–74
Innovation: in modern art, xxiv

Javacheff, Christo, 66; *Running Fence*, 42; *Surrounded Island*, 44; *Valley Curtain*, 42
Judd, Donald: *Untitled*, 3–4, 17, 21

Kali (Indian deity): compared to Gorgon, 96–97
Kircher, Athanasius: Gnostic interests of, 115–18, 126, 128–30; influence on Alexander VII, 115, 125; *Oedipus Aegyptiacus*, 115, 130
Kitao, Timothy K.: on design of Piazza San Pietro, 112–14, 129
Kleinman, Arthur, 178
Knowledge: and experience, xxiv–xxv
Kosuth, Joseph, 22n, 23n
Kroeber, Alfred: on mental illness, 144–45
Küchler, Susanne, 54

Latour, Bruno, 181, 197
Lavin, Irving, 135
Lawrence, T. E., 155
Lévi-Strauss, Claude, 55
Lévy-Bruhl, Lucien, xxv, 6, 59–60
Ludolph of Saxony: *Vita Christi*, 133–35

Man Who Mistook His Wife for a Hat, The (Sacks), 53–58, 134
Martin, Emily, 186
Mary: as archetype, 130; cult of, 133, 135; Gnostic interpretation of, 118–19, 121, 128–30

Mauss, Marcel, 7, 17, 32, 69, 158, 167, 170n, 171, 179
Medawar, Peter, 174
Medicine: as warfare, 172–73
Meditation, 133–34
Medusa. *See* Gorgon
Memory, 49; and culture, 193; Freud on, 180–81; and homospatial process, 192–94; and meditation, 133–34; memory palaces, 55–57, 135; and mnemonics, 134–35; nature of, 53–57, 191–92
Memory Palace of Matteo Ricci, The (Spence), 55
Mendeleev, Dmitri, 54
Ménétrier, Claude, 126
Mental health care: poor state of, 143–44, 146, 150
Mental illness: and culture, 138, 142, 144–47, 151; Kroeber on, 144–45; nature of, 142–43, 150–52. *See also* Neurosis
Metaphor: and disease, 146, 148–49, 151, 165, 172, 180–81, 185–89, 196; and dissociation, 180, 187, 192, 199; and immunology, 180–82; nature of, 181, 184, 192; in science, 180–82, 189
Metaphysics, Greek, 7
Metaphysics, Judaeo-Christian, 26–27, 38, 45, 48, 50, 65–66
Metaphysics, post-Enlightenment, 8, 184, 194
Metropolitan Museum of Art (New York), 74; Michael Rockefeller Wing, 1
Microcosmos/macrocosmos, xviii, xxi–xxii, 45, 49–50, 75–76, 118n, 128, 133–34, 146n, 152–53, 166
Millennialism: and American culture, 146n, 166–70; and capitalism, 170; in democracies, 156–57; and foreignness, 167, 172; and hysteria, 157, 170; and pioneer culture, 165–66
Minimal art, 11n, 17–18, 54
Mirrors. *See* Reflection
Mithraism, 121
Monotheism, 153
Morality: and ontology, 139
Musée d'Art Brut (Lausanne), 144
Museum of Modern Art (New York), 16, 26
Museum of Primitive Art (New York), 1
Mycenae (Greece): ruling house of, 80–83, 86–87
Mylonas, 79
Myth: foundation, 77–78; pioneer, 170;

social and cultural dimensions of, 77–78, 171, 189–91, 193

Navajo: blankets, 11; sandpaintings, 6–7; and symbolic thought, 13–14, 58–59; worldview, 11–14, 16, 27
Naven (Bateson), 194
Needham, Rodney, xv, 49, 54
Neurosis: and connectedness, 50; creative functions of, 196; cultural functions of, 144–47, 151. *See also* Mental illness
Noguchi, Isamu, 1, 6
Noland, Kenneth, 3
Normalcy: nature of, 141, 146, 150, 154, 161, 187–88, 198

Obelisk: Gnostic interpretation of, 115, 118; as *omphalos*, 124
Objectivity, xxii–xxiii, 48, 58–59, 62–65, 183; and freedom, 139–40
Oedipus Aegyptiacus (Kircher), 115, 130
Omphalos: obelisk as, 124
Ontology, 158, 163; and morality, 139
Orientation, 39–40, 49, 153, 167–69
Otherness, xxvi, 50, 79, 188, 190; and definition of self, 75, 140–41, 154–57, 178, 185, 192; and freedom, 153–55; and science, 189. *See also* Foreignness
Oxford, xv–xvi

Panofsky, Erwin, 64
Paranoic Face (Dali), 59
Parkinson, Sidney: nature drawings by, 9
Participation, xxv, 51n, 59–62, 65
Pathology: nature of, 145, 188–89, 196; and normalcy, 141, 150, 187–88, 198
Patriotism, 171
Pausanias, 86–87, 121
Peiresc, N. F. C. de, 118, 126, 129
Performance art, 18–19, 21–24, 54; and ritual, 69–70
Perseus: as historical figure, 79–80
Perseus myth, 77–89, 101–2, 104, 105, 111, 132; and Greek identity, 78–81, 89, 106–11; iconographic elements in, 87–89
Personhood: Freud on, 177–79; selective dissociation and, 190, 198–99; self-conscious cognition as condition of, 161–62, 176–78, 181; theory of, 179, 194
Peter, Saint: Gnostic interpretation of, 121
Piazza Minerva (Rome): Gnosticism and design of, 118

Piazza Obliqua. *See* Piazza San Pietro
Piazza San Pietro (Rome), xxvii; Bernini and design of, 112–14, 120–26, 128, 135–38; Gnosticism in design of, 114–15, 118–24, 120–22, 129–30; symbolism in design of, 112–14
Pioneer culture: and freedom, 167–68, 170; and millennialism, 165–66
Pisistratus, 107–11
Platonism, 8, 11, 26, 32, 45, 49, 75
Pocock, D. F., 182
Pollock, Jackson, 6–7, 9, 11, 27; *Autumn Rhythm*, 3
Portable Fish Farm: Survival Piece 3 (Harrison), 34–36
Postmodernism, 48, 50. *See also* Reflexivity
"Primitive" art, 1–2, 6, 7n, 16, 22, 24, 28–31, 72–75
Primitivism in art. *See* "Primitive" art
Prinzhorn Collection (University of Heidelberg), 144
Psychoanalysis, 68, 145–46, 158, 162, 178, 183, 190, 192, 194–97
Psychoneuroimmunology, 161, 193

Reagan, Ronald, 166
Reality: and symbols, 53–57, 65, 75–76, 86, 129, 183
Reflection, 32; mirrors and, 85, 103, 132, 136–37, 174
Reflexivity, 14n, 49, 182–84
Ricci, Matteo, 55, 134
Right and left, 49, 56–58, 64, 68–70, 98, 99n
Ripa, Cesare, 130
Rites of passage, 85, 167–68, 190
Ritual, 36, 104, 173–75; in ancient China, xvi; in Bali, 68–74; boundaries in, xv–xviii, xxvi, 36–37, 69, 198; in Hinduism, xvi–xviii; in India, xviii; and myth, 77–78; and performance art, 69–70; and symbols, xviii, 60–63, 69–70; and theater, 85, 107; transformations, 22
Ritual behavior: autism as, 173, 175; and individualism, 173–74
Rockefeller, Nelson, 1
Rome (17th century): and cultural revisionism, 75, 185
Rosenberg, Harold, 3
Ross, Charles: *Star Axis*, 39
Rothenberg, Albert, 192–93
Royal Society for the Prevention of Cruelty to Animals, 34, 36

Rubens, Peter Paul, 118
Rubin, Edgar: and figure/vase reversal, 59
Running Fence (Christo), 42

Sacks, Oliver: *The Man Who Mistook His Wife for a Hat*, 53–58, 134
St. Peter's Basilica (Rome), 112, 120–21, 138
Scheper-Hughes, Nancy, 186
Schliemann, Heinrich, 80
Science: metaphor in, 180–82, 189; and otherness, 189
Self, 7–8, 19, 173; and absence of connectedness, 11–13, 32, 66, 140; and environmental art, 45; loss of, xxvi, 163–64, 181, 190, 196–98; in modern art, 11, 16, 19; and not-self, 19, 32, 86, 104, 108, 154, 165, 172, 177, 185, 189; otherness and definition of, 75, 140–41, 154–57, 178, 185, 192; pluralism of, 172–73; "social," 179–80; and soul, 160
Self-awareness: and the body, 141–42, 153, 158; and society, xxii, 13n
Self-consciousness, 14n, 32, 58, 60, 143, 150–51, 177, 179, 182, 197; and cognition, 161–62, 184, 191, 196; as condition of personhood, 161–62, 176–78, 181; and immunology, 179
Self-evidence, 65–66
Self-reference, 11n, 22, 155–56, 176–77
Self-sacrifice, 21–22, 26–27
Sentimentalism, 48, 51
Serra, Richard: *Tilted Arc*, 42–44
Simmel, Georg, xxii; on foreignness, 139–40; on freedom, 140
Singer, Michael, 44
Sixtus V (pope), 125
Smithson, Robert, 19, 41, 45
Smithsonian Institution, 44
Somatic disorders. *See* Disease
Sonfist, Alan: *Time Landscape*, 44
Sontag, Susan, 150, 186
Soul: Balinese concept of loss of, 158–60, 162; and self, 160
Space, symbolic. *See* Symbolic space
Spence, Jonathan D.: *The Memory Palace of Matteo Ricci*, 55
Spiritual Exercises (Ignatius of Loyola), 133
Star Axis (Ross), 39
Strangeness. *See* Foreignness; Otherness

Stress: and hysteria, 161, 163–64; nature of, 160–61
Suicide, 21–22, 26–27, 146, 175
Sun Tunnels (Holt), 39, 41
Superficiality, xxvii, 120, 151, 159, 172
Surrounded Island (Christo), 44
Sylvie and Bruno Concluded (Carroll), 45
Symbolic images, xviii–xxi, 45, 130
Symbolic imagination, xxi, xxvi, 70–71; of children, xix–xxi
Symbolic language, xviii–xxi; Balinese and, 70–71, 160; disease and, 141, 147–49, 151–52, 172, 180–81, 197
Symbolic space, xv–xviii, 18–19, 36–37, 45, 135n, 136. *See also Axis mundi;* Microcosm/macrocosm
Symbolic thought, xxi, xxiii, xvi–xviii, 13–14, 26, 28, 58–59, 75, 198; and abstraction, xxi, 152–53
Symbols: animistic, 148, 149; and the foreign, xxiii–xxiv; in Hinduism, xvi–xviii, 152–53; in Navajo worldview, 13–14; and the real, 53–57, 65, 75–76, 86, 129, 183; ritual and, xviii, 60–63, 69–70; in Perseus myth, 83–86

Tantrism, xxi, 69, 128, 133
Tao Te Ching, xv
Theater, 109, 130, 135–36, 152, 174; and divine stage, 114, 124, 136; and ritual, 85, 107
Theocritus, 86
Thespis, 107
Tilted Arc (Serra), 42–44
Time Landscape (Sonfist), 44
Tiryns (Greece), 80–81, 106; archaeological history of, 86
Tobey, Mark: *Edge of August*, 6
"Total prestation," 13–14n, 17, 158, 167. *See also* "Gift"
Trompe l'oeil, 58
Turner, J. M. W., 9, 11
Tylor, Edward B., 51–53, 55, 158

Untitled (Judd), 3–4, 17, 21
Upaniṣads, 98–99
Urban VIII (pope), 130
U.S. Department of the Interior, 44
Uterus: as Gnostic image, 114, 118–22, 124, 129, 136–38

Valley Curtain (Christo), 42
Vernant, Jean-Pierre, 103
Virgin Mary. *See* Mary

Visualization, xxi, 53–59. *See also* Memory
Vita Christi (Ludolph of Saxony), 133–35
"Voodoo Death" (Cannon), 148, 171
Vygotsky, Lev Semenovitch, xix, 54

Warhol, Andy, 48
Way Station (Acconci), 37–38
Webster, T. B. L., 7

Whorf, Benjamin Lee, 32
Witherspoon, Gary, 11, 58
Wittgenstein, Ludwig, 54
Womb. *See* Uterus

Yates, Frances, 56–57
Yoruba esthetics, 29–31

Zimmer, Heinrich, 101

Designer:	Barbara Jellow
Compositor:	Wilsted & Taylor
Text:	10 × 13.5 Bembo
Display:	Bembo
Printer:	Malloy Lithographing, Inc.
Binder:	Malloy Lithographing, Inc.